Steveli

The Philosophical Series of the Higher Institute of Philosophy,
University of Louvain, Belgium

EPISTEMOLOGY

by

CANON FERNAND VAN STEENBERGHEN,
PH.D. (Agrégé), S.T.D.

*Professor of Philosophy at the Higher Institute of Philosophy,
University of Louvain, Belgium*

TRANSLATED BY

REV. MARTIN J. FLYNN, PH.D. (LOUVAIN), S.T.D.

*Professor of Philosophy, Immaculate Conception Seminary,
Huntington, L. I., N. Y.*

*Translated from the
Second Revised and Corrected Edition*

NEW YORK CITY

JOSEPH F. WAGNER, INC.

LONDON: B. HERDER

Nihil Obstat:

JOHN M. FEARNS, S.T.D.
Censor Librorum

Imprimatur:

✠ FRANCIS CARDINAL SPELLMAN,
Archbishop of New York

NEW YORK, July 26, 1949

TRANSLATOR'S PREFACE

THE demands of modern critical philosophy make it imperative that Thomism prove itself to be an *organic system* of philosophy, capable of satisfying the most stringent requirements of modern thought. Canon Van Steenberghen's *Épistémologie* represents a masterful effort in that direction; consequently its translation into English appeared to promise a useful contribution to American philosophical life. It was for this reason that the present work, translated from the second French edition, was undertaken.

Since Canon Van Steenberghen's *Épistémologie* differs considerably in scope from English treatises bearing corresponding titles, careful consideration of the author's introduction is necessary to appreciate properly the true scope and aim of his work.

Throughout the translation I have used the term *critique* to signify a "critical evaluation of knowledge." I have tried in this way to avoid the misunderstandings which might possibly arise from the Kantian connotations generally attributed to the term *criticism* in current philosophical literature (see Dagobert Runes, *Dictionary of Philosophy*, Philosophical Library, N. Y., 1942, p. 71).

It is a pleasant duty to express my grateful appreciation to the many persons who have assisted me in the preparation of this translation. For their valued critical comments and suggestions, my thanks are especially due to Professor Harry McNeill, Ph.D., of St. John's University, Brooklyn, N. Y.; the Reverend James F. Coffey, Ph.D., D.D., the Reverend Francis X. Glimm, S.T.L., and the Reverend Francis M.

Tyrrell, Ph.D., all of the Immaculate Conception Seminary, Huntington, N. Y.; and the Reverend Thomas J. Kelly, Ph.D., D.D., of Cathedral College, Brooklyn, N. Y. My gratitude is also owed to Miss Catherine Griffin and several others for help in typing the manuscript, to Kevin Sullivan, M.A., Ph.L., for his care in editing the text, and to Mr. Thomas J. Kennedy for many stimulating suggestions and for his assistance in the preparation of the index. I gladly express my thanks also to the Rev. David J. Lynch, S.T.D., of the Diocese of Brooklyn for many kindnesses which facilitated this work.

I wish also to thank Messrs. Sheed and Ward, N. Y., for kind permission to quote several passages from Rousselot-O'Mahony, *The Intellectualism of St. Thomas.*

Canon Van Steenberghen's companion text, *Ontologie,* will constitute the further extension of the present critical approach to the fields of General Metaphysics and Theodicy. It is now in the process of translation.

MARTIN J. FLYNN.

AUTHOR'S INTRODUCTION

AT THE present time all philosophers agree on the prime importance of the problem of knowledge. But a great number of really embarrassing differences of opinion arise as soon as there is question of elaborating a theory of knowledge and of fixing its object, its place among the other branches of philosophy, its method and its results. The situation remains almost as confused even when we restrict our investigation to philosophers who belong to the same historical tradition, or who profess definite allegiance to the same school. Present-day Thomists, for example, in spite of the fact that they are in substantial agreement on certain general points, are still very far from agreeing on the manner in which the problems relating to knowledge should be placed and solved.[1]

We should not be too much surprised by a situation of this sort. It is due both to the nature of the case and to certain historical circumstances. It is due in the first place to the very nature of the case because, as we shall show in the course of this work, human knowledge is an extraordinarily complex reality which gives rise to many difficult problems. It is due secondly to certain historical circumstances, because in no field has the thinking of philosophers gone astray so frequently and so gravely as in the basic study of knowledge.

Furthermore, although a considerable number of scientific monographs have been published on different aspects of the theory of knowledge, and although many Thomistic thinkers have contributed to these investigations, we must still admit

1. See G. Van Riet, *L'épistémologie thomiste. Recherches sur le problème de la connaissance dans l'école thomiste contemporaine* (Louvain, 1946).

that not very much has been done on the level of popularization. Professors in Seminaries and Scholasticates who have the task of instructing numbers of young philosophers complain bitterly about the lack of good textbooks, notably in the field of epistemology. They have rightly appealed to the professors on the graduate level to meet this need. If a university school of philosophy is to exercise a proper influence and fulfill its function, its research must lead to periodic rejuvenation and improvement of instruction as given in hundreds of undergraduate schools.

We have published this treatise on epistemology in response to frequent requests of this kind. In it we shall try to arrange in logical fashion all the problems relating to knowledge which arise at the threshold of a genuinely systematic philosophy. We are not underestimating the difficulties involved in such an undertaking, and we recognize better than anyone else the gaps and defects still extant in this attempt. But it seemed better not to put off publication indefinitely while we tried to reach an impossible perfection. Much more help in correcting and completing the work can be expected from the suggestions and criticisms of readers than from any such timid abstention.

What is the basic motive for the work? What sources does it use? We have tried to consider the whole philosophical tradition, and to avoid neglecting any noteworthy contributions made by philosophers to the solution of the problems of epistemology. This sketch, however, is primarily the result of continuous reflection on the thought of St. Thomas Aquinas. Our principal motive for choosing this master, in preference to so many other possible ones, was not primarily extrinsic; rather it was because long-continued contact with his thought has brought home to us its astonishing solidity

and inexhaustible fecundity. Furthermore, genuine fidelity
to the principles of St. Thomas excludes all mere servility to
him, for the Universal Doctor counsels his disciples to give
absolute submission to the truth, but to be independent of all
human authority: "Studium philosophiae non est ad hoc quod
sciatur quid homines senserint, sed qualiter se habeat veritas
rerum" (*De Coelo*, I, *lect*. 22). This volume does not aim at
giving a literal reproduction of medieval themes on knowledge, rather it will try to report the fruit of a sincere effort
of personal reflection, doubtless nourished by the reading of
St. Thomas, but determined principally by the nature of the
problems raised and by the requirements of genuine philosophical criticism. Among those contemporary thinkers who
have exercised the greatest influence on our thought, we take
especial pleasure in citing Monsignor Leon Noël, our former
professor, whose works will be frequently quoted and used.
Our other references will show that we are indebted to a
number of secondary sources for various ideas. We wish to
express our gratitude finally to all our colleagues, friends and
students, who by fruitful exchanges of opinions have helped
us to state more precisely the delicate problems which we have
tried to treat. Our colleagues M. F. Renoirte and M. J. Dopp,
who kindly undertook the task of checking the work in gal-
leys, have a special claim to our gratitude.

In the face of the unprecedented confusion which afflicts
our contemporary world in the realm of ideas, the promoters
of the Thomistic renaissance have tried to help clarify the
intellectual atmosphere by restoring and rejuvenating the
traditional philosophy. The task which faces the Thomistic
school in the field of epistemology is very considerable. If it
can succeed in combining a more profound knowledge of
the realism of St. Thomas with a sympathetic but critical

appreciation of the solutions offered by later periods, it will contribute effectively to a much-needed modernization, reformulation, and rejuvenation of critical realism. The importance of this task cannot be overemphasized, since not only all philosophy but also theological speculation presupposes a clear, balanced and genuinely human answer to the problem of knowledge.[2]

Before re-publishing this volume we have examined again the various problems of epistemology and have tried to profit by the criticisms and suggestions occasioned by the first edition. This has resulted in a considerable number of changes in detail which we hope will help in clearing away some misunderstandings and in bringing out better the essential theses of the book. The essential theses have not been changed; consequently this second edition of the work does not differ radically from the first.[3]

In the course of the book we have abbreviated the bibliographical references to those publications which will be found listed in the bibliography given at the end of the volume.

Louvain, September 8, 1947.

INTRODUCTION TO THE ENGLISH TRANSLATION

IN INTRODUCING this treatise on Epistemology to English readers, we wish to point out once again the aim uppermost in our mind when writing the work.

2. See L. Noël, *Notes d'épistémologie thomiste*, pp. 1-18; *Le réalisme immédiat* (Louvain, 1938), pp. 1-20; E. Gilson, *Réalisme thomiste et critique de la connaissance* (Paris, 1939), passim.

3. To eliminate discussion which would merely encumber our present treatment we have examined some general difficulties in an article entitled "*Problèmes épistémologiques fondamentaux,*" in *Revue Philosophique de Louvain* (Nov., 1946), pp. 473-496.

We believe that up to the present time it has not been sufficiently shown that Thomistic philosophy is far more than a mere collection of philosophical doctrines grouped in orderly fashion about theology and serving that sacred science. Thomism is a strict philosophical system, well able to face up to the most brilliant systems of modern philosophy. It is possible, and today it is absolutely indispensable, to expound Thomism in a way which will satisfy the strictest requirements of a critical and systematic philosophy. In an exposition of this sort epistemology must occupy the first place. It must devote itself to a positive constructive study of knowledge, rather than to refuting errors concerning knowledge. Finally, it should limit itself to the treatment of those problems which actually arise at the start of philosophical research and which can be properly solved at that point. We would like the reader to note especially the sections in which these points are expressly developed: "The Primacy of the Theory of Knowledge" (pp. 8-12); "The General Plan of Epistemology" (pp. 19-22); and above all "Further Problems" (pp. 261-67).

A well-constructed epistemology will give us a clear understanding of the way in which Thomism differs from other philosophical systems, and it will help us evaluate the erroneous conceptions which have appeared in the history of thought. The reader will find all the elements he needs for this work in the "Historical Survey" provided at the end of Part One (pp. 51-74), and especially in the chapter devoted to "The Principal Errors in Epistemology" (pp. 268-83).

Louvain, March 7, 1949.

TABLE OF CONTENTS

PART FOUR

EPISTEMOLOGY

Part One

INTRODUCTION TO EPISTEMOLOGY

LIKE all scientific work, philosophical reflection is just one part of the integral activity of man, and is governed by a human purpose which antedates science itself. Since, as we shall see, epistemology forms the very first stage of the philosophical journey, we must at the very beginning of this discipline show the place it occupies in the whole domain of human activities. We must also determine its object at least briefly. We must offer some preliminary justification (as yet only provisional and extrinsic) of our approach to the problems to be considered.

Our objective in this chapter, then, is to *introduce* the reader to epistemology. And since we shall be dealing with notions which are still prescientific, we must not expect to find in them all the critical accuracy and technical vocabulary required in the later development of our study. An introduction of this kind has a psychological or pedagogical function. It serves to focus the attention of the reader on the problems to be studied, and to bring him into contact with them. The "reasons" that are offered in an introduction of this kind do not claim to be scientific: they are borrowed either from the judgments of common sense, or from the experience of philosophers, but we do not here attribute any definitive value to them, and they do not predetermine in any sense the later development of the study.

One must not for this reason conclude that this first chapter has no importance. On the contrary, it has a very es-

1

sential role from the psychological point of view. It helps to assure the transition from popular knowledge to scientific knowledge, and it serves to put the philosopher (especially the beginner) in a proper frame of mind to grapple with epistemological problems. It also furnishes epistemology with a satisfactory starting point.

From this point of view, then, we can group the questions which are to be discussed here around the following main points: (1) After having determined the *place* which epistemology should have in a systematic philosophy, (2) we shall try to give some indication as to the *general method* of procedure to be followed in developing this science; (3) these suggestions will lead up to a description and examination of the *beliefs of common sense* in such a way that we shall be able to determine thereby the starting point of epistemology; (4) an *historical survey* of the evolution of the problem of knowledge will complete the reader's preparation for the study of epistemology.

CHAPTER I

EPISTEMOLOGY IN A SYSTEMATIC PHILOSOPHY

§ 1. *The Systematization of Knowledge*

GROWTH in knowledge is an essential element in the development of man's personality as well as, on the level of society, of human civilization. The educated man strives not only to extend his store of knowledge, but also to organize and evaluate the data of popular knowledge. It is this effort which gives rise to scientific life.[1] In his desire for knowledge man thus seeks an *ideal of unity*. Incapable of a unique intuitive act that would satisfy his whole appetite for knowledge, he admits that human knowledge can arrive at unity only through the unity of a synthesis.

But how should he conceive of this synthesis? What kind of order is it possible to establish among different kinds of knowledge? What principle of order should be employed?

On this point there is no agreement, especially if we consider "philosophical" knowledge as distinct from "scientific" or "positive" knowledge. First of all, we can note in certain thinkers tendencies which we may call *non-rational*, either because they derive from a distrust of reason (a distrust which is stressed more by some and less by others), or because they arise from a positive preference for some value distinct from reason. In both these cases we shall see that the arrangement of knowledge is dominated by some ordering principle other than rational. For example, certain forms of empiricism may

---

1. See De Raeymaeker-McNeill, *Introduction to Philosophy* (New York, Wagner, 1948), pp. 3-19.

use an order suggested by the spontaneous evolution of experience; Bergsonism will use an order suggested by the laws of intuition; certain forms of Augustinianism will use an order suggested by the laws of love.[2]

On the other hand, the organization of knowledge is, in many cases, influenced by *pedagogical* reasons; instructors seek an order of graded difficulty in which each branch of knowledge would be taught so as to attain the best results in the minds of their pupils. At other times we find that the dominating interests of some thinkers are primarily *esthetic*. Thus, for example, in the Middle Ages sciences were readily classified according to the dignity of their respective objects, or according to the degree of certitude that the sciences attained. Most often, however, the attempt at scientific synthesis followed "principles of order" which were intellectual in nature; in other words, it followed methods which were properly *rational*. This remark, however, calls for further explanation, at least in a provisional sense.

Take, for example, a science such as the geometry formulated by Euclid, which received its definitive form very early. This science is a synthesis of items of knowledge concerning a determined object: space as defined by the postulates of Euclid. These items of knowledge are expressed in judgments, and these judgments are stated in the form of propositions. But what determines the grouping of these propositions? As far as possible, they are linked up with each other according to the order of *logical derivation*; that is, we start from postulates and basic definitions, then we study the figures and their properties according to an order of increasing complex-

2. See É. Gilson, *Introduction à l'étude de saint Augustin,* Études de philosophie mediévale, XI (Paris, 1929), pp. 294-297; 2nd. ed. (1943), pp. 312-314. Idem, *La philosophie de saint Bonaventure,* Etudes de philosophie médiéval, IV (Paris, 1924), pp. 452-473; 2nd. ed. (1943), pp. 379-396.

ity. The requirements of this kind of knowledge make such an order necessary, for the propositions bearing on the more complex figures are *deduced from* previous propositions bearing on more simple figures. However, let us note that even in geometry certain theorems can be displaced, or even interchanged, without invalidating the deduction.

The characteristics of the science of geometry are found to some extent in all human knowledge. Every science that bears on a specific object can be set forth in a series of propositions which will always have certain logical relations among themselves, either immediately (for example, when one proposition is deduced from another), or through the agency of the object studied (natural classifications, relations of succession, etc.). Among the propositions which make up any science we can distinguish principles and conclusions, general conclusions and particular conclusions, and so forth. Consequently, we can always synthesize a body of knowledge according to rational principles, to some degree at least.

These rational "principles of order" are of different kinds, and they do not all impose themselves on us with equal force. In certain cases they are absolutely indispensable: thus, postulates must necessarily come before the theorems which use them; the study of the triangle must necessarily precede that of the pyramid. In other cases, the principle of order will be a principle of economy: thus, as between two procedures which are equally legitimate from the point of view of strict logical coherence, we shall choose the one which avoids repetitions, the one which passes from the more simple to the more complex, from the general to the particular. In this case we can see that the principle of order is already less strictly rational. It may frequently happen that several ways appear to be equally commendable, either because each one has its own advantages and disadvantages, or because they all offer the same assurance. Scientific classifications, then, may be arbitrary or the result of convention.

What we have just said about any science taken by itself, can also be said about all human sciences taken together. Hence arises the idea of a general synthesis of knowledge, in which all the branches of knowledge would be arranged in as rational an order as possible. Throughout history scientific and philosophical endeavors have always been accompanied by an effort at a *rational systematization;* this effort has tried to link up segments of knowledge in such a way that one part would as far as possible flow from the other. In any event, the parts would be connected one with the other, starting from certain basic items of knowledge. They would start from immediately given elements whose value would force itself upon us and which would therefore act as the basis for the formation of a science. For a long time it was thought that the Middle Ages had not felt this need very much, but today we know that such was not the case at all. Problems concerning the classification and subordination of the sciences, questions dealing with the starting point of knowledge (first evidences, first principles, the general laws of inference and reasoning, the formation of concepts) were constantly recurring topics in medieval philosophy.[3]

Scientific systematization strives toward the ideal of a rational order of *methodical discovery* as opposed to the gropings of spontaneous research and discovery. The procedure

3. On the problem of the systemization of knowledge, an historical survey and simple bibliographical information can be found in our article, *"Réflexions sur la systématisation philosophique,"* in *Revue Néoscolastique de Philosophie* (May, 1938), pp. 185-216, pp. 191-199. On the work done on scientific systemizations during the Middle Ages, see our *Siger de Brabant d'après ses oeuvres inédites,* Les Philosophes Belges, XII-XIII, vol. II (1942), pp. 568-575.

which we have outlined is in fact an *order of discovery*, that is, a succession of discoveries, a progressive enriching of the field of knowledge, starting from certain basic items of knowledge. But the mind's spontaneous searching, involving as it does innumerable deviations, can hardly be a model for scientific systematization, for the story of collective or of individual scientific research tells of an infinite number of trials and attempts which were often unsuccessful. We can avoid these by making use of the experience of preceding generations. The order of discovery, therefore, exemplified in scientific construction is not the order of *psychological* discovery —we should rather speak of the disorder of psychological discovery—but the order of *methodic* discovery. In other words, we must try to arrange the problems and their solutions in the sequence which naturally forces itself upon the mind (more or less imperiously) when the mind undertakes a systematic study, that is, when it tries to follow rules which promote simplicity, coherence, and harmony in the system. It is clear that in the expression "methodic discovery" the word "discovery" does not quite have the meaning usually given to it, for a "methodical" organization of knowledge presupposes that spontaneous research and discovery have already been carried out by the mind. Here the word "discovery" signifies only progress, the progressive enrichment of knowledge, the passage from known to unknown, starting from elements immediately given and known by themselves. It is not, then, a question of conducting an inquiry along paths yet to be explored; rather it is a question of systematic "exposition" of a familiar route—possible only to one who has already some knowledge of it.

§ 2. *The Primacy of the Theory of Knowledge*

These are the facts which are recorded in the history of human thought. As soon as we ask ourselves what this attempt to unify knowledge is worth, or whether any such systematization of the various branches of human knowledge is possible, we see that these questions immediately raise grave problems concerning the very nature of knowledge in general and the nature of philosophical knowledge in particular. Can I know anything with certitude? Can I really express what I know in language, or at least can I express it to myself in internal mental "diction"? Do I have any knowledge which deserves to be called "philosophical," and in what sense? Granted that I have various kinds of philosophical knowledge, can they be unified and made into a synthesis or system? Even if that is possible, is it desirable, is it necessary? What is systematic philosophy? Can philosophy be systematic? Should it be systematic? Under what conditions should it be systematic?

All these questions depend on another question which is still more basic: What is "knowing"? The sense and scope of all the other questions depends on the answer that is given to this. In other words, if we reflect at all on the most elementary definition of scientific elaboration (namely, that it is a "synthesis of human knowledge"), we shall see that at the basis of every synthesis of this kind there must be a doctrine which determines, to some degree at least, what we mean by "human knowledge," its nature,[4] scope, and general condi-

4. This term, like all the terms used in epistemology, should be taken in a *psychological* sense. It refers to an immediate datum of consciousness. We are not speaking, then, of nature in the metaphysical sense of the term, but only in the very general sense of "that which characterizes an object," and consequently distinguishes it from others. See *"Problèmes épistémologiques fondamentaux,"* in *Revue Philosophique de Louvain* (Nov., 1946), pp. 473-96.

tions. Until we have solved these problems, the whole system remains suspended in air, waiting for a solution not yet given.

Here again history confirms our position. As soon as science emerged from the shadows and attempted to shape itself into a synthesis, one finds at the basis of each system some sort of theory of knowledge. This is the case in Plato and Aristotle, in Plotinus and St. Augustine, in medieval Augustinianism and medieval Aristotelianism, in nominalism and in all modern systems.

However, the idea of having a theory of knowledge as the starting point of philosophy meets with strange opposition in certain Thomistic circles. How can we explain this opposition? Does it rest on solid arguments? A study of neo-scholastic literature suggests the following observations:

1. Many authors confuse the *philosophical* problem concerning the critical foundations of knowledge with the *pedagogical* problem concerning the order which should be followed in the elementary teaching of philosophy. The arrangement of most textbooks of philosophy is determined by pedagogical considerations; the textbooks do not start with a study of knowledge, because authors believe that such a study cannot be undertaken by beginners.

Now, in reality, the problem of what should be the starting point of a systematic philosophy is not at all the same as the practical problem of the order to be followed in teaching. The first problem does not depend on the second in any way. On the contrary, it seems that the answer to be given to the pedagogical problem should be determined by the attitude we take to the other problem. We think that in so far as possible the systematic order of philosophy ought to be followed, even in the teaching of philosophy. The pedagogical problem of how to give a gradual introduction to philosophy should not be solved by upsetting the natural order of questions in philosophy.[5]

2. Other authors reject the idea of beginning philosophy with a critique of knowledge. They hold that this sort of critique involves a process of reflection on a philosophy and sciences which are already constituted.[6] This sort of attitude seems to reveal several points of confusion. First of all, there is confusion again between the *logical* order which problems have among themselves, and *psychological* conditions on the part of the person who begins to study them, between the order of methodical discovery and the psychological conditions of the investigation—"Fabricando fit faber." The apprentice-philosopher begins by making a trip "just for the ride." He begins philosophy without knowing what he is doing; he may believe that he understands it, but he is being satisfied with words only, he is not yet acclimated to the work. Only at the end of this first initiation will true philosophical work begin, work which implies at every step a critical and methodical investigation, and which must therefore necessarily begin with a critical reflection upon knowledge.

But at this point new confusions may arise. Critique in the broad sense (the only sense in which critique can be employed at the start of philosophy) may be confused with the more specialized critical reflection which must be carried out in every part of philosophy and in all scientific effort. Or again, the first study of knowledge, made *in the light of the immediate data of consciousness,* may be confused with the later interpretation of knowledge given *in the light of an al-*

5. See our article already cited, "*Réflexions sur la systématisation philosophique,*" pp. 212-216.

6. See, for example, J. Maritain, *Distinguer pour unir ou les degrés du savoir* (Paris, 1932), pp. 153-155.

ready established metaphysics. It has not been proved, then, that we cannot make *any kind* of critical examination of knowledge at the beginning of philosophy. If this were the case, we should have to stop trying to give any critical justification of our scientific knowledge, and we could not give it any other basis than the evidence of common sense.

3. Very often those who hold that epistemology should be the basis of philosophy encounter an opposition which springs, not so much from the idea of having a critical study of knowledge at the start of philosophy, as from a *certain opinion as to what that study should be and how it should be carried out.* This is the case with Professor Gilson who recognizes the need of an epistemology at the threshold of Thomism, but declares that all "critical realism" is contradictory, because he holds that this form of realism adopts an initial attitude which implies idealism.[7] This point of view will be discussed later on. It is not necessary for us to examine it here and now because it does not question the legitimacy of epistemology as such.

We take epistemology to mean a preliminary study of knowledge undertaken at the very beginning of the work of scientific systematization. No one has ever made out a good case against the proposal to have such an epistemology. Since science is by definition a system of knowledge, the starting point of this system can only be found in the *immediate data of consciousness.* Consequently, it is only by making an attentive analysis and reflective examination of these immediate data that we can hope to show the eventual possibility and the basic conditions of any scientific knowledge or elaboration.

7. See É. Gilson, *Réalisme thomiste et critique de la connaissance* (Paris, 1939), passim.

At the threshold of philosophy, then, the mind must first examine knowledge itself, as it first appears to consciousness, and the general conditions of science, in so far as they can be determined at this time. This first inquiry will very properly be called "epistemology," that is, a theory of knowledge (in the broadest sense of the term), a science of science, a *Wissenschaftslehre*.[8]

Let us see how a study of this kind can be developed.

8. See L. Noël, *Le réalisme immédiat* (Louvain, 1938), pp. 114-117, 162-167, 259-266. The builders of our present day Thomistic renaissance, have not always taken sufficient pains to show that Thomism involves a true philosophy, a system of philosophy. Until we prove that there exists, at least virtually, in Thomism a living organism of this sort, we shall hardly offer any serious opposition to the powerful and influential syntheses of modern philosophy. Until that is done, Thomism will still seem to our contemporaries to be a sort of mosaic of philosophical fragments which have been more or less coordinated among themselves by the external influence of theology.

Chapter II

GENERAL METHOD OF EPISTEMOLOGY

§ 1. Survey of Models

How can we organize the problems of epistemology methodically? We could study and discuss a number of "models." Since our aim here is to present an epistemology inspired by Thomism, we shall limit ourselves to the Thomistic tradition. Here we find several works of great value. We shall examine three of them briefly: the *Critériologie* of Cardinal Mercier, the *Critica* of Paul Gény, S.J., and the *Critica* of Joseph de Vries, S.J. These works are sufficiently representative of different neo-scholastic circles.

The *Critérioliogie générale ou Théorie générale de la certitude* will remain the capital work of the illustrious founder of the Thomist school of Louvain. It appeared in autograph form in 1884, was printed for the first time in 1899, and has been republished many times since then. This *Critériologie* of Cardinal Mercier showed the very new and very modern orientation which was to distinguish all his philosophy. In the work, the theory of certitude is developed as a branch lifted out of psychology. Its object is the "analysis of our certain knowledge and the philosophical inquiry into the foundation on which certitude rests." [1] The work was to include a general criteriology and a special criteriology, but this second part has never been published.

After a preliminary chapter dealing with certitude as a psychological fact, general criteriology was divided into four

1. Eighth edition (1923), p. 1.

13

books: (1) the position of the problem of certitude (truth, evidence, certitude); (2) the initial state of the intelligence when confronted with the problem of certitude (universal doubt, exaggerated dogmatism, rational dogmatism); (3) the objectivity of propositions belonging to the ideal order, or the solution of the first problem of epistemology (unsuccessful attempts at solution, the supreme motive for certitude, discussion of criticism and positivism); (4) the reality of the terms of the judgment, or the solution of the second problem of epistemology.

The *Critériologie générale* of Cardinal Mercier is rich in all sorts of suggestions which may prove very profitable to us, but still it leaves itself open to criticisms which are rather basic. In the first place, the emphasis is put on *certitude*. But certitude is only a psychological state which results from a certain quality or perfection of the knowing act itself. Now, if we look at epistemology as a science and therefore as an impartial investigation, its principal object should be that of determining the nature and value of knowledge. The question of certitude can be only a corollary to that.

In the second place, the *Critériologie* is so conceived that it depends strictly on the *modern way of putting the problem* of knowledge, from Cartesianism to positivism. Now, while it is necessary to take this modern statement of the problem into account, and while the direct discussion of the modern answers is both very relevant and very fruitful, we must not allow ourselves to be strait-jacketed by one way of looking at the problem, and by the prejudices that it involves. Epistemology should first establish its own theses, assert its own principles and prove its own positive conclusions, before undertaking to answer the errors incidental to modern philosophy.

In the third place, to what extent can we defend the distinction which Mercier established between two basic problems, namely, the *objectivity* of the propositions of the ideal order and the *reality* of the terms, and especially the fact that priority is given to the problem of objectivity? The position taken by Cardinal Mercier seems to imply that the ideal is independent of the real, and that the abstract is independent of the concrete. On this score it gives rise to very serious objections.

A final remark may be offered: Whereas in the Aristotelian epistemology *logic* occupies a very important place, the criteriology of Cardinal Mercier (which is an appendage to his psychology) is developed entirely independently of the logic. The question then arises as to what should be the relation between epistemology and logic.

The *Critica de cognitionis humanae valore disquisitio* of Paul Gény, S.J., was privately printed in 1914 for use by his students. A posthumous edition was published in 1927, based on a copy of the 1914 version which had been annotated by the author. At the starting point of a systematic philosophy, Father Gény puts a *Logica* comprising two sections, *Dialectica* and *Critica*.[2] The first of these two disciplines teaches the correct method to be followed in knowing (*rectum modum sciendi docet*); the second proves the value of knowledge (*valorem scientiae in tuto ponit*). The "critica" arises from the fact of error, for it was error which created the demand for a criterion of the true and the false, and, in a more general sense, the need for a critique of knowledge. The "critica" included a general part and a special part. The "critica generalis" first treats of certitude as opposed to scepticism (truth, certitude);

2. The third part of the *Logica* (Logica scientiarum) is, on the whole, a critique of the sciences and does not belong at the beginning of the system.

it then treats of the objective value of knowledge as opposed to idealism (value of experience, and the value of universal concepts). The "critica specialis" determines the validity of reasoning (deduction, induction, the appeal to testimony), and then discusses the "methodology" of the sciences (physical, mathematical, philosophical and historical).

If we compare this work with the preceding one, we immediately note several interesting advances. The "critica specialis," which had remained in the state of promise in the work of Cardinal Mercier, is actually undertaken. The distinction between the two fundamental problems does not stand out as strongly; the problem of *objectivity* is absorbed into the problem of certitude in general and into the refutation of scepticism, while the problem of *reality* is considerably developed and becomes the genuine problem of the "objective" value of knowledge. An attempt is made to determine the relations between logic and critique. The author does not bind himself so much to the modern statement of the problem, and he takes more account of the Aristotelian and Thomist tradition.

In addition, we can also make the following remarks about the *Critica* of Father Gény. Here too the emphasis is still being put on certitude, on security of knowledge. Critique is presented as a sort of accidental discipline, arising from the fact of error, as if the problem of the nature and scope of knowledge would not in any event have to be examined at the beginning of an attempt to systematize knowledge. His view of the nature of critique apparently prevents the author from seeing the true relation between dialectics and critique, as well as the distinction between the methodology of the sciences and the critique of sciences. In this investigation, the problems should be attached to the immediate data of consciousness. Further, a strictly epistemological terminology should be used, excluding notions borrowed from ontology and philosophical psychology. For such notions cannot be properly used at this phase of the investigation. Father Gény was not sufficiently careful in these matters.

The *Critica in usum scholarum* of Joseph de Vries, S.J., dates from 1937. The author himself presents it as *Metaphysica quaedam fundamentalis* in the sense that it aims, above all, at proving that an affirmative answer can be given to the problem of Kant: Is it possible to have a metaphysics which would be a science? However, the object of the *Critica* of Father de Vries is in fact the more general problem "of the possibility and limits of true and certain human knowledge." The author declares that he has abandoned the plan followed in most textbooks, because he wants to develop his treatment in logical fashion starting from data which are really immediate. Consequently he divides his work into three parts which discuss: (1) the possibility of having true and certain knowledge *in general*; (2) the possibility of attaining knowledge which is *transcendent* (with respect to consciousness); (3) the possibility of attaining *scientific* knowledge.

In the first part, Father de Vries treats of the immediate certitudes of consciousness, of the concepts which express immediate experience, of the first principles, and finally of those systems of philosophy which have been refuted already by the solution given to these first problems. The second part presents the doctrine of realism, first as a postulate, and then as a proven truth; it then determines more precisely the value of concepts which serve as expressions of this transcendent reality. The third part shows the possibility of the natural sciences, of historical science, and of metaphysical science.

When compared to the two preceding works, the *Critica* of

Father de Vries resembles each of them in turn. Like Cardinal Mercier, Father de Vries is strongly influenced by the modern statement of the problem, especially as found in Kant; like Cardinal Mercier, he puts the problem of the principles before the problem of the real. On the other hand, the place which he gives to critique in philosophy reminds us more of the views of Father Gény; again, the third part of his *Critica* corresponds to the "critica specialis" of Father Gény.

The work of Father de Vries merits praise because of the order, clarity and precision of the treatment, and because of its very high critical standards. But sometimes there seems to be evidence of an excessive criticism. Perhaps the author was immoderately influenced by Kant; at any rate, we cannot agree with him in his view of indirect realism. This basic difference of opinion will also show itself in a difference of opinion regarding the order in which questions should be treated.

There is finally a fault which is common to all three works. An epistemology which is well thought out cannot start the critique of knowledge without further preliminaries because, before criticizing, we must have an object to criticize. Epistemology should begin, then, with a precise psychological study of the elements which are given in every conscious act, or, in other words, with an exact *description* of the conditions which go to make up human consciousness.

It was because of their neglect of this preliminary work that famous thinkers led the critique of knowledge into blind alleys. When we study the great historical systems which have tried to solve the general problem of knowledge, we are struck by the fact that the most basic and harmful disagreements have arisen not so much in the *interpretation*, or the *evaluation*, of the immediate data of consciousness, but rather in the preliminary *description* of these data.[3] None of the three works which we have mentioned devotes sufficient space to the preliminary inquiry.

§ 2. *General Plan of Epistemology*

Critical observations such as we have just made on the works of Cardinal Mercier, Father Gény and Father de Vries, together with similar reflections on other works of epistemology, have led us to distinguish three principal steps in the development of the general theory of knowledge which should serve as the starting point for a systematic philosophy.

1. *Analytical or Descriptive Epistemology.* Epistemology studies knowledge. Its object must necessarily be provided for it by popular or prescientific knowledge, since epistemology represents the first step in scientific inquiry. When this first object of inquiry is given to him, the philosopher will try to grasp it in all its complexity, subject it to a careful analysis, and describe it with the greatest possible accuracy. This first inquiry will be expressed in a series of factual statements, which we shall call "affirmations of presence." My consciousness testifies to the presence of such and such elements.

3. This opinion is not, however, shared by all. Thus, one of my correspondents wrote to me: "It is quite evident that all these philosophers (Kant, Brunschvicg and so forth) agree with you on the psychological description of our knowledge. This is also the reason why they do not talk about it." Here we must distinguish. These philosophers agree in their description of the beliefs of common sense, but they do not agree at all in their description of the immediate data of consciousness. This is something entirely different. There is an enormous gap between the philosopher who, after the fashion of Kant, does not admit any other immediate data besides the *phenomena* (abstracting from all ontological value) and the philosopher who recognizes in *being*, or the ontological value, the first indisputable datum of consciousness. See *"Problèmes épistémologiques fondamentaux,"* pp. 480-485.

2. *Critical Epistemology.* Analytical epistemology establishes a factual situation; it determines what are the actual data that make up my human consciousness. So, it has the effect of *stating* the problem of the value of knowledge in an exact way, in the light of precise data. Critical epistemology attempts to *answer* this problem. It reverts to the elements which make up human consciousness, tries to judge them, and to determine their role or finality. It expresses this evaluation of the immediate data in *judgments of value.* It is led to distinguish in the knowing activity different possibilities, modes of knowing which are very different in value and in scope.

3. *Logical Epistemology.* We have already asked what place logic has in systematic philosophy, and what relation it bears to epistemology. Critical epistemology fixes and defines the object of logic, when it shows the validity of the reasoning activity of the mind. The life of the mind is one of movement and progress, and if this progress depends in part on the widening of the fields of experience, it depends just as much on the intellect's reasoning activity, which consists in linking thoughts together. Critical epistemology shows this reasoning activity is not merely a matter of chance, but is subject to laws. The object of logic is to determine the general rules for progress in thought. Thus, this discipline belongs *after* critical epistemology. If, however, we consider that logic, like analytical and critical epistemology, also studies the general conditions of human knowledge, then it seems reasonable to look on logic as being the third step of epistemology or general theory of knowledge.

Long before any attempt was made to systematize the analysis and critique of knowledge, this third phase was already a distinct branch. It keeps its independence to the present day, and it is not usually made a part of epistemology properly so called. We shall follow this tradition for practical reasons, and so shall restrict our treatment to the first two steps of the theory of knowledge.

However, this practical arrangement of the materials should not cause us to forget that these basic disciplines, which we group here under the general title of "epistemology," form a unit. Many modern scholastic authors who have written essays on "Major Logic," "Criteriology" and "Critica," have not seen the true relations which exist among these disciplines. The use of the term *epistemology* is still indeterminate [4] enough to justify our proposing this precise usage. This usage is in complete agreement with the etymology of the term, and it may serve to emphasize the organic unity of the problems which belong to analysis, critique and logic.

An epistemology conceived along these lines will have the *objectivity* and *unity* that a genuine science must possess; it will be essentially positive or constructive:

(a) Epistemology is an *objective* and *disinterested* inquiry; it studies the nature, conditions and value of knowledge without deciding beforehand what the results and consequences of its study will be. It is not merely trying to restore the peace and quiet of certitude to a troubled mind.

(b) Epistemology possesses a true *unity*; all its efforts concern the same object (that is, human knowledge as it exists at the threshold of philosophy), and all its efforts have the same end (to determine the nature of science, and consequently the potentialities or value of science).

4. Lalande takes epistemology to mean the philosophy or critique of the sciences, but according to English usage epistemology means a theory of knowledge. (See A. Lalande, *Vocabulaire technique et critique de la philosophie*, 4th ed., 3 Vols. [Paris 1932]). Many neo-scholastic philosophers understand epistemology to mean the general critique of knowledge.

(c) Epistemology should be *positive* and *constructive;* its principal objective is not to fight error, nor to refute the prejudices and mistakes of modern thought concerning knowledge, but to give a positive solution to the problem of knowledge.

§ 3. *Terminology and Method of Treatment*

Here we must consider another general question of method —the question of terminology and manner of treatment. Nothing is easier in philosophy than to appear profound. All that is needed is to be obscure, and obscurity can be easily obtained by using a series of recipes which have long since become classical. Because of undisciplined thinking, many philosophers apply such recipes freely: for example, adoption of a novel vocabulary, without defining the new terms invented; disregard of the laws of reasoning—by omitting essential links in the progress of one's thought, or by making use of complex and derived notions to explain first notions; submergence of thought in imagination by the abuse of metaphors; confusion of thought by formulae which are radically inexact and which cannot stand up under logical analysis.

But this kind of profundity brings discredit on philosophy in the eyes of thinking people, especially in the case of those who, through scientific work, know the requirements of precise, methodical and rigorous research. If they happen to read or to hear the lucubrations of certain obscure thinkers, philosophy will necessarily appear to them to be an impenetrable gnosis, a kind of verbiage bordering on the domains of poetry and mysticism, or a kind of inexpressible and incommunicable knowledge. Clearness, precision and method can only be obtained by an unceasing intellectual asceticism. The more complex, delicate and subtle the object to be studied (and this is especially true in the mystery of human knowledge), the more necessary it is to begin our investigation in a strictly methodical fashion.

What kind of a vocabulary should be used in epistemology? A common-sense vocabulary, or a technical vocabulary? A vocabulary which is borrowed from an existing philosophy, or one which is entirely new? The difficulty which has to be faced is quite evident. Words have a conventional meaning, which is often rather indeterminate. Frequently they have several senses. How can I indicate to others the precise meaning that I am attaching to a certain word in this study? If I coin a new term to describe an original experience, which I believe I have had, or some element which I have discovered among the immediate data of my consciousness, I shall have to appeal to older terms, already known, to define my new term. Otherwise I shall not be understood. If I use a term which is already in use, then my reader runs the risk of understanding it in a sense different from the one which I am giving to it. What, then, is to be done? New terms are sometimes useful, if they really refer to a new object of knowledge, to some "new" shade of meaning, or to some unexplored aspect of things. But the multiplication of new terms only complicates and obscures thought without necessity. Ordinarily it will be better to use a vocabulary which already exists, whether it be the vocabulary of ordinary life or the technical vocabulary of a particular philosophical system. In this last case we must avoid changing the sense of words, so as not to create confusion. To avoid ambiguity we must try in every case to *define* as well as possible the meaning of the terms used, and to set aside meanings which are not intended.

Now, since epistemology is the very first study of knowledge, and is logically prior to all scientific or philosophical elaboration, it is clear that all the technical terms of epistemology must refer to elements which are *immediately present* to consciousness. The vocabulary of epistemology, then, will be the vocabulary of descriptive psychology. We must not introduce any metempirical vocabulary into it, except in so far as the existence of certain metempirical values has been established.

Our way of developing epistemology must follow the natural progress of reflection, by proceeding always from the better known to the less known, from that which is evident of itself, and therefore a "principle of knowledge," to that which is not evident, but needs to be demonstrated or at least pointed out and explained. We must not propose anything which has not been previously given or established. We must avoid anticipations and confirmations borrowed from much later metaphysical theories, whose scientific validity rests entirely upon the conclusions of epistemology itself. If we do anticipate something in order to clear up a misunderstanding, we must be careful to note that it is a parenthetical statement whose role is exclusively psychological and pedagogical.

All too often we meet ambiguity and obscurity in the terminology and development of works on epistemology. This is due to a lack of method more than to the difficulty of the object. If authors were willing to study *human* knowledge such as it is given to us in reflection before any metaphysical elaboration, instead of occupying themselves from the start with problems which are much more complex and much less immediate (as, for example, the ontological conditions of our knowledge, the comparison of our human knowledge with divine or angelic thought, the essence of thought whatever it be, and so forth), they would not only avoid equivocation and confusion, but also other logical errors which are much more grave, including the vicious circle and the *petitio principii*.

§ 4. Methods of Research

Is it possible to carry out the program which we have just outlined? Can we conceive of any *method* which might promise some chance of success in the study of knowledge? Things seem easy enough at first sight, but if we look closer, we shall see that the route bristles with difficulties.

In the first place, is a study of one's own knowledge possible? Can I observe my knowledge in conditions which will allow me to describe it exactly and precisely, as the botanist can observe a living cell, or as the astronomer can observe the movements of the stars? And even if we suppose that I can analyze my knowledge, can the judgments expressing this analysis serve at all to describe a consciousness other than mine? But if my description does not go beyond the limits of my personal knowledge, if it concerns only my particular case, can this analysis claim to have a genuine scientific character? Is it not evident that if the "science" of knowing wishes to be a true science, it must study the conditions of *every* act of human knowledge, and not merely of *my* acts? There is also another difficulty. When I begin to study my knowledge, I am no longer in the condition of the child in the cradle whose consciousness awakes for the first time, and who by a perhaps enviable privilege could see clearly the first steps of his knowledge. The epistemology of this new consciousness is no longer within my reach. My human experience has grown continuously in the course of an already considerable span of existence. I have undergone thousands of influences and reacted to them; I have been fashioned and perhaps warped by my teachers; I have acquired a vision of the world which I cannot shed merely by an act of my will. Under such conditions is it possible for me to discover once again the virgin soil of my consciousness beneath this tropical growth of ideas, principles, prejudices and theories? Can the educated adult hope to find, in the depths of himself, the consciousness of the child as it was in its first awakening? If he cannot do this, what sense will the analysis of the *primitive data* of consciousness have? How can we distinguish that which is primitive from that which is elaborated?

We can give at least a provisional answer to difficulties of that sort, by showing the apparent possibility and necessity of constructing epistemology according to a method which is reflective, personal and interrogative.

1. *A Reflective Method.* For epistemology to be possible, I must be able to "know knowledge."

Is it a question of studying knowledge possessed by a *consciousness other than mine*? Is it, for example, a matter of observing the knowledge of a "subject of experiment," as we might observe the reflexes of a frog or the conduct of a spider? This evidently is not the case, for from the very start knowledge appears to me as being a hidden mystery, a sort of interior and secret life. It is true that it can be manifested in some way by outcries or gestures, and then by language which assigns to certain sounds a determined and conventional meaning. But these manifestations of consciousness are only a poor translation of it to the spatio-temporal world. They may perhaps suffice to show me that other consciousnesses are present around me, but only on condition that I am capable of interpreting this conduct as the expression of a consciousness. And this evidently supposes a previous knowledge of my own consciousness.

I am, therefore, forced to acquire a knowledge of *my own consciousness*. Evidently I cannot observe it as I might observe an "object" placed "before" me. There can be question then only of a return on myself, of a "reflection" of my knowledge on itself. Now, is such a thing possible? Yes, it is because it actually exists. I am aware of precisely this sort of a process. I know that I know. I know myself as knowing, at the very moment when I know. My knowledge is in some way "transparent" to itself. There is then *some* possibility that I may be able to describe it and to analyse it, since I have the power of studying it from within at the very moment when it is taking place. In brief, I can "reflect" on my own acts of knowledge.

This power of reflection provides epistemological analysis with an efficient instrument. This reflection is carried out by means of the *reflective method,* that is, attentive examination on the part of consciousness to see clearly what is taking place in itself, in order to draw from this examination every conclusion which may serve to determine the nature, conditions, finality and validity of knowledge.

In what exactly does this reflection consist? What value does it have? The answers to these questions can only be given by epistemology itself. For the present, it is enough for me to know that epistemology is possible *at least in a certain measure,* and that it is possible by means of reflection. An approach to epistemology is thus opened to me. I shall see later how far this road can lead.

2. *A Personal Method.* Science makes universal claims. The chemist claims that he can formulate laws which not

only hold for all intellects (for all chemists), but which also describe the conduct of all the bodies of a given class, not merely the conduct of some specimens that he has studied in his laboratory. We can call this twofold universality of science *subjective* universality (science is common to all subjects, or to all scientists) and *objective* universality (science formulates general laws which hold for all the objects of a given class). Now, can the philosopher who studies cognition make any similar claims?

First of all, we have to distinguish carefully between the question of the subjective universality of science and the question of its objective universality, for these are two different problems.

As far as subjective universality is concerned, the position of the philosopher seems, at first sight, to be much worse than that of the scientist. For the same particle of matter (for example, a given drop of mercury) can be observed by all the chemists in the world, whereas, as we have just seen, my knowledge can be properly known only by myself. Thus on the one hand, it seems that science can be universal, and common to all scientists, because the object studied is within the reach of all, while on the other hand, it seems that philosophical knowledge must remain something strictly individual.

In reality, the difference between these cases is only accidental. All genuine scientific knowledge is at the same time individual and universal, personal and impersonal. To explain this we must for the time being anticipate something which will be shown later. There should be no objection raised to this, because it is simply a question of setting aside a preliminary objection, of clearing up a possible misunderstanding, and not yet of properly constructing an epistemology.

All scientific knowledge is essentially *personal*, and as such incommunicable. Chemical "science" properly exists only in the mind of the chemist. It exists in chemistry books only in the form of symbols, in a potential state, and only an intellect capable of interpreting these symbols can reconstruct it. In the same way but to an even greater degree, philosophical reflection exists in the mind of the philosopher and not outside. Philosophical work is eminently personal and incommunicable. Each one does it on his own account and lives it in himself. We have said "to an even greater degree," because the knowledge of the scientist generally concerns those aspects of things which are controllable, and objects which everyone can easily observe. But the knowledge of the philosopher concerns essentially his own consciousness and those characteristics of the real which go beyond sensory perception as such and even beyond instruments. "Communication" between scientists is, therefore, relatively easy, while language offers to the philosopher only a very imperfect instrument for the expression of his inner vision.

On the other hand, all scientific knowledge is *universal* because it is expressed in true judgments, and a judgment that is true, is true for everyone and for every consciousness. Hence supposing that the analysis of my knowledge allows me to formulate this true judgment, "A human consciousness (mine) knows a corporeal reality," this judgment will be true for everyone, even if, in fact, no one but myself thinks of formulating it or is able to formulate it. Similarly, the judgment of the chemist, "Water (which I have observed) boils under certain conditions," is true for everyone. It is understood, of course, that for this universality of scientific knowledge to be *realized,* the problem of communication of thought (the problem of language) must be accepted as solved.

Let us pass on now to *objective universality.* If we consider the object which is known, can we again say that scientific knowledge has a universal value? Can the chemist say, *"All* water boils under certain conditions"? Can the epistemologist say, *"Every* human consciousness knows corporeal reality"? Or even, *"All my acts* of knowledge have (and will have in the future) the characteristics of the act I am analyzing at this time"? Questions of this sort raise the problem of induction and cannot be answered here. But this answer is not absolutely essential now, for at the start of epistemology we can be content with a purely *hypothetical universality.* As we shall see, epistemology can be summed up as the description and critique of a complete act of human knowledge, stripped down to its essential or component elements. The conclusions of epistemology will have the following provisional value: the conclusions will hold for my other acts of knowledge and for another consciousness, to the degree in which my other acts of knowledge are constituted like this act, and to the degree in which any other consciousness is constituted like mine.

The *verification* of this hypothesis will raise new problems. When these problems concern my own acts, they will be easy to solve. When these problems concern another consciousness, the solution will be more difficult. If by any chance my conscious life discloses to me in the future acts of knowledge which do not fit the description of the act which served to construct my epistemology, then all the work will have to be done again for these novel acts. In the same way, if some one of my readers, upon analyzing his own consciousness, fails to find the distinctive elements that I describe on the basis of my own personal experience, then he will have no other alternative than to construct an epistemology for himself which fits his own condition.

In brief, then, the study of my knowledge is a personal

work. It does not make any universal claims beforehand. The results of this study will tell me how far any claims of that sort can be justified.

3. *An Interrogative Method*. My consciousness is filled with all the knowledge that I have acquired up to the present time, with all the convictions and opinions which go to make up the educated adult's "picture of the world." How can we unravel this confused tangle? How can we distinguish the primitive elements in it from later constructions, primary data from subsequent elaborations, the stable from the shifting, the solid from the fragile, the essential from the accidental? Shall I attempt to go back over the course of my conscious life, to reach its source in the past, and to live once again the *historical genesis* of all the various parts of my knowledge? It is clear that this method would offer me no guarantee at all. The memories of my childhood are, for the most part, confused and uncertain; and I am aware that I can not write the story of my conscious life from its beginnings with any chance of the account being exact and complete.

Shall I try to get a fully conscious experience of the *actual genesis* of an act of knowledge, or of the way in which I pass from unconsciousness to consciousness when, for example, I awake from sleep? This would be merely a new illusion, because I cannot obviously know the absence of knowledge as such. As soon as I begin to know, knowledge is already constituted, and the "passage" from unconsciousness to consciousness has already been made. The most I can do is to observe the discovery of a new object, or the progress of knowledge as it becomes more and more precise, more and more clear. Besides, the acquiring of new acts of knowledge and the perfecting of previous acts of knowledge are only episodes in my conscious life which blend immediately with the whole content of that life. Thus it is always the same complex situation which I must try to unravel.

If I had some direct intuition of the essence of cognition, or of knowledge realized in its most perfect state, then this intuition could serve as a standard or guide in analyzing my human knowledge. But it is clear that I do not have access to anything of the sort. There is only one way to carry out my inquiry, and that is to start from my actual knowledge, with all its complications and uncertainties, and with all its common sense convictions and thought habits. To guarantee a solid starting point for our theory of knowledge, I must find a *method of analysis,* or *discernment,* which will enable me to dissociate in my actual knowledge what is solid from what is fragile, what is elaborated from what are real data, what is given contingently from what is given as a necessary component of every modality of my knowledge.

The method of analysis which we are seeking has been, in fact, practiced from the beginning of philosophical reflection. It was already implied in the Socratic irony; it found explicit application in the works of Plato and Aristotle, and since that time it has become a classical procedure of scientific inquiry. It is the *interrogative method* or the *methodic doubt.*[5]

When faced with the task of solving a problem or constructing a science, Aristotle always began by examining the opinions commonly accepted by the people and by the philosophers who had preceded him. He subjects these opinions to a process of discussion, doubt and judgment. He notes

5. In the first edition of this work this method was called the critical method. We have now dropped this expression in order to avoid the danger of confusing this method with that proper to critical epistemology, or with critique as the term is ordinarily understood since Kant (the study of the value of knowledge).

the questions suggested by this discussion and tries to gather from the discussion solid elements which will serve as materials for the solution. In a celebrated passage of the *Metaphysics*, Aristotle states that, at the start of the most universal science, we must undertake a very careful analysis of all the difficulties that the study of being as being will suggest.

Scholasticism made constant use of this method of doubt. It was crystallized especially in the celebrated method of *sic et non*, the opposition of *pro* and *contra*. The thinkers of the Middle Ages began all their discussions and almost all their inquiries in this way. In his *Commentary on the Metaphysics of Aristotle*, St. Thomas discusses the function which the doubt can have as an introduction to science, and he requires at the very start of the science of being a "universalis dubitatio de veritate."

Descartes dramatized the scientific doubt. In reality, the scientific doubt is a *methodical* doubt, which can therefore be really universal without any difficulty, since it does not imply in any way even a provisional abandonment of moral and religious convictions. Besides, the scientific doubt can be *real* in a number of cases, since a number of problems are really debatable or even insoluble.[6]

In the field of epistemology, the interrogative method will consist of placing in doubt the statements of common sense or the spontaneous convictions of my consciousness. Certain of these convictions will not be able to stand up under criticism at all; others will appear to be more or less uncertain; still others perhaps will resist every attempt to shake them. On this basis we can distinguish and classify the elements of my

6. We shall see that the doubt cannot be universally real, for the doubt encounters first evidences that consciousness cannot contradict. See J. Maritain, *Distinguer pour unir*, pp. 150-153.

consciousness. Perhaps this classification will enable me to determine the conditions which make up this consciousness.

By the "conditions which make up this consciousness" we do not mean the state of my consciousness at its first awakening in my early childhood. At the present time I am not interested in knowing what materials I could have used to construct an epistemology when I was six months old. Furthermore, it could be that my consciousness was only imperfectly formed at that time, either because my physiological development was inadequate, or because of lack of practice and experience, or because of lack of reflection. I want to know what actually constitutes my consciousness at the present time, what elements are essential and indispensable in the sense that without them I would have no consciousness, or one of a different nature.[7]

Let it be said once again that we do not have to decide beforehand what potentialities are latent in the method of doubt or the methodic doubt. The very use of the method ought to reveal its fertility.

7. On the method of doubt, see D. Mercier, *Critériologie générale*, 8th ed., (Louvain, 1923), pp. 54-91, 114-124; M. D. Roland-Gosselin, *Essai d'une étude critique de la connaissance* (Paris, 1932), pp. 14-18; L. Noël, *Le réalisme immédiat*, pp. 97-103, 134-146; É. Gilson, *Réalisme thomiste*, pp. 50-68; L. Noël, "Le réalisme critique et le bon désaccord," in *Revue Néoscolastique de Philosophie* (1940), pp. 47-54.

CHAPTER III

DISCUSSION OF THE CLAIMS OF COMMON SENSE

To FIND the starting point of epistemology each person must attempt a reflective examination of his own consciousness as it is before any scientific study of knowledge has been made. But it is clear that this "prescientific" condition will vary from one person to another, depending on their natural dispositions, their education and their previous experiences. As the present description aims at helping the reader to carry out this personal examination for himself, we shall take as our example a human consciousness which has received a minimum of scientific or philosophical training. In short, we shall take the consciousness of the average man, of the "man in the street."

§ 1. The Claims of Common Sense

What is roughly the conception of the world which this sort of man will have? We can easily find out by observing the way in which ordinary people speak.

1. The man in the street is aware of his own individuality. His own person holds first place in his cares and interests. For him, the "self" means, first of all, his own body with its needs, its appetites and its dislikes. If we were to ask him whether he is certain that he has a body which possesses organs of sight, hearing, touch, and so forth, he would find the question absurd. Nevertheless he never says, "I am a body," but always, "I have a body." This seems to imply that he sees a distinction between the "I" and the "body," at

least in a confused way. Again, if this same man in the street believes in the existence of the soul, he will not say, "I am a soul," but, "I have a soul." It seems to follow, then, that this man looks upon himself as an "*I*," which "possesses" a body and a soul. All this clearly implies a claim to have a certain *knowledge of himself*, of his own nature, capacities, and inclinations. This knowledge also embraces his past through his *memory*. He remembers his own history, he recalls going through a certain evolution, but he is sure that he has remained himself throughout that evolution.

2. The man in the street knows many other things besides himself. By means of his "five" senses he is in contact with the *external world*, which is made up of a multitude of persons, animals, plants, and inanimate things. By means of his senses, he perceives all these beings with their characteristic properties, their forms, colors, movements, parts, and the sounds which they make. In these respects he does not believe himself too superior to the animals, for animals appear to have the same kind of knowledge in a more or less developed state (often more developed than in man). Certain animals seem to have very remarkable instincts and marvelous cunning. Some appear to be fairly "intelligent." But when all is said and done, men are far more intelligent than animals. The fertility of human intelligence is shown in all the products of civilization: buildings, works of art, machines, books, artistic life. The man in the street believes that he is "intelligent." For him, that means being able to do a certain number of things, such as reading, writing, counting, solving problems, understanding a mechanism, explaining "why" there is an eclipse of the sun, "how" clouds are formed, "how" one makes paper, "why" the world exists, and so forth. So, the man in the street believes that he can know the *nature*, or the

characteristic properties of a number of things. He can distinguish iron from copper, marble from granite, wood from horn, the beech tree from the oak tree, the cat from the dog, the motor of an automobile from the mechanism of a clock, planets from stars, the cube from the cylinder. . . . Furthermore, he possesses dictionaries which give him the "definition" of every word, and the definitions of all the things to which these words apply.

3. The man in the street knows that his own personal experience is very limited, and he admits that great numbers of things exist which he himself has never seen. Here he profits by the *experiences of others*. He believes the historians, the geographers, the astronomers, the physicists, who tell him of the existence of an infinite number of different objects and events. Frequently he will believe in people who claim to have had more extraordinary experiences, such as diviners, clairvoyants, mediums, prophets and mystics. He will make use of *reasoning* to convince himself that certain things exist. He will admit that certain geological remains show the existence of a prehistoric humanity. He will admit that the resemblance between two languages can show their kinship or their common origin. He will admit that we can prove the existence of God starting from the marvelous order of nature. He will admit that a miracle shows a divine intervention in the world.

4. The man in the street has certain "principles." The experience of life has taught him how to evaluate men and events. He distinguishes what is good from what is evil, what is useful from what is harmful, what is timely from what is untimely, what is correct from what is incorrect. So, for example, a man will condemn capitalism and approve universal suffrage and the democratic form of government. He will

preach free trade and universal disarmament. He believes that homicide is an evil and compassion a virtue. He will admit that the whole is greater than the part, that 6×8 always equals 48.

5. Sometimes it happens that the man in the street is mistaken, and he is aware of this. He had faith in a certain friendship, and he was deceived. He expected dictators to provide order and peace, and he was misled. For a long time he confused Oceania and Australia. At times his short-sightedness has played him mean tricks. He has had tragic dreams and charming dreams, all of which disappeared before commonplace reality. His memory is not always trustworthy, and he sometimes makes a mistake about even his own birthday. However, these experiences have not made him a sceptic, but only more prudent, less sure of himself, and less absolute in his affirmations. In brief, the man in the street would readily agree to the following formulae, which attempt to sum up his elementary epistemology.

First, *man is a knowing subject*. This subject exists permanently, but he does not always know (for example, when he sleeps or has fainting spells). He knows by means of his sense organs, his imagination, his memory and his intelligence.

Secondly, *confronting the subject are objects which are known*. The knowing subject knows directly the corporeal world which surrounds him. He knows himself. He knows in an indirect way other corporeal things and certain realities that are called "non-corporeal" (such as the soul, God, spirits), also certain general truths or principles.

Thirdly, *it is possible to have discrepancy between knowledge and its object*. This is called error.

§ 2. *The Objections of Common Sense*

Let us see now how much the application of the methodic doubt can shake the idea of the world which the "man in the street" possesses.

1. When the man in the street tells us that he sometimes makes mistakes, he himself gives us the first sign of a weakness in the structure of his knowledge. What is *error*? How is it possible? What is truth, of which error seems to be the privation? I am aware that at times I have been mistaken. But it may be that I am mistaken more often than I think. It may be that I am always mistaken, at least in some measure. How can I know whether I am mistaken? How can I distinguish truth from error? May not knowledge be always an illusion, at least in part?

Perhaps the *problem of error* is not the basic problem of epistemology. This point will be cleared up later, and at the present time it makes little difference. But the *fact of error* has played a capital role in the history of the theory of knowledge, because it has developed men's critical sense. Error is a fact which is both disturbing and encouraging. On the one hand, the fact that I am aware of having, at times, erred causes fear that I may always be in error. But, on the other hand, the fact that I do at times become aware of my errors means that there is some way of distinguishing the true from the false.

However that may be, let us take up some questions which are less general and more precise. Let us examine more closely the different spheres of knowledge mentioned by the man in the street. We may start with those which are furthest removed from experience and which seem to be more vulnerable to attack.

2. First of all, there is the sphere of *principles*. Ordinarily it is the easiest thing in the world to undermine a principle either by opposing a contrary principle to it, or by asking some artful "whys." It is easy to show the merits of democracy and the excellence of liberty against the proponent of dictatorship. Or we can shake his beliefs in a direct fashion by asking some innocent questions: Why is a dictatorship better than a liberal government? Does history show many "good" dictatorships? What can we do if the dictator abuses his power? Does dictatorship suppress favoritism? Does it do away with embezzlement, secret accusations, injustices, wars?

However, there are some principles which seem to be considerably more solid. For example, I say: "Homicide is an evil." It would seem paradoxical, indeed, to hold that homicide is a good. Men agree more easily on this principle than on the superiority of a dictatorship. But even so this kind of principle must be made more precise and must be demonstrated. First it must be made *more precise*. Is homicide always an evil in every circumstance? Or is it licit to kill an unjust aggressor, the enemy in a just war, the criminal who is condemned to death by a legal court? The principle should be *demonstrated* or *established*. Why is the act of killing a man evil, as a rule? Why should the life of my neighbor be respected? Why is that life a good? What is a good? Why must I respect a good? Why *should* I do this rather than that? Am I obligated? In short, even when the principles seem undeniable, they ordinarily stem from other more fundamental principles through the intervention of a longer or shorter series of intermediary propositions or principles. So, we can ask what each of these intermediaries is worth. We can also ask what the connection between them is worth, and what guarantees the operation by which we go from one to the other.

Finally, certain principles seem to be completely fundamental or primary. We can scarcely reduce them in turn to principles which would be more simple. They seem to impose themselves. "The whole is greater than the part." "6 x 8 = 48." "One straight line and only one can be drawn between two points." What do such principles mean? Where do they come from? What value do they have? Are they really primary, and in what sense are they so? Are they based on experience, or are they independent of it? History, as we shall see, shows us an unending conflict between the Platonic idealist view, which holds that the transcendent world of Ideas is independent of experience, and the Aristotelian empiricist view which bases the principles on experience.

3. Let us now look at the realities which are known in an *indirect way*. If they are known by means of reasoning (existence of God, the existence of prehistoric man, and so forth) we find ourselves faced with the problems which we have already raised. What is the value of the principles which we use in such reasonings? What is the value of reasoning itself, that is, of the operation by which I link up my judgments? If these realities are known by appealing to the experience of other people, then a new problem arises. What is the value of *testimony*? Under what conditions does it have value? How can we measure its value? Men have deceived me at times, whether deliberately or not. May it not be that they always do so? The problem of error here involves two unknown factors: first, the knowledge of the person who testifies, and secondly, the knowledge of the one who accepts and interprets that testimony.

4. Then we have instances of *immediate* knowledge. Will

they escape all doubt? The man in the street sees the exterior world through his "five" senses. Is their testimony infallible? Certain perplexing experiences, as old as humanity itself, raise doubts about that point. A certain sick person, for example, may find tasty meats insipid. Another who is feverish thinks that the temperature is low when it is actually above seventy degrees. Another hears a continual buzzing which no one around him hears. A ruler which is partially immersed in water seems to me to be bent, when it really is straight. A gray disk appears to me to be pinkish, when placed on a green background. A certain small-sized body seems to me to be much heavier than another larger body, when in reality the weight is the same. What can we say about certain experiences which are even more perplexing? There are, frequently, "nocturnal visions," dreams, which mislead us to the extent of causing anguish and may even cause the sleeper to break into a sweat. What can we say about the morbid states of hallucinations, delirium, hysteria, in which consciousness seems to escape almost completely from the influence of "reality"?

The man in the street believes that he is *intelligent*, and therefore claims to go far beyond the animal in this respect. He believes that he can comprehend what he sees, that he can discover the relations that the perceived objects have among themselves (thus "solving problems" and explaining the "why" of things). In this way he believes that he will finally come to know the "nature" of things. What should be said about these claims? If it is a question of things of which he himself is the author, well and good. If he has made a clock, he can take it apart; he can know the how, the why, the nature, the "quiddity" of it. But what about the rest? Doubtless he can get to know the more apparent properties of objects, the "sensible" properties of iron and copper, of a cat and of a dog; but to what extent do these reveal the "nature," the real "how" and "why" of the objects? The cat can be "taken apart" as the clock can, but if after doing that we try to put it together again we find that the cat is no longer a complete unit, no longer "lives." The piece of copper is far more difficult to "take apart." Only the scientists have succeeded to some extent in doing that, as we shall soon see. All that the man in the street can do is to reduce it to powder or to melt it, but this does not reveal the "nature" of the copper to him any more clearly.

5. Finally, the man in the street is faced with the *mystery of himself*. He claims to know himself and to be able to preserve his past experiences in the treasury of his memory. But we may ask, first of all, what value memory has, since it is so often undependable. To what extent can man depend on it, as a source of knowledge and as a witness of the past? As for the present, how can we unravel the often confused tangle of perceptions, images, sentiments, passions, judgments and volitions which fill the consciousness of the man in the street? Can the latter say that all these are clear for him? How can we clarify the vague domain that we call the "inner life"? What is the "nature" of the common root source of all these states of consciousness? Is it the body, or is it some hidden organ of the body, such as the brain, the heart, or the nervous system? Is it something different from the body, something that is more subtle, the "spirit," the "soul," or the "self"? Is it the body and the soul taken together, the "living body"? What does the mental construct, "man," mean? Does it really show a "nature," a "how," a "why"?

§ 3. *The Objections of the Scientist*

Up to this point our discussion with the "man in the street" has remained on the level of common sense, that is, on his own level. Now let us listen to what the scientist has to tell us about the latest discoveries of physics and experimental psychology.

1. In the field of psychology, the scientist's description of the way in which his "subjects" react in the laboratory is, at first sight, rather baffling. The organs of perception are more numerous, more varied and infinitely more complex than the man in the street suspects. We are now told that certain perceptions like those of space, relief, depth—in short, perceptions of the third dimension—are by no means as simple as they may appear.

Perceptions obey numerous laws, such as the laws of structure. In other words, in his perceptions the subject manifests certain constant tendencies: for example, the tendency to synthesize the elements which occupy his field of perception at the same time; the tendency to fix his attention on the whole rather than on parts; his actual perception is influenced by previous perceptions, by expectation, by desire, by fear and so forth. Other parts of psychology which deal with the laws of association, memorization and learning, give us a very new outlook on the biological and physical conduct of man as a knower, and so they also give us new insights into the complex conditions under which human knowledge is achieved.

2. In the domain of physics also, the scientist describes for us a world unsuspected. His observational procedures enable him not only to measure all the phenomena which the senses perceive (that is, to reduce them to differences of size and

number), but also to reach phenomena on the scale of the "infinitely small" and "infinitely large" (that is, phenomena far beyond the limits of ordinary perception). Seen in this new light, the corporeal world takes on an aspect very different from that which is the result of natural perception. It is seen to be a fantastic whirlpool of particles whose physical properties are now described by means of concepts which are more and more removed from our imaginative representations. And this picture of a physical world, so "different" from the world of our ordinary perceptions, immediately raises many problems. What relation is to be established between these two worlds? What is the value of my "natural" knowledge of the corporeal world? What is the value of my "scientific" knowledge of the same world? To what degree is my "natural" picture of the world dependent on biological and psychological factors? Does "scientific" knowledge escape these conditions? And, on the other hand, to what extent do physical laws condition and perhaps disturb, or at least complicate, the play of our perceptions? What influence, for example, do the laws of the propagation of light have in the sphere of visual perception?

We can easily see how the more exacting and more developed study of the world of phenomena made by the positive sciences can bring out numerous difficulties regarding knowledge which almost completely escape common sense. These difficulties concern especially our knowledge of the corporeal world, and the biological conditions entailed by that knowledge in the knowing subject. This investigation could easily be extended in other directions, into physiology, chemistry, astronomy, and so forth.

§ 4. *The Objections of the Philosopher*

There is also the philosopher. "Philosopher" here means the man who claims to get to the bottom of things, as far as that is possible. He claims that he does not neglect any of the "whys" which can be asked. His critique will deal the final blow to the theory built up by the man in the street; it will sum up in itself all the difficulties so far encountered, and its doubt will penetrate to the very heart of the mystery of knowledge.

The critique of the philosopher first of all embraces all the doubts we have listed. What is the value of reasoning? of principles? of the testimony of others? of my perceptions? of my ideas? All these questions are only variants of a question which is still more basic, namely, What is the value of my knowledge? And this question in turn rests upon an even more primary question, What precisely is "knowledge"?

Here doubt penetrates to the core of my every cognition; it affects "knowing" as such. It affects the fundamental claim of common sense, the claim to be a "subject" which, barring some accident, is able to "know," that is—to possess, to penetrate and to understand objects which are distinct from itself; the claim to be a subject which is, at the same time, capable of "knowing itself;" in brief, the claim to be able to get "true" knowledge (knowledge which conforms to the object known) which is recognized as such. Now, this basic claim gives rise to objections which are just as basic.

1. Is cognition a matter of "acting" or of "submitting," of "producing" or of "assimilating," of "giving" or of "receiving"? Or is it something altogether different? Is there a difference between "to know" and to "know oneself"? Does cognition consist in anything more than feeling oneself alive

and subject to change? Is it anything more than a biological state, a factor in the conduct of a living being?

To what degree are the known object and the knowing subject distinct? How can I possess in myself an object distinct from me, or other than myself? Is it not a contradiction in terms to speak of knowing an object which is exterior to the subject? Must we not then either admit that there is no *external* object, but only an object which is *interior* to the subject (a certain "content of consciousness"), or say that there are two objects: the object in itself (the external object) and the known object (the internal), which is a simple "representation" of the first? But, in that case, how can we pass from one to the other? How can I be sure of the existence of the object in itself? Is it not wrong to call it "the object," if it is "unknowable"? Or rather is it not wrong to speak of it at all?

2. If it is wrong for me to talk about an unknowable, I am reduced to the known object, "interior" to consciousness. May we not suppose that objects will have "reality" only in the subject, and through the subject? Does not this apparent independence of "things" merely mask a basic dependence? This may not be a dependence on the fragile and mortal "subject" that I am, for I am (myself and my body) only a "thinking reed." But perhaps there is a dependence on a more basic Subject, common to all the apparent subjects. In this case, cognition would be (or at least would imply) "action," "production," a "positing" of the object by the Subject.

3. But is it not rather naive to proclaim offhand that this subject, to which we claim to reduce everything else, is the source of all light and the font of intelligibility? For, first of all, can the subject really "know himself"? The wisdom of

mankind declares "nemo judex in propria causa." What can be more obscure than consciousness bent back on itself and isolated from other things? "I would know nothing of myself, I would not know that I know and I would not know that I exist, if the evidence from without did not arouse me to consciousness of myself and of my acts." [1] Furthermore, does this knowing subject necessarily obtrude itself as something distinct from the "objects"? Is it not merely one object among other objects? Is not knowledge merely an epiphenomenon, that is, an accompanying phenomenon, a superficial condition of the nervous system, somewhat like the presence of a magnetic field? Are human brains anything more than cells which secrete images, or antennae which intercept waves?

4. What happens to the value of cognition in the face of this avalanche of doubts? What happens to the distinction between the true and the false, between truth and error? Does the distinction retain any meaning at all? Nevertheless, when I pick up my neighbor's hat instead of my own, when I dream of falling into a river, when I drink white lime water instead of milk, when I give someone a ten instead of a one-dollar bill, in such cases the expression "I have been mistaken" certainly has a very definite sense.

This is doubtless true, but the question still remains whether the distinction between truth and error retains the meaning popularly given to it, as the conformity or nonconformity of subject to the object, of the knower to the known. Or should we not rather define truth as a *social* value (meaning that which is *accepted* in certain circles, or that which is *declared* true by the Minister of Propaganda, or

---

1. A. D. Sertillanges, *Les grandes thèses de la philosophie thomiste*, Bibliothèque catholique des sciences religieuses, 52 (Paris, 1928), p. 13.

that which is *useful* to a given society or nation)? Or perhaps we should rather define truth as a *biological* value
(meaning that which is *useful* or *agreeable* to the subject).
If we still insist on retaining something of the popular conception of truth, in what will this conformity of the knower
with the thing known consist? Will it be an identity, or a
resemblance, or an approximation? Can we appraise it, measure it, control it? Will it be in the object or in the subject?
What will be the norm of truth?

Here we have reached rock bottom. Every stone in the
edifice has been taken from its place and provisionally set
aside for the purpose of examination. We can see immediately a first result of the universal methodic doubt: It gives
us valuable hints on the method we must follow in studying
knowledge, and it rules out in advance certain ways which
would end only in blind alleys.

(a) First of all, it becomes clear that the question of the
value of my knowledge depends on other questions which are
more fundamental, questions concerning the nature and purposiveness of this knowledge. It is doubt about these latter
points which causes doubt regarding the value of knowledge.
Thus, to solve the problem of the value of knowledge, we
must first discover how knowledge is constituted and what is
the goal at which it aims.

(b) Our discussion of the beliefs of common sense allows
us to distinguish the *actual knowledge* of an *immediately
given object* from all indirect knowledge. In indirect knowledge, a number of factors distinct from the immediate presence of the object intervene, for example, memory, the
testimony of others, reasoning, principles. The epistemological analysis must first consider the most simple and fundamental case, that of actual and direct knowledge. We are

constantly talking about objects which are not given to us immediately. Thus, for instance, oxygen is an object which became known only after a series of laborious experiments and research enabled chemists to discover and define it by a series of properties. If we consider the planets as distinguished from the stars, they are not immediate data either; they are rather the result of scientific study. All such instances should be set aside at the beginning of epistemology.

(c) Most of the elements immediately present to my consciousness are evidently *contingent* in the sense that they can disappear without destroying consciousness itself. Thus, a given landscape can disappear completely from my field of consciousness, without my consciousness ceasing to exist. On the other hand, there are other elements which are indispensable in the make-up of my consciousness; what they are in general will become quite clear at the end of this discussion. But evidently there can be no question about the fundamental reality of consciousness itself, since it is the *sine qua non* of any discussion at all. Two irreducible poles stand out in consciousness, the *subject* and the *object*. Each has its own characteristics, and each constitutes a *complexity* which must be so simplified that the basic structure of consciousness will be set in bold relief. The *purposiveness* which belongs to knowledge will then follow naturally from this structure, and thus we shall immediately obtain a precise statement of the critical problem. This then is the general direction which descriptive epistemology will take; how the critical problem will tie in with its conclusions will become clear as we proceed.

Chapter IV

HISTORICAL SURVEY

Before concluding this introductory section, we must consider a final question. It also concerns a point of general method. What use may we make of history? How much attention ought we to pay to the problems which have been raised concerning knowledge in the course of time, and the solutions proposed to them?

The most elementary sort of common sense tells us that we ought to profit by the efforts and experiences of the past. By so doing we may gain an enormous amount of time. We shall avoid detours and blind alleys. The many different aspects which these problems have will be drawn to our attention. On the other hand, the great variety of answers proposed in the past will protect us from getting only a one-sided acquaintance which might cause distortion in judgment and many insidious prejudices. A brief historical survey of the theory of knowledge throughout the ages will serve as a very useful mental preparation for work in epistemology. The survey will be purely descriptive, not critical, because criticism would imply that a solution had already been obtained. Surveys of this kind can be found in good textbooks on the history of philosophy. Readers who are sufficiently trained can read very profitably the well-known work of J. Maréchal, S.J., *Le point de départ de la métaphysique: Leçons sur le développement historique et théorique du problème de la connaissance*.[1] The following pages will give a brief historical

1. Part I, *De l'antiquité à la fin du moyen âge: la critique ancienne de la connaissance*.

survey of the principal problems and the most characteristic
answers given to them.

§ 1. The First Period

A first period of reflection on human knowledge extends
from the origins of philosophy down to the time of Aristotle.

The first thinkers of Greece, the so-called "physiologists,"
did not concern themselves with knowledge as such, nor with
the knowing subject. Their attention was directed rather to
the object, that is, to nature, whose secret they tried to discover. Soon, however, the paradoxes which nature manifests
gave rise to interpretations regarding the inner constitution
of the universe that were radically opposed. Thus, Heraclitus
saw only multiplicity and movement in reality, while Parmenides and Zeno ignored becoming and the multiple in
favor of the identical and unchangeable. Both these views
disregarded certain spontaneous affirmations of common sense,
and the calm dogmatism of the first cosmologists gave place
to a more reflective and more critical attitude.[2]

A more radical reaction to dogmatism soon developed in
the *scepticism* of the sophists. Certitude's first crisis was apparently provoked by the multiplication of cosmological systems, and especially by the irreducible oppositions that existed

---

Part II, *Le confiit du rationalisme et de l'empirisme dans la philosophie mod-
erne avant Kant.*

Part III, *La critique de Kant.*

Part IV, *Le système idéaliste chez Kant et les postkantiens.*

Part V, *Le Thomisme devant la philosophie critique,* is an attempt to go beyond Kantianism with the help of the principles of Thomism. Because of the
death of Father Maréchal, which occurred at Louvain on December 11, 1944,
Part VI, which was devoted to contemporary epistemologies, will not appear.

2. *Dogmatism* is the attitude of one who does not bother to subject the spontaneous affirmations of his reason to any critical examination.

among the first attempts to solve the paradox of the one and the many. The absolute evolutionism of Heraclitus already implied a genuine *empiricism*, akin to *phenomenalism*,[3] because it did away with all objective unity and stability, and saw in the real only an everchanging flow of concrete and transient sensory data. The sophists went further in their denial of the intellect. They professed a universal *relativism*, ending in complete scepticism. Man is incapable of attaining absolute truth and certitude. No statement can be affirmed in absolute fashion, not even the first principle or principle of non-contradiction. Man is the measure of all things: the value of the true, the good, the beautiful depend on the judgment of each man.

The reaction against the empiricism of Heraclitus and the scepticism of the sophists was begun by Socrates. It reached its greatest force in Plato, who professed a *radical intellectualism* and laid the foundation for *ancient idealism*.[4] In fact, it is to Plato that we owe the discovery of the intelligence, for it was he who brought out fully the characteristics proper to thought, in opposition to those of sensation. But he pushed the disjunction of the sensible and the intelligible to extremes, and far from grounding intellection on sense experience he took intellection to be a sort of independent contemplation of the world of intelligibles or Ideas. These Ideas are eternal,

3. *Empiricism* is the doctrine which limits human knowledge to concrete experience, and ignores the role and value which general principles and universal concepts have. *Phenomenalism* is the doctrine which holds that the only objects of knowledge are "phenomena," that is, the objects of experience as they appear to our senses.
4. In a very general sense, we call *idealism* that philosophical tendency which reduces all genuine knowledge to thought, ideas, or intellectual activity, to the detriment of sensory experience. Ancient or Platonic idealism reduced science to an intellectual contemplation of the Ideas which were objectively present to the human mind.

necessary and unchangeable; they form a world which is in the highest sense real and perfect. Of it the corporeal and changing world is only a fleeting shadow. He solved the old paradox of the one and the many, the stable and the shifting, by juxtaposing two worlds—the world of Ideas which recalls the unchanging universe of Parmenides, and the material world which reminds us of the everflowing universe of Heraclitus.

Aristotle returned to a more balanced position, which shows more respect for the data of consciousness and tries to reconcile the partial truths in both empiricism and idealism. He constructed for the first time in history a genuine theory of knowledge, whose richness and depth explain its long-lasting success. We refer especially to the analyses of sensation, imagination and thought, in the *De Anima*, to the monumental intellectual construction represented by the *Organon*, and to the numerous studies concerning knowledge in the *Metaphysics*. Aristotle professed an *intellectualist and rational realism*, in which all the previous tendencies of Greek thought reappear in an harmonious unity. It formed the basis for a philosophical synthesis powerfully constructed by the intellect and solidly based on an all-embracing experience. In the epistemology of Aristotle we must especially emphasize his refutation of scepticism; his criticism of Platonic idealism and his decided return to *experience* in reaction to Platonism; his doctrine of *abstraction*, which safeguards the bond between thought and the real, while at the same time protecting the transcendence of the immaterial intellect with respect to the organic activity of sensation: his *moderate realism*, which affirms the objective apprehension of reality, but recognizes at the same time the inadequate character of conceptual knowledge, and guards against identifying the logical order and the real order; his doctrine of *analogy*, which allows him to go beyond the monism of Parmenides and makes it possible to know transcendent realities; finally, the penetrating studies in the *Organon* on the discursive activity of the human intelligence.

We shall not dwell any further here on the Aristotelian epistemology, for we shall meet its essential points again in Thomism.

§ 2. The Second Period

After the death of Aristotle, the Peripatetic school went into a rapid decline. On the whole, it tended toward a materialistic interpretation of his philosophy. For that matter, all the schools of the time entered a period of decadence, in which the fundamental problems of philosophy were neglected in favor of secondary questions that had more immediate interest and could be more easily treated.

This comparative eclipse of philosophical reflection was to allow philosophy to spring up again with renewed strength and to re-examine the eternal problems in a fresh light. In the domain of knowledge, the old paradoxes were to reappear, now with added nuances (materialism-spiritualism, empiricism-idealism, scepticism-dogmatism). And these were to prepare a way for a new expression of intellectualist realism, which would be richer and more profound.

Among the philosophies which depreciated human knowledge, we must list the materialist tendencies of several disciples of Aristotle, the materialism of the Epicureans and Stoics, and finally and especially the rebirth of scepticism which manifested itself from the third century before Christ (Pyrrho). This scepticism continued its solvent action to the end of the period of antiquity. In his youth, St. Augustine himself suffered a severe attack of scepticism under the influence of the New Academy.

But soon an intellectual reaction took place, and like every reaction it was excessive. Stoicism already marked a rebirth of *intellectualism*, both in its metaphysics and in its ethics. In certain respects the Stoic movement recalls the work of Socrates in the preceding period. Soon *radical intellectualism* returned under the aegis of Plato, in the vast movement of ideas known by the name of Neoplatonism. The most celebrated names in this movement are Philo, Plotinus, Porphyry, St. Augustine and the Pseudo-Dionysius.

The general tendencies of Neoplatonic epistemology are clear: a return to Platonic idealism, a distrust and disregard for the sensory, a tendency to mystical speculation. The deeper study of this doctrine and the comparison of this ancient idealism with the different forms of modern idealism are very illuminating. The literature written about 1930 to commemorate the fifteenth centenary of the death of St. Augustine (430) brought out the dominant traits of Augustinian Neoplatonism; his critique of scepticism leading to the celebrated "Si enim fallor, sum" (a striking anticipation of the "Cogito, ergo sum" of Descartes); his analyses of consciousness; his keen sense of the weakness of the human mind; his critique of ideas and the judgment, which tried to show that there was a transcendent object revealing itself in the qualities of eternity, unchangeability, necessity and universality possessed by the true judgment (the doctrine of the divine Ideas and Illumination). Augustinianism is, then, a *radical intellectualism* or an *idealism*. It opposes sensory experience and thought, and it tries to make thought as independent as possible of sense data.

Neoplatonism runs through all the medieval period—

among the Jews, the Arabs, and the Christians. In the Latin
world of the West, we find it in the system of John Scotus
Erigena (Dionysian Neoplatonism), in St. Anselm, in the
school of Chartres, in the Augustinian theological school, and
in general among all the defenders of exaggerated realism,
who give genera and species (or universal concepts) a greater
or lesser independence with respect to the individual realities
of sense experience. But very soon these Neoplatonic philosophies felt the influence of Aristotelianism, and this influence
continually grew. It is found in Porphyry; it is very important among the Jews (Avicebron) and the Arabs (Avicenna); by degrees it grows more marked among the Latins
(in the Victorines, William of Auvergne, Robert Greathead,
Alexander of Hales, St. Bonaventure, and all the Franciscan
School up to John Duns Scotus and Henry of Ghent). The
theories of knowledge found among the Augustinians toward
the end of the thirteenth century are often very subtle. At
times they show a remarkable critical sense, but this current
of ideas is still not too well known.

The revival of Aristotelian *realism* followed closely upon
this idealistic reaction. The beginning of the Christian era
witnessed numerous commentators on Aristotle (Alexander
of Aphrodisias, Porphyry, Themistius, Simplicius, John Phil-
oponus). Aristotelianism inspired the theology of St. John of
Damascus in the East, and penetrated into the West with the
work of Boethius. Among the Jews it reached its climax with
Moses Maimonides, and among the Arabs with Averroes. In
the Latin world the work of Peter Abelard marks the triumph
of Aristotelian realism in the twelfth century. However,
Aristotelianism reached its zenith in the thirteenth century
with Albert the Great, Siger of Brabant, and especially
Thomas Aquinas.

Undoubtedly Thomistic realism is the ripest and most perfect fruit of the moderate realism of Aristotle. An almost complete theory of knowledge is incorporated in the work of the Universal Doctor, and continued study of his work helps us to discover profound thoughts hidden under the hard crust of expressions which are at times naive, and often baffling. A superficial reading of St. Thomas has misled many people regarding the exact meaning of doctrines like abstraction, the immediate and infallible apprehension of "quiddities," the infallibility of the senses, and so forth.[5] We can list here briefly the principal positions taken by Thomas in the field of epistemology.

St. Thomas did not leave any synthetic statement of his philosophy, or even of his theory of knowledge. Consequently, we have to reconstruct his system with the help of fragmentary statements scattered through his philosophical and theological works. Furthermore, when he treats of knowledge, he almost always neglects properly *epistemological* problems for *ontological* problems. Finally, following the custom of his time, he does not draw a sufficiently clear distinction between the *conceptual* order and the *real* order. It is often necessary to make a transposition to determine the exact meaning of certain expressions in which he seems to be talking about the real order, but is in fact expressing only conceptual relations.[6] This state of affairs makes every at-

---

5. Some have gone so far as to confuse the Thomistic doctrine of knowledge with the epistemology of common sense, or "popular realism." But surely the doctrine of abstraction (*species sensibilis, phantasma, intellectus agens, species intelligibilis, verbum mentis*), and the doctrine of judgment, the doctrine of *reflection* and the theory of *truth*, the criticism of the *first principles* and the *universals*, the doctrine of quiddities and all the Thomistic logic, are not merely doctrines of common sense.

6. For example: "The form is individuated and multiplied by the matter." It is clear that this formula is concerned with real form and real matter. In de-

tempt to reconstruct the Thomistic epistemology a rather delicate undertaking.

But is not the very idea of an epistemology, and especially the idea of a critique of knowledge, completely foreign to the viewpoint of the medieval scholastics? Many philosophers of our own day are quite convinced that the Middle Ages never felt the need for a critical study, at least prior to the appearance of nominalism with William of Occam. Now, in reality, a complete lack of interest in this problem would be very surprising on the part of people trained in the doctrine of Aristotle and the thought of St. Augustine. They had inherited from Aristotle, in addition to the *Organon* (or "instrument" of knowledge), a critique of ancient scepticism, a theory of truth, the technique of doubting and discussing accepted opinions. Aristotle's commentators had raised the problem of the universals (that is, the problem of conceptual knowledge), and all the early Middle Ages had tried to solve it. For his part, Augustine, after freeing himself from the snares of scepticism and materialism, had handed on to the Middle Ages the affirmation of the primacy of consciousness, a new refutation of the absolute doubt, a critique of sensation, and a remarkable transposition of Platonic idealism. An examination of the philosophical writings of the Middle Ages completely confirms the surmise we have just made. If we limit ourselves only to St. Thomas, we can find in his work a num-

---

scribing this real relation of matter and form in the composite, St. Thomas apparently states that the matter intervenes to "multiply" and "individualize" a form which was previously "unique" and "universal." In reality it is the universal *concept* of the species which is participated in by multiple, numerically distinct individuals. However, it is true that the real foundation of these conceptual relations is found in the fact that the individuals are composed of matter and form, and not of subsistent forms.

ber of different elements which can be used to construct an epistemology.

In the first place, Thomas takes logic to be the first philosophical discipline. His opinion on the point is well known: "Oportet in addiscendo incipere a logica, non quia ipsa sit facilior scientiis ceteris; habet enim maximam difficultatem, cum sit de secundo intellectis; sed quia aliae scientiae ab ipsa dependent, in quantum ipsa docet modum procedendi in omnibus scientiis. Oportet enim primum scire modum scientiae quam scientiam ipsam, ut dicitur II° *Metaphysicae*." [7] Thus, logic should be first even in teaching in spite of the great difficulty of its object, because logic is the science of science, the theory of science, epistemology. Now, this logic of the Scholastics goes considerably beyond the limits of a simple formal logic; it includes the doctrine of the *universals* —that is, a critical evaluation of concepts, a vital part of critical epistemology. To form a complete Thomistic epistemology, we have only to group around the traditional logic accepted by Thomas a certain number of related themes which are scattered throughout his works. Among these complementary themes, we may mention different elements of psychological analysis (on apprehension, sense perception, abstract notions, judgment, reflection, and so forth); the universal doubt bearing on the notion of truth, and therefore on science in general; the theory of truth; the critique of the first principles and of quiddities. The epistemology thus constituted would, in fact, be only a broadening of logic as it was understood in the time of St. Thomas. [8]

7. *Super Boethium de Trinitate*, qu. 6, art. 1, ad 3ᵐ. See *In Metaphysicam*, II, lect. 5ᵃ, (ed. Cathala, no. 335).
8. For practice one could examine and discuss the theses of Father L. M. Régis, O.P., in his study "*La critique néothomiste, est-elle thomiste?*" in *Philosophie*,

What are the principal features of the moderate realism, or better the critical realism, that St. Thomas professed? First of all, it is a *realism,* and even an *immediate realism.* Thomas holds that human consciousness opens on a material world, existing independently of this consciousness. Through sensation, the knowing subject is in immediate contact with reality itself without any conscious intermediary. The intellect acts in close connection with sensation; the abstract concepts formed from the sensory data are authentic representations, even though not adequate, of the concrete reality, and the judgment which restores them to the real completes a knowledge of the real which is true and certain. The sense is infallible when grasping its own proper object; the intellect also is infallible when apprehending quiddities, and when it affirms the first principles, particularly when it affirms the principle of non-contradiction which is the supreme law of thought.

But this Thomistic realism is a *critical* realism. Knowledge is a human *activity;* even more, it is an *immanent* operation, which comes from the subject but remains in it. It exists for the subject, and it inevitably bears the mark of the subject: "Cognitum est in cognoscente *ad modum cognoscentis.*" This subjective stamp appears at every level of the act of cognition, in sensation, in the image, in the concept, in the judgment, and in all the reasoning activity. Sensation already implies a certain immaterial presence of the object in the subject; the image (or phantasm) is freed still further from the material conditions of the object, while the concept is not material in any way. The concept is abstract and universal; all the activity of the intellect is occupied with the universals. The

II (Ottawa, 1938), Studies and Researches published by the Dominican College of Ottawa.

judgment is, par excellence, the act of the subject; in it the subject adopts a position with respect to the object, and therefore error becomes possible on this level. Finally, all logical reasoning is the work of thought. It is, no doubt, not an arbitrary work, but still it is a personal and original work ruled by laws which are *sui generis*. It sets up a logical order which is quite different from the real order. We can easily see, then, that this doctrine involves a whole critique of knowledge.

§ 3. *The Third Period*

The short but brilliant period extending from the death of Thomas Aquinas (1274) to that of John Duns Scotus (1308) gives us a picture of intense philosophical activity, about which we still have much to learn. The conflict between Augustinian Platonism and Aristotelianism became acute in the field of knowledge. A number of first-rate thinkers took part in these discussions; some of them emphasized the opposition of the two doctrines, others attempted to reconcile them.

Before long the appearance of nominalism marked the beginning of a profound decadence in philosophical speculation and again upset that balance which had been reached for the second time in history in *intellectual realism*. The rapid eclipse of Thomism and Scotism by nominalism, which sprouted triumphantly in most of the universities in the fourteenth century, is far from fully explained. The fourteenth and fifteenth centuries remain the least-known eras in the history of philosophy. Perhaps this intellectual collapse was due more to the religious and social decay of the period than to philosophical causes, for in a disturbed and profligate society it is usually an easy negative philosophy that is successful. The blast of independence and reform which began to stir Europe at about this time likewise favored the *nominalist critique*. Among the intellectual causes of the decay of Scholasticism are usually mentioned the abuse of dialectics, degenerating into a sterile verbalism, and the steady crumbling of the ancient physics with which the philosophy of Aristotle seemed to be united. However that may be, this decay fortunately cleared the way once more for a new revival and caused a fresh examination of the problems of epistemology.

Dating from the old controversy over universals, a kind of nominalism had already been defended from the twelfth century. It was a reaction against exaggerated realism. But it soon gave place to a more balanced doctrine, the moderate realism of Peter Abelard. Genuine nominalism dates from the fourteenth century. It owed its success to the Franciscan, William of Occcam, the Venerable Inceptor, who introduced Scholasticism to the *via moderna*.[9] This nominalism was the natural corollary of the empiricism to which the masters of Oxford had long since tended: experience is the only authentic source of knowledge; it is the fruit of a sensible intuition and an intellectual intuition together; abstract and universal concepts are pure symbols, signs or labels, by which the intelligence groups and classifies individual objects; however, these symbols are not arbitrary or conventional, like the words of a language; they are natural signs "after the fashion of smoke naturally signifying fire." In short, Occam rejected any real or ontological likeness among things which might serve as a foundation for the universal signification of con-

9. *Nominalism* is the "doctrine which holds that there are no general *ideas*, but only general signs." (A. Lalande, *Vocabulaire de la Philosophie*, Vol. II, p. 517). Nominalism denies the objective value of the intellect's concepts and reduces them to names, that is, to symbols or signs which have a function analogous to the function of words in language.

cepts; or at least he denied that the human mind could really attain such a likeness. This anti-intellectualist attitude brought along in its train very unfortunate consequences in all branches of metaphysics, because when there was a question of knowing anything outside of experience, it led to a complete agnosticism.

Nominalism destroys irremediably the unity of human knowledge, because the intellect's universal concept can no longer be a faithful representation of an objective form given by sensibility. Only a very fragile bond is left between experience and conceptual thought. This point of view influenced all modern philosophies, for once the balance of realism was upset, it was inevitable that all the old paradoxes should reappear in new shapes and forms. A new crop of one-sided systems appears—pushing their biased views of the nature of human knowledge to ever greater extremes. Finally, the very excesses of these views caused a return for the third time to a more balanced view.

During the last centuries of the Middle Ages the anti-intellectualist current was dominant. It showed itself in a group of related trends such as scepticism, criticism, empiricism, all of which aimed at depreciating intellectual knowledge, and at questioning the possibility of a metempirical knowledge. This agnosticism was already apparent in Scotism. It received much greater emphasis in the nominalism of Occam. It becomes almost absolute in the phenomenalism of Nicholas of Autrecourt, and in the fideism of Nicholas of Cusa.[10] On the other hand, the progress made in scientific research gradually discredited the ancient physics, and caused

10. For *phenomenalism* see above, p. 53, n. 3. *Fideism* is the tendency to subordinate reason excessively to faith. In a more general sense, it is the tendency to trust in the blind inclinations of nature, rather than to seek truth in objective evidence.

a certain scepticism regarding the objective value of sensation. This progress was especially effective in sharpening men's curiosity to know the mysteries of nature, and in reinforcing the empiricist and positivist trends already present in the thirteenth century in Robert Greathead, Roger Bacon, Albert the Great, and others.[11]

The same currents of ideas continued in the sixteenth century. The scientific movement reached its high tide (Copernicus, Kepler, Galileo): scepticism appeared in the work of Montaigne, and in that of Charron; empiricism received its magna carta from Francis Bacon, and continues in various forms throughout all the modern period. We meet it again in the materialist nominalism of Hobbes, in the subtler nominalism of Locke, in the empiricist idealism of Berkeley, in the phenomenalism of Hume. English philosophy in the eighteenth century showed sceptical trends which were only the natural consequences of empiricism. Empiricism and scepticism soon passed over to France, where the eighteenth century is marked by the sensationalism [12] of Condillac and the ideological school, and by the even coarser materialism of the Encyclopedists.

Empiricism continued in the nineteenth century in numerous systems: positivism and scientism, materialism, utilitarianism and pragmatism, agnosticism, intuitionism, and neopositivism are the principal forms of this widespread empiricist movement. These doctrines differ a good deal in other respects but they share the common characteristics of empiricism, that is, the *appetite for concrete fact* and *distrust of the*

11. *Positivism* is the doctrine which reduces all scientific knowledge to a knowledge of facts. It is a form of empiricism.
12. *Sensationalism* is a doctrine which tends to reduce all knowledge to sensation. It is another form of empiricism.

mind's abstract constructions, or more generally distrust of all claims of the mind that are not controlled by immediate experience. As a frequent reaction to idealism and rationalism, empiricism emphasizes what it believes is one of the essential notes of our knowledge, namely, that knowledge is *receptive* or *assimilative.* Therefore, human thought cannot remain in a state of splendid isolation, but must be entirely subject to the real, which dominates its act in every respect, both in objective experience and in internal experience. But empiricism overlooks another aspect of man's knowledge, that is, the productivity peculiar to thought. This is why every empiricist affirmation, every agnostic or sceptical attitude, soon causes a spontaneous reaction on the part of the intellect. We must now examine this new reaction.

Platonism has always appealed to minds which are under the spell of the "intelligible world." We have met Platonism in the West in Augustinianism, in the Neoplatonist system of John Scotus Erigena, and in the school of Chartres. At the very moment when Aristotelian realism triumphed for the second time in the work of Thomas Aquinas, Neoplatonism was beginning a new growth. Thus, in spite of his connections with Aristotle and in spite of his attraction to the positive sciences, Albert the Great stands at the beginning of a genuine Neoplatonist movement which developed especially in the German province of the Order of Preachers. And, for his part, Henry Bate was strongly influenced by Neoplatonism. Neoplatonism runs through all the Renaissance with Nicholas of Cusa and a considerable number of thinkers of this epoch (Ficino, Bruno, Boehme, and others). However, this Neoplatonist current lacked originality and power, it showed itself incapable of successfully challenging the anti-intellectualist tendencies of those troubled times.

The credit for starting the modern intellectualist movement and for restoring the rights of thought belongs to Descartes. His philosophy represents a vigorous reaction against scepticism, eclecticism and empiricism. But Descartes' work was carried on under conditions that caused him to lead modern intellectualism in the direction of rationalism and idealism. First of all, his historical information was very limited. He was not acquainted with Aristotelian and Thomistic realism. Under the name of "Scholastics" he summarily lumps together Augustinians and Aristotelians, Scotists and nominalists. He knew only the decadent products of this blurred Scholasticism, and he seems to attribute to the Scholastics a crude sort of empiricism which is very close to sensationalism. In the second place, Descartes was strongly impressed by the discoveries of science. Physics had furnished much new and precise data on the nature of bodies. But instead of using these data to correct the traditional doctrines about sense perception, Descartes fell into complete scepticism regarding sensation. He no longer sees in sensation an immediate contact of consciousness with the external world; he regards human consciousness as a closed consciousness, without any direct relation with realities foreign to the self. Its only contents are representations or images of things. In this way he introduces into modern thought the "representationist" conception of knowledge and the "principle of immanence," [13] which will become the basic dogmas of modern idealism. Finally, Descartes believed that he could transfer the deductive method of geometry into philosophy. He

13. It can be formulated as follows: "Every object of thought is immanent in thought." Or according to the formula of É. Le Roy: "Anything beyond thought is unthinkable." Later we shall see just how equivocal these formulas are.

marks the beginning of the period of *dogmatic rationalism* which dominates European thought to the time of Kant.[14]

Even though the Cartesian system had within itself the germs of *idealism,* the purpose of Descartes was still realist.[15] No doubt unconsciously, he restores several traditional doctrines. His "Cogito" is Augustinian, his methodic doubt is Aristotelian (at least in its scientific aspects), his proof of God is inspired by St. Anselm, and many other elements of his system recall Augustinian Platonism or nominalism. The originality of Descartes has been exaggerated by many who, like him, are not too well acquainted with medieval thought. The most characteristic theses of Cartesian epistemology originate from the representationist conception of knowledge. Descartes denies the experience of the corporeal world. He revives the Platonic theory of innate ideas which are not abstract concepts but rather principles for an intuitive knowledge of essences.

With Malebranche, Cartesian Platonism soon becomes an even more radical Platonism—ontologism. This doctrine recalls the Augustinian doctrine of divine illumination.[16]

Spinoza accentuates the opposition of the sensory and the intelligible. He professes a *metaphysical rationalism,* which is on the whole dogmatic, for the identity of the ideal and the real order is affirmed without being critically proved. Otherwise, the great merit of Spinoza is to have restored the properly metaphysical values.

14. *Rationalism* here refers to a philosophical position which gives a predominant role to discursive reason, as it operates by deduction, starting from rational principles which are fully intelligible. Pre-Kantian rationalism was called *dogmatic,* because it put blind trust in the statements of reason.

15. See L. Noël, *Le réalisme immédiat,* pp. 39-46, on Cartesian "realism."

16. *Ontologism* is the doctrine which admits a certain intuition of the Divine Being, or of the Ideas in God.

The epistemology of Leibnitz is fundamentally idealist, and his conception of human knowledge recalls the Thomistic doctrine of angelic knowledge *(per species infusas)*. It is here that Cartesian "angelicism" and rationalism find their complete expression.

Finally, Wolff utilizes the principles of Cartesian rationalism in constructing a metaphysics of possibles or essences, which is partially inspired by the Scholastic tradition. Nowhere is the loss of the "sense of the real" so evident as in this *a priori* construction which has no foundations in experience.

Kant put at the service of philosophy a penetrating and methodical intellect, persevering labor and excellent intentions. However, his historical information was limited, and his thought was often shackled by the cadres of the eighteenth-century systems. The Kantian criticism is a work of patience, but it is complicated and often obscure. It has thus given rise to quite different interpretations.

The ambition of Kant was to end once and for all the "dogmatic slumber" of reason (which had too much confidence in its own value), and to institute a genuine critique of knowledge. This critique would try to determine the conditions under which scientific knowledge was possible, and thus fix the limits of human science. At first sight, Kantianism seems to be an effort to reconcile empiricism and idealism, a patient attempt at reconstruction intended to restore unity to the edifice of knowledge. But in reality the value and function which he attributes to the *datum* are so reduced that the whole weight of reconstruction must be borne almost exclusively by the *activity of the knowing subject*. Kant ends by positing the principles of an *idealism* which is much more radical than that emanating from Descartes. His *critical idealism* is, in fact, a *subjectivism;* it contains in germ the *transcendental idealism* of his successors.[17] Kantianism, then, belongs to the line of radical intellectualism and stands at the beginning of contemporary idealism.

Under the influence of Hume's phenomenalism, Kant depreciated the objective datum. He sees it as a "pure diverse," which cannot be a fertile source of determinate knowledge. Thus, he completely overlooks the notion of an abstracting intelligence, and sees no possible intermediary between an *intuitive* intelligence which would create its object, and an *informing* intelligence which would impose intelligible forms on a matter furnished by sensibility. This last is the case for our human intelligence. In this way Kant arrived at his famous "Copernican revolution," which completely upset the usual notion of knowledge. Just as the heliocentric conception of Copernicus eliminated the geocentric views of the ancients, so Kant shifted the center of gravity of human knowledge. The real is no longer *knowable in itself;* now it is the subject's activity which constitutes the object and *makes it knowable.* The real no longer informs thought; it is thought which informs the datum. New prerogatives are attributed to the knowing subject: *a priori* forms of sensibility, *a priori* categories of understanding, synthetic *a priori* judgments, and so forth. To know a datum is to make an object of it by imposing on it *a priori* forms. To conceive an object means to represent it to oneself in a concept produced by the spontaneous activity of the intelligence. The synthesis made in the judgment attaches this concept to the datum. This doctrine had as consequences the ruin of metaphysics and the triumph of agnosticism.[18]

17. *Subjectivism* is the doctrine which rejects the objective norm for truth, and tends to make the knowing subject the measure and judge of knowledge.
18. On Kant see L. Noël, *op. cit.*, pp. 49-96. See also the works of Father

The Kantian system was a collection of incongruous pieces, and so it had to disintegrate. By his phenomenalism and agnosticism, Kant exercised an enormous influence on the positivist currents of the nineteenth century. By his critique of practical reason, he prepared the way for *voluntarism* and *pragmatism*.[19] Finally, his critical idealism soon gave rise to *transcendental idealism* (Fichte, Schelling, Hegel). In these systems the so-called "Copernican revolution" reached its final consequences: the primacy of the subject becomes absolute, the object results entirely from the subject, and the real is totally subordinated to thought. But the "subject" of which these philosophies speak is no longer or even principally the human subject. It is the absolute Ego, or the absolute Mind. In this sense, transcendental idealism tends to rejoin metaphysical realism and emanationist pantheism.

The idealist movement which received its impetus from Descartes was reinforced by Kantianism and transcendental idealism. It pursued its career under various forms throughout the nineteenth century. Frequently, especially under the influence of Hegel, it took on a metaphysical appearance. In other cases (for example, with Brunschvicg) Kantian "formalism" is carried to the extreme.

While the university circles of the fourteenth century were allowing themselves to be led down the easy descent of

---

Charles, S.J., and Father Joseph Maréchal, S.J., which are listed in Noël's study (p. 79).

19. *Voluntarism* is the doctrine which for any reason defends the superiority of the will over the intellect, or the superiority of the act of the will over thought. More particularly, it is the doctrine which stresses the role of the will in the acquisition of knowledge or certitude. *Pragmatism* is the doctrine which stresses the role of activity and practical life in the discovery of truth, or even in the constitution of truth. Pragmatism tends to confuse "truth" with "utility," "success," or "effectiveness."

nominalism, the realism of St. Thomas still kept some faithful disciples. From the end of the thirteenth century, some remarkable minds (Peter of Auvergne, Godfrey of Fontaines, Giles of Rome, not to mention the members of the Dominican school) had resumed and reconsidered the Thomistic doctrines. Up to the present this first Thomistic school has not been studied very well and we cannot say as yet how far it developed the principles of the epistemology of St. Thomas. The Thomistic school enjoyed a new growth about the beginning of the fifteenth century with John Capreolus. The sixteenth century witnessed a brilliant Thomistic renaissance which is adorned especially by the names of Cajetan and Suarez. In the following century the name of John of St. Thomas adds lustre to it. But the teaching of Thomism hardly extended outside theological circles, and, shorn of contact with lay thought, it did not at all adapt itself to the scientific interests of the period. As a result it had no noteworthy influence on modern thought. On reading the principal Scholastic treatises subsequent to the fifteenth century, we are astonished to see how much ignorance of contemporary science is revealed in otherwise solid and penetrating works. After a further eclipse in the eighteenth century, the Thomistic movement took on new strength at the beginning of the nineteenth century. The Encyclical *Aeterni Patris* (1879) gave it an official mission and marks the beginning of a world wide revival of Thomistic studies.

The return to St. Thomas has been, first of all, a return to *critical realism*. For sixty years considerable effort has been made to bring out the fundamental theses of this traditional realism, a realism which offers a solution to the time-honored paradoxes of sensationalism and idealism, empiricism and rationalism.[20] Outside Thomistic circles we can see in contemporary thought different signs of a return to the equilibrium of realism.

The brief summary which we have just given sought to bring the complexity of the problem of knowledge to the reader's attention. It also tried to furnish a preliminary idea of the different forms that the answer to this problem can take.

One fact seems to dominate the history of epistemology. It is the almost universal recognition that there are two basic aspects to human knowledge: receptivity and spontaneity, passivity and activity, experience and an *a priori* element. All forms of *empiricism* emphasize the first aspect; *idealism* and *rationalism* emphasize the second aspect; *realism* tries to reconcile the two elements.

This is a first ground for disagreement, but there are also several others which are more or less basic. These differences explain why philosophers express their views on knowledge in so many different ways.

§ 4. Conclusion

We can now recapitulate the results obtained in this section.

1. Some sort of examination of knowledge should be made at the beginning of systematic and critical philosophy, unless we want to run the risk of building without solid foundations. This inquiry should determine, at least to some degree, the nature and value of knowledge, the nature and value of

20. See G. Van Riet, *L'épistémologie thomiste: Recherches sur le problème de la connaissance dans l'école thomiste contemporaine* (Louvain, 1946).

science. We shall call this first study of knowledge "Epistemology."

2. Epistemology should include, first of all, an analysis of the immediate data of consciousness, a description of the elements which make up consciousness (*analytical* or *descriptive epistemology*). Then a critique of knowledge, aimed at establishing the value and potentialities of human knowledge, can be undertaken on the basis of this description (*critical epistemology*). This analysis and critique will furnish the object for a third discipline which will try to determine the general laws of the discursive activity of the mind (*logical epistemology*). We must exercise the greatest care in choosing our *vocabulary* in epistemology, and the development of the theses should follow strictly the *natural sequence* of thought. It seems that we can and should carry out our study of knowledge by the help of a method which will be *reflective, personal* and *interrogative*. The advantages of this three-fold method will appear progressively as we use it to construct an epistemology.

3. The discussion of the claims of common sense regarding knowledge helped us to bring out quite clearly the elements which make up consciousness and the starting point of epistemology, properly speaking.

4. The history of the theory of knowledge showed us the complexity of the problems which have to be considered. It also furnished useful suggestions regarding possible solutions to these problems.

These preliminary reflections have shown us the task we face. It is time now for us to enter the field of epistemology, properly so called.

Part Two

ANALYTICAL OR DESCRIPTIVE EPISTEMOLOGY

CHAPTER I

OBJECT AND METHOD

THE ancients declared that no science proves its own object. This is but a common-sense principle, for if I undertake to study a certain object, this implies that the object is already given me in some way. Thus the object of analytical episte-mology is given to me in my prescientific knowledge, and it must be, since this science is first in the system that I propose to construct. We must not, however, conclude from this that the value of epistemology depends necessarily on popular knowledge. As we shall see shortly, epistemology has its own working methods which allow it to determine its own object scientifically and to bring out the value of that object.

This object of epistemology is my *actual knowledge* or my *actual consciousness,* which has been purified of every ques-tionable and even contingent content and reduced to its component or essential elements. In this first study (de-scriptive epistemology) I propose simply to observe, analyze and describe this knowledge, or this consciousness. In terms of traditional terminology we would say that the *material* ob-ject of analytical epistemology is my knowledge, and the *formal* object is the description or analysis of this knowledge. Or, if we prefer to put it another way, it is this knowledge in so far as it is the object of description and analysis. The classical distinction between the material and formal objects comes from the fact that an object of human knowledge almost always lends itself to different kinds of study. We must, therefore, determine the point of view (the aspect or "form") under which we are going to study the object.

At the start of analytical epistemology, we do not have to say very much about the *method* which will be used in this inquiry. Our prescientific reflections have given us a hint of the direction our work must follow. Since knowledge cannot be examined from the outside, the only thing that the epistemologist can do is to examine his own consciousness (the reflective method, which is therefore *personal*). This examination must begin with the adult's actual consciousness taken in all its complexity. We have to use some method of analysis or distinction to bring out the stable elements of consciousness, and among them those elements which are the essential components of consciousness (the *methodic doubt*). Applying that method we saw that the methodic doubt left us only consciousness itself as the irreducible synthesis of subject and object. This is the point from which our description will start. We must be very attentive and precise in our description, particularly in the vocabulary. To better satisfy the requirements of rigorous method we shall, at each step of our description of consciousness, distinguish the condensed precise statement of the propositions—listing the elements forming consciousness, and the commentary or explanation of the statement. In the commentary we shall use notions foreign to our inquiry, but this will be done only for pedagogical reasons, namely, to bring out more clearly the meaning and importance of the formulated propositions.

To avoid all misunderstanding, we must fix at once the

exact significance of the description we propose to give. It will be a case of describing a *factual* situation as accurately as we can with the help of a preliminary methodic doubt. The factual situation as such is undeniable and nothing can shake it. But a further problem concerning the *value* of the knowledge which has been described still remains. The answer given to that problem will necessarily affect the value of the description itself, since the description involves the activity of knowing (reflections, judgments, and so forth). Thus, the conclusions of analytical epistemology acquire their full value only after critical epistemology has ruled on the value of knowledge itself.[1]

1. This situation does not in any way involve a vicious circle, for as we shall see, the absolute norm which gives knowledge its value imposes and justifies itself. Logically then, critical epistemology is not built on analytical epistemology. We put the description before the criticism for psychological reasons, because it helps the philosopher better to set up the problem in his own mind.

Chapter II

CONSCIOUS REALITY OR REAL CONSCIOUSNESS

At the outset of the description of my actual knowledge, I must affirm a twofold presence. There are two inseparable parts to this affirmation. I must affirm a reality, and I must affirm a consciousness. I must affirm a conscious reality. I must affirm a real consciousness. This consciousness is both *becoming* and *perduring*—an extremely complex reality.

§ 1. State of the Question

I am seated at my desk in my study. I have succeeded in casting doubt on all my common-sense beliefs. What still remains? There still remains the *consciousness that I am, with everything that actually constitutes that consciousness.* Let us explain this a bit further, for we must carefully eliminate every common-sense prejudice as to what "constitutes" this consciousness. Consciousness certainly involves an "attitude of the self," an "act" (and even a complex act in which we shall shortly distinguish several elements: perception, attention, affirmation, and so forth), but it implies equally well "gray walls," a "white ceiling," a "desk," "chairs," and other objects besides. There can be no doubt that here and now all this constitutes my consciousness, provided that I use the terms in a purely *descriptive* sense and do not say anything about the basic nature, origin, independence or dependence of these various objects.

Consequently the consciousness that *I am* involves a sub-

jective pole and an objective pole, or, more briefly, the subject
and the object. These are inseparably united. But before describing these two poles separately I must focus my attention
first on a datum which is more simple and more basic, that is,
consciousness taken in its unity. We must note well that it is
the unity which is prior, because the subject and object are
only two aspects of one and the same consciousness. Consciousness does not result from a synthesis of a subject and
object, which are first given separately.

Having clarified the situation in this way, I can now say
that every attempt to doubt or deny will encounter this evident affirmation: *A consciousness exists*. If in spite of all
evidence I still try to deny that a consciousness exists, I see at
once that epistemology itself vanishes, and with it all knowledge including the consciousness of my own existence. I de-
base myself to the level of the plants. The existence of
consciousness then "*necessarily* stands at the beginning of any
description of my knowledge as it actually is." There is a
double reason for this: first, because this existence is *undeniable* or *unavoidable*, and I cannot sincerely doubt it; secondly,
because the affirmation of this existence is the *indispensable*
condition for every further affirmation.

This affirmation can be analysed still further. It can be
analysed into two simple statements: "something exists," and,
"that which exists is consciousness." Like the preceding statement, these two statements are both evident and indispensable, for all further description depends on them. If we
reject the first statement (that is, if we deny that something
exists), then we destroy everything including the second statement; for, if nothing exists, no consciousness can exist. If we
reject the second (that is, if we deny consciousness), this is
equivalent to destroying the first *as an affirmation*, for if

there is no consciousness, no one "knows" that "something exists," no one can affirm it. Affirmation implies consciousness. These two affirmations then are inseparable; the one implies the other, they express a twofold basic evidence.

Now let us examine more closely this twofold basic evidence, the evidence of the *real* and the evidence of *consciousness* which affirms itself as real. It is wise to begin with consciousness, because the real can be affirmed only by consciousness.

§ 2. *Consciousness*

I am conscious, I am a consciousness. As Descartes said, "I think." This is undoubtedly the first immediate incontestable fact found at the starting point of all knowledge, all science, all scientific systematization.

Consciousness is an original datum which cannot be reduced to any other. It is a first datum which, strictly speaking, it is impossible to explain, define, or describe in terms which might be clearer or better known. To know what consciousness is, we must live it, we must be "conscious" ourselves. We can try to throw more light on this indefinable datum by appealing to certain analogous ways of being. We can say that "to be conscious" is "to be known by oneself," "to be transparent to oneself," "to appear to oneself," "to be present to oneself," "to be possessed by oneself," "to be affirmed by oneself." All these formulas try to suggest what consciousness or a conscious being is.

Note that when I say "I am a consciousness," this term means the whole concrete reality which is given originally as "transparent to itself," with everything that it contains before any opposition or division is introduced into this primitive unity, and even before the opposition of subject and object. In short, it refers to the *conscious being* with all the contents of its consciousness.

Consciousness is then a primitive and irreducible datum, a *primum cognitum*. In epistemology we can neither construct, deduce, nor derive the essence or nature of consciousness from anything else; every such attempt is illusory and conceals a basic defect in method. Consciousness forces itself upon us as a fact; I affirm that a consciousness (my consciousness) exists, I do not know why it exists.

As it offers itself to me for analysis, this consciousness presents several aspects which we must describe. Consciousness implies, first of all, experience, intuition or realization. Here "experience" means every sort of knowledge which is direct and without an intermediary. Consciousness is an experience, because it implies an immediate knowledge of the self. It involves an original and unique presence of the self to itself, an intimacy with oneself, an immediate grasping of oneself.[1] Consciousness also implies affirmation. Affirmation means that consciousness adopts a position. It is a complex act by which one element of consciousness (the predicate) is referred to another (the subject). Affirmation thus appears to be the fruit or the expression of experience. Thus, since I have the experience of my own consciousness, I affirm that "a consciousness exists." Why this complex act? Why can I not stop at the experience? What does the term "exist" add to "a consciousness"? These questions raise the problem of the nature of judgment. We shall come back to this later. At present we are content to note this fact, that consciousness expresses its experience in judgments, in affirmations. We can

1. The very penetrating study by F. Grégoire, *"Note sur les termes intuition et experience,"* in *Revue Philosophique de Louvain* (1946), pp. 401-415, can be very profitably read.

say that analytical epistemology will consist of a series of affirmations expressing the experience which I have of my own consciousness and its component parts. Finally, consciousness implies evidence, that is, clarity or self-transparency. We have said that consciousness is a reality which is transparent to itself, which reveals itself to itself. It obtrudes on itself with overpowering force, compelling, invincible, and undeniable. The clarity which belongs essentially to consciousness pervades both the experience and the affirmation. It pervades, first of all, the immediate and undeniable presence which constitutes the experience, and immediately it expresses itself in the judgment because of the necessity of consenting, admitting, recognizing, submitting—in brief, of affirming that which imposes itself with so much evidence. Evidence is, then, the clarity with which being reveals itself to itself in consciousness.

§ 3. Reality

Consciousness clearly implies reality. Descartes recognized this in his "Cogito ergo sum," but he did not know how to make use of this basic experience of the real. The experience of consciousness implies the experience of being, and this is expressed spontaneously in the affirmation that "something exists," "aliquid est." "Something," "reality," "existing," are all terms which express (with certain nuances, which we must make more precise later on) the same fundamental experience, the experience which is the most simple, most general and the poorest possible—the experience of "being" or of the "real." [2]

2. We use the terms "real" and "reality" as synonyms for "existing," "being," or "something." This is the basic sense of these terms in the Thomistic tradition,

This experience has an object which cannot be explained or defined. Being is the most primitive datum. It is par excellence the *primum notum*. It is impossible to analyze it or to reduce it to anything more elementary. Being is strictly *per se notum*. It is a principle of knowledge; it is not known by anything else. Nothing is clearer or simpler or more evident than being, as apprehended in our very first experience or act of consciousness. This is why we cannot ask what is the essence or nature of being. For essence and nature are already "ways of being." It is the essence of being not to have any essence, because it surpasses and includes all essences. Consequently, it is impossible to construct, derive, reduce or define being in terms of anything other than itself.

In a word, being imposes itself in the same way as consciousness itself does, as a fact which is mysterious and brutal. I perceive that something exists, just as I perceive that a consciousness exists. But I cannot say, at least at present, *why* something exists. The first evidences which human knowledge acquires are evidences of fact. To demand at the start *de jure* evidence or evidence of absolute necessity would mean ignoring our human status. Such a demand could not be met.

As we can see, the very first affirmation of epistemology goes beyond phenomenalism in so far as the latter takes the contents of consciousness or consciousness itself to be only pure phenomena, that is, objects which have no ontological properties. An object lacking all ontological value would be a contradiction in terms; it would coincide with non-being

---

where *ens, res, aliquid* are equivalent terms. In this primitive sense, "real" does not mean "independent of consciousness," and it is not opposed to "ideal" or "mental," since the "ideal" or the "mental" is also a way of being, a modality of the real.

pure and simple. The first step of epistemology introduces me at once into the sphere of ontology.[3]

§ 4. *Reality and Consciousness*

At the beginning of epistemology, reality and consciousness are not distinct or juxtaposed. Everything which is given as reality is given as an element of consciousness, otherwise this reality would not be affirmed. Inversely everything which is given as consciousness is given as real or as being. Otherwise this consciousness would not exist, it would be nothing, it could not assert itself. This is why our first proposition can also be stated as "the affirmation of a conscious reality," or "the affirmation of a real consciousness."

This primitive identity of the real and consciousness, which we see at the beginning of the epistemological analysis, has great significance. It implies that "real" is not opposed either essentially or primitively to consciousness (or to thought or to the ideal). There is not then an initial phase of juxtaposition, separation, opposition, duality of the real and consciousness, but on the contrary there is unity and identity.[4] Thus the critique of knowledge never has the task of proving that any element of consciousness is real. That point is evident; it is given beforehand, for the non-real, non-being, cannot be an element of consciousness. There will, however, be a need of determining more precisely the *kind* or *degree* of reality that we must recognize for this or that element of conscious-

---

3. See *"Problèmes épistémologiques fondamentaux,"* pp. 480-485. Also M. D. Roland-Gosselin, *Essai d'une étude critique de la connaissance,* pp. 52-55, where he shows that the notion of "being" is even more fundamental than the notion of "object" in general.

4. See A. De Coninck, *L'unité de la connaissance humaine et le fondement de sa valeur,* 2nd. ed. (Louvain, 1947), pp. 26-31.

ness. Thus, for example, among the actual contents of my consciousness there is a certain extended gray object which I call in ordinary speech a "wall." In this fact there are given two immediate evidences: this extended gray object *exists,* and it is *known*; it is real, and it is an element of consciousness. What is not immediately evident is the *how* and the *why* of this object. How does it exist? Why does it exist? Does it exist only as known, as a content of consciousness? Does it exist independently of consciousness—and of every consciousness?

At this point a difficulty naturally arises: if there is identity between being and consciousness at the outset of our epistemological analysis, why distinguish these two terms? Is not this distinction premature at least? It is true that the experience which provides the start for our analysis is truly one, and so from this point of view there is no reason to introduce any distinction between being and consciousness. At this phase of my reflection, I do not yet know whether it is possible to be, without being conscious, or even whether anything else exists besides my consciousness. But I find it impossible to express this first experience by means of only one term. Neither being nor consciousness suffice to express all its richness. This results from the nature of language. To express my basic experience I have to use ordinary terms if I wish to make myself understood.[5] In ordinary language, the term "being" expresses the object of any experience at all; it expresses the basic value which is *common* to all, while the term "consciousness" refers to a *particular* way of being, a way of being distinct from other ways of being (since common sense believes, rightly or wrongly, that there are nonconscious beings). If this is the case, then neither of these

5. See above, p. 22.

two terms is sufficient by itself to express the initial experience that I am speaking about here. The term "being" would neglect the original aspects of the experience of consciousness, and the term "consciousness" would neglect the capital experience of being. We must, then, make use of the two words, but it should be clear that they refer, at least for the time being, to one and the same reality.

§ 5. Becoming and Duration

The conscious reality or the real consciousness is both becoming and duration. These are new characteristics of consciousness which are absolutely primitive. Consciousness is very evidently a becoming; it is not fixed in a state of immobility. It evolves and changes, it is a perpetual flux, a succession of states or ways of being; but it is also duration, that is, unity, continuity, permanence, identity in spite of the change and throughout the change. Consciousness has a history, a past, which remains in the present. The present is not a completely isolated and unstable instant, a flash which vanishes immediately; it is a duration and a permanency which, to a certain extent, dominates the becoming.

The relative survival of the past in the present is called "memory," and the elements of the past which are conserved in this way in consciousness are "remembrances." These can be more or less clear and precise. Usually their reliability diminishes as they get further away from actual consciousness. In epistemology it is the immediate past of consciousness that is of most interest, for, thanks to the continuity of the immediate past with the present, the present has the duration and consistency without which there could be no epistemological reflection or analysis.

The identity of the self appears as a fact of conscious

experience which is both undeniable and unexplained. When I awake in the morning, I have to admit that my remembrances of previous knowledge or of my past belong to the very same self that I am now. I see that this identity is the reason why I can synthesize the past and present. But in itself it remains an unexplained fact, a simple datum of my personal experience. Furthermore, this identity did not always exist, because fifty years ago I did not exist. At least for the moment, I have no assurance that this identity will continue in the future.[6]

§ 6. *Complexity of Consciousness*

When analyzed, consciousness shows an inexhaustible complexity and richness. Even when we leave aside the past or memory and consider only actual or present consciousness, even when we leave aside the more obscure regions of consciousness (subconsciousness, semiconsciousness and inattention) to consider only the regions which attention can make completely clear, consciousness is still a world in itself.

Consciousness is not chaotic. It may have been at its first awakening in my early childhood. But today, however new the elements may be which make up my consciousness at any given moment, I spontaneously recognize different structures among them, I can see different groupings of elements. Among these structures and variations there is one which appears to be completely fundamental and undeniable—a basic structure which seems to constitute my "real consciousness." This is the "object-subject" structure, or the presence of two "poles" in this real consciousness, the objective pole and the subjective pole. We shall study this new fact in the second step of our description.

6. In other words, the immortality of consciousness is not immediately evident.

CHAPTER III

THE SUBJECTIVE POLE AND THE OBJECTIVE POLE

IN THE unity of my real consciousness I can see a real undeniable duality of subject and object, of knower and known,
of self and non-self. This duality shows me that knowing is
a modality of being.

§ 1. *The Two Poles in Consciousness*

By taking the term "consciousness" broadly, we have seen
that there is a first sense in which "real" and "consciousness"
are equivalent. Everything which is given as real is an element of consciousness, an object which is experienced and
affirmed. But in this real consciousness there are clearly two
poles which cannot be interchanged, the objective pole and
the subjective pole, the known and the knower. It is true
that I cannot claim that this duality belongs essentially to *every*
consciousness. I do not know anything about that, since at
present I do not know any other consciousness but my own. I
do not even know whether another consciousness exists or
whether it is possible.[1] But I do see that this duality is essential
to *my* consciousness and that it constitutes my consciousness.[2]

1. In metaphysics we will show that an infinite creative Consciousness exists
from which all duality of subject and object is excluded.
2. At the present time it is readily admitted that the consciousness of man is
always "a self in the world"; it is never a self cut off from every non-self.
But this expression can not be used at the start of epistemology, for to speak
of the "world" already implies a realistic interpretation of knowledge.

§ 2. *Discovery of This Duality*

How does this duality of subject and object manifest itself? Here we do not have to bother with the question of the origin of this duality, or how this duality arose psychologically when consciousness first awoke in the child. In my actual consciousness this duality shows itself as another undeniable fact, as another first datum. In my consciousness there is a "one-way street," a direction, an irreversible orientation going from the subject pole to the object pole, from a knower to a known. The self shows itself to be a real tendency, a real appetite for knowing (and enjoying by knowledge). It shows itself to be an active center of knowledge directed towards the objects and the thing known. On the other hand, objects are presented as data which impose themselves and oppose the self. They are presented as *contents* of consciousness which the self does not dominate, with which it clashes, which resist it, which it cannot arbitrarily suppress.[3]

The self which knows the objects also knows itself and thus it too is something "known." On the other hand, the objects are *only* something "known." They cannot become "knowers" (at least so far as they are contents of *my* consciousness). Here again a careful analysis of consciousness goes beyond the position of phenomenalism, which sees in the subject or knowing self only the unity of a phenomenal flux, or a phenomenal synthesis of phenomenal objects. But consciousness shows the self to be a real center of unity and permanence and a real tendency directed toward the objects.

3. See L. Noël, *Le réalisme immédiat*, pp. 31-33.

§ 3. *Nature of This Duality*

What is the nature of this duality? To what extent is it *real*? Considered as an immediate datum, this distinction of subject and object in my consciousness is quite mysterious. We must be very careful to avoid reckless and premature statements in this matter. The duality is real in this sense, that there are really two elements in my consciousness: a *known* reality and a *knowing* reality, and these two realities really oppose one another in the unity of my consciousness. But whether these two realities are separable, and to what extent, is an entirely different question which we cannot immediately answer. For in reality, it is precisely the union of object and subject that constitutes my actual consciousness. To suppose that we could destroy one or the other of these poles of consciousness, or to suppose simply that we can separate one from the other, is actually to destroy consciousness. In my consciousness there can never be question of a pure object without a subject, or of a pure consciousness without objective content. When I undertake this epistemological analysis of my consciousness, I can legitimately *presume* that the objects do not cease to exist when they cease to be present, and I can also suppose that the subject does not cease to exist when it ceases to know (for example, in sleep or coma). However, it still remains true that in those hypotheses consciousness, as such, disappears. Thus all the objects of my actual knowledge are real (perhaps in different degrees) and really distinct from the self which knows. But I cannot tell whether this real distinction implies a more or less complete independence of objects and subject. This question remains in its entirety.

It is true that I can easily see that most objects are contingent in the sense that they can disappear from my consciousness without it vanishing or ceasing to be itself. This leads me to suppose that they could have an existence independently of my consciousness. But this is only a conjecture, for I do not know what happens to these objects when I no longer know them. In short, the subject and object are two essentially correlative elements of human consciousness, and whatever be the proper value of the objects—a problem which we have still to examine—those objects are of interest to the subject only in so far as they are in consciousness as known objects or as contents of consciousness. And on the other hand, whatever be the proper value of the subject, whatever be its natural powers of knowing, these powers will show themselves only when an objective datum is present.

§ 4. *Knowing as a Modality of Being*

Through this duality of subject and object in my consciousness I can see that knowing is a modality of being. When I begin my epistemological analysis, the real consciousness is given to me in its concrete unity and in such a state of indistinction that there is identity between consciousness and the real, between "to be" and "to know." [4] But the distinction which I can make within consciousness between an objective and subjective element enables me to foresee that a certain dissociation between consciousness and the real is possible. Thus the objective pole of my actual consciousness is composed of "walls," "furniture," "tables," and so forth. These objects undoubtedly are contents of consciousness, but they are not given to me as conscious subjects, and so I can

4. See above, pp. 84-86.

legitimately consider them as real, without considering them as "conscious" or "knowing." Furthermore, it is not completely clear to me that these objects would cease to exist if I stopped knowing them. That is sufficient to enable me to distinguish between the sense of "being" and the sense of "knowing," and to see in knowing a mode of being, a way of being which, at least apparently, sets itself off from other ways of being. It also gives me sufficient reason for distinguishing in consciousness, as such, the reality or the being of the consciousness and the knowledge or consciousness of this reality. In short even without affirming that one can *exist* without being *conscious*, that is, without being a *subject* of knowledge, or that one can *be* without being actually a *content* of *consciousness*, that is, an *object* of knowledge, I can still dissociate in my real consciousness the aspect "to be" and the aspect "to know."

Now, if I compare "to be" and "to know" with one another, I shall soon see that "to be" is prior from the psychological point of view. In fact "to know" clearly implies "to be," while "to be" does not clearly imply "to know." I can conceive of a thing existing without being a consciousness, but I cannot conceive of a thing being a consciousness without existing. From this it follows that being is necessarily the *primum notum,* the object of our first experience and our first affirmation, for it is implied and presupposed in every other experience and in every other affirmation. Consciousness is also a *primum notum* in the sense that it is a datum which cannot be reduced to any other, but it is not a *primum notum* in every respect, for the apprehension of consciousness implies another apprehension which is even more simple and more fundamental, that of being. And consciousness appears to me at once to be a mode of being, a manner of being.[5] This recognition of being as the *primum notum* is one of the deepest insights of the Aristotelian-Thomistic doctrine. It is also one very frequently overlooked. "Aliquid est" has logical priority over "cogito," since the *cogito* even when taken in its strictest sense (self-consciousness) implies *aliquid* three times: "ego" (*aliquid*); "cogito" (*aliquid*); "meipsum" (*aliquid*).

5. It is for this reason that, when we try to determine the profound nature of knowing and to develop an "ontology of knowledge" in special metaphysics, we try to reduce "knowing" to "being"; in other words, to situate "knowing" among the modes of being.

CHAPTER IV

THE OBJECTIVE PRESENCE

CONSCIOUSNESS always implies a certain objective content. The object known is present to consciousness as a datum which forces itself upon the subject, dominates the subject and measures its knowledge. This fact shows us the primacy of *being* over *cognition*.

§ 1. *The Objective Pole*

The presence of an objective pole in consciousness is a new immediate datum. We have already seen that the conscious self cannot be completely isolated. There must always be a non-self to help make the self a knowing self. To have "consciousness" a certain apprehension of objects is required. In other words, I have to know *objects* to be aware that I know at all, to know myself as a knowing subject, to be conscious.[1]

§ 2. *Dominating Character of the Object*

The dominating character of the object is another undeniable fact of consciousness. Not only is the object the indispensable condition for awakening consciousness but it also

---

1. Some authors use the term "object" to indicate not the conscious objective term of the act of knowing, but rather the ultimate term to which the intellectual dynamism tends, that is, the Absolute Being. They call the conscious objective term a "representation." But this deflection of the word "object" from its natural and customary meaning is a most effective means of misleading readers. The object of knowledge is that which is "cast before" the subject (*ob-jectum*), that to which its attention is turned—in brief, "that which is known" by the subject (*id quod cognoscitur*).

orientates and specifies the attention or consideration of the knowing subject. Far from feeling that I constitute the object as object, or specify it by knowing it, I am conscious of being dominated by its objective presence. It is true that I can turn my attention away from the object, I can close my eyes so as not to see it, but when I open my eyes, it does not depend on me whether I will see this or that. The immediate analysis of consciousness shows me an evident subordination of the subject to the object, of the knowing reality to the known reality. On the plane of the immediate data of consciousness, it is not the conscious subject as such which "places" or which "determines" the object, rather it is the object which actuates or determines the knowledge of the subject. Whether a certain object is present or not, does not depend on the subject. The object's presence obtrudes. At times it may be even violent and painful for the subject. It may even go so far as to destroy his capacity for knowing—in the case of a burn, or something deafening, blinding, and so forth.[2]

The object not only dominates the subject, it measures and limits the knowledge which the self can have of the non-self. Whatever is beyond the objective datum is unknowable. To talk of something as being genuinely beyond the objective datum has no meaning for my consciousness. Any further progress which my consciousness may make will consist either in the enlarging of the objective datum or in the further

2. We shall see later that the subject can "represent" at will objects which were previously perceived, and even "manufacture" imaginary objects with the help of images that it has acquired. In these cases it is clear that the presence of the object is no longer compelling. But on the other hand, the past acts of the subject and the subject himself, as contained in memory, form part of the "objective datum" and by that fact impose themselves on the subject which is actually knowing.

development of the implications of the objective datum and the subjective function. It is well, in order to avoid any misunderstanding, to specify just what this primacy of the object means. We have already mentioned that we do not intend to assert at this point that the "object-reality" is ontologically independent of the "subject-reality." It may be that in some *non-conscious* phase of its duration the subject created the object. (In that case the object would exist only as dependent on the subject, its efficient cause.) It may be that the subject and object are two correlative realities coming from a common root, from a common real principle, somewhat after the fashion of the modes of the unique Substance in the pantheism of Spinoza. (In that case again, there could be no ontological independence of subject and object.) At the present time we are merely stating that on the plane of my actual consciousness the object dominates the subject and specifies it.

§ 3. *Primacy of Being over Cognition*

This psychological primacy of the object over the subject in my consciousness shows me an extremely important characteristic of knowledge, that is, that cognition is subordinate to being, or the primacy of being over cognition. This subordination follows from the very nature of cognition, *as it is given in my consciousness*. From the very start, cognition appears to me to be a certain original way of seizing or of possessing being, as an original presence of being to consciousness, as a revelation or appearance of being to consciousness. Knowledge has the characteristic property of evidence, that is, a certain clarity arising from this fact that when being reveals itself to consciousness, it forces itself upon it in an absolute fashion. That is why consciousness must submit, consent to being, and in short affirm the real.[3] We need only reflect on these single characteristics to see that knowledge, as given to us, is essentially a *submission to the real* and that cognition is essentially *subordinated to being*. Consciousness does not posit being, or create it by knowing it; rather it is being which forces itself on consciousness and determines it.[4] Every object of knowledge has this essential property of independence with regard to knowledge as such. The object is known because it is, it does not exist because it is known.

In critical epistemology we will inquire whether this subjection to the real which appears to be the ideal of knowledge is really possible, and to what extent. For the time being, we can content ourselves with underlining this essential characteristic of knowledge, as it appears on the level of the immediate data of consciousness.

Étienne Gilson has realized this primacy of the real over thought, and we believe that he is right in putting the evidence of the real at the starting point of epistemology. But he is wrong in taking "real" to mean something *ontologically independent of consciousness* and opposing it on that account to the *cogito*. Everything is real, including the *cogito*. The distinction of an objective real from a subjective real is given just as immediately as the dominating character of the object.

3. See above, pp. 81-82.
4. Let us note in advance that this is true for every consciousness, even for the divine consciousness. The divine Thought does not "posit" the divine Reality, it "possesses" it, it "grasps" it *as it is*. If the creative Thought "posits" creatures, it does so not as thought, but rather as cause. As thought it is still subject to the real, for it knows creatures *as they are*; it knows them moreover in itself: *omnia cogniscit Deus in seipso*. The divine knowledge involves a perfect possession of self including the creative power.

But the ontological independence of the objective real, with respect to the subject, is not at all evident.[5]

Jacques Maritain also recognizes the primacy of being, and he expresses the first step of his critical epistemology by the proposition *scio aliquid esse* ("I know that something exists"). But he seems to err when he takes this affirmation to be an affirmation of the *principle of identity*—"I know at least one thing, that that which is, is"—and when he at once sees in it the *necessary possibility* of being. Now all that is by no means so immediate. That which is first of all is the experience of the real, "something exists." [6]

5. See E. Gilson, *Réalisme thomiste*, passim.
6. See J. Maritain, *Distinguer pour unir*, pp. 137-158. Professor Maritain was probably misled by his anxiety to put a *de jure* necessity rather than a factual truth at the base of his critique. This in our opinion is an error, for the first evidence which we get is factual evidence. See above, p. 83.

CHAPTER V

THE SUBJECTIVE FUNCTION OR ACTIVITY

THE knowing subject appears to consciousness as a real tendency or real appetite for knowing, that is, for becoming, possessing, or being the objects as much as possible (in the unique and indefinable way that is called "knowing"). The subject is, therefore, a function or capacity for objects. At the same time it is the knowledge of self or consciousness. This double knowledge (of objects and of self) makes up one act of the subject, an immanent activity.

We have already noted that there is a subjective pole in my consciousness and we have described it briefly. We must now undertake a methodic analysis of the characteristics of the knowing subject as such.

§ 1. Tendency or Appetite of Cognition

We have said that the subject or self shows itself to be an element of consciousness which is not reducible to the object, because it shows itself to be a conscious tendency, an appetite, a desire, a need which has to be satisfied, a tendency which gives to consciousness a certain irreversible direction or orientation from the subject to the object, that is, toward that which is alone the content of consciousness, the term of knowledge. This experiencing of a tendency is again a primitive, original, irreducible, and therefore indefinable datum. "To tend" or "to desire" is a certain "way of being" that I find in myself. It implies a certain "lack of being" and a certain capacity for more being to fill up this privation.

The knowing subject is a conscious tendency toward objects. So we have privation (or ignorance) and the capacity for "becoming" the objects, "possessing" the objects, "being" the objects as much as possible. This capacity manifests itself by fulfilling itself in my actual consciousness. Its term or goal is a certain unique "possession" of the objects by the subject. This possession appears to be a partial realization at least of an appetite. The subject as such shows itself to be a true capacity or function for knowing.[1]

We have seen above that the presence of the object stimulates the subject, that the object forces itself on the subject, that it limits and measures the subject's actual knowledge.[2] These facts do not in any way exclude the spontaneity of the subject, which we have just described. The subject's curiosity constantly tends to something beyond the object apprehended. The subject not only wishes to explore all the aspects of the object, but its experience with the frequent appearance of new objects gives it a "premonition" of something beyond its actual knowledge. Of course, this premonition is verified only to the extent to which the presumed "outside" becomes the object or content of consciousness.

The singularity of the knowing subject as compared with the known objects is a classical theme in philosophy. Thus, for example, in Aristotelian philosophy the subject exercises a function in the act of knowledge which is exclusively proper to itself. However, the moderns, especially after Descartes, have placed more emphasis on the role of the subject and its consequent implications from the view-point of the critique

1. Aristotle used the expression "clean tablet on which nothing is written," and again "potency for knowing." The Aristotelians of the Middle Ages spoke of the *tabula rasa in qua nihil est scriptum, potentia cognoscitiva.* But for these philosophers such formulas had a metempirical sense.
2. See above, p. 94.

of knowledge. Kant especially relied on the characteristics of the knowing subject to overcome phenomenalism. The subject is an active function, a spontaneity, the *a priori* [3] condition of knowledge, the principle which remains the same throughout the evolution of knowledge, the function of synthesizing or unity. All this is quite similar to the traditional ideas; consequently it would be contrary to the data of history to claim that Kant discovered the self as the "subject" or "function" of knowledge.

§ 2. *Consciousness*

In my actual consciousness the "capacity for knowing" which characterizes the subject is always satisfied to some extent by the presence of an object. It is enough that the subject know any object whatever, for it to *know itself*. In other words, the subject becomes actually *conscious* of itself at the same time and by the same instance that it is given actual *knowledge* of the object. This is a most important fact, as will be shown later in this study.

Let us note that this fact is not an entirely new element in our epistemological analysis, since we have seen from the start that the existence of a real consciousness or a conscious reality must be the necessary starting point of the analysis.[4] But in the first phase of our inquiry before we had made a clear distinction between the two poles of consciousness, the term "consciousness" was taken in a broad sense, in which the distinction between knowledge (the knowledge of the object) and self-consciousness (the knowledge of the self) had not yet appeared. Here we are talking about a new refinement.

3. An *a priori* condition is a condition presupposed by objective experience; it is independent of experience and not constituted by it.
4. See above. pp. 78-79.

Within consciousness (taken in the broad sense) there now appears self-consciousness (taken in the strict sense) as the knowledge which the knowing subject has of itself, the knowledge of the self by the self.

In the next place let us note how inseparable "knowledge" and "self-consciousness" are in my human knowledge. There can be no consciousness for me, as long as there is no knowledge or perception of an object. But on the other hand, a knowledge of an object which would exclude all consciousness of myself would have no meaning for me; "to know" without knowing that I know, without knowing myself as knowing, makes no sense for me. In brief, my knowledge is completely conscious.[5]

What is this self-consciousness like? It is ordinarily described as a "reflection," a "return on oneself," a "reditio completa in seipsum." We can see immediately that these expressions conceal a rather crude spatial image, that of an orbit described by a centrifugal movement from the subject to the object, followed by a centripetal movement back to the subject. Now, self-consciousness is something entirely different. If we must make use of images, we can describe the process of "becoming aware of oneself," when knowing an object, as a

---

5. De Coninck brings out this capital fact very well, and he goes so far as to identify "consciousness" and "knowledge." "To have consciousness of something, to be conscious of it, and to know it, is identically the same thing." This is a logical consequent of his preceding statement: "Our initial knowledge is identically the consciousness that we have of ourselves as relative." See De Coninck, *L'unité de la connaissance,* 2nd. ed., pp. 18-23, 105-122 (especially p. 121.) We are in fundamental agreement with the author, but the last formula quoted ("ourselves as relative") shows that within "consciousness," taken in a broad sense, it is still licit to distinguish between "consciousness" in its strict sense (that is, knowledge of the subject by the subject), and "science" (that is, knowledge of objects, the knowledge of that to which the subject is relative). This is so provided that we stress the point that these two aspects of "consciousness" are not juxtaposed, or external to each other.

sort of luminous field spreading progressively from the object to the subject without abandoning the object. This self-consciousness is not, at least at first, a distinct act in opposition to the knowledge of the object. Rather it is the same act in so far as it is transparent to itself. Furthermore, by this self-consciousness the subject does not properly become an "object" of knowledge like other objects because the subject knows itself as subject, that is, from within, within the act of direct or objective knowledge. This is why self-consciousness does not interfere in any way with the knowledge of the object or the non-self, even though the attention of the subject can be focused at one time more on the object, at another time more on itself. We can see now how "consciousness" or "reflection" makes it possible to have a rigorous epistemological analysis, since this reflex knowledge does not *take the place* of direct knowledge, but accompanies it and perfects it as knowledge. In short, self-consciousness and the knowledge of objects are originally only two aspects of one and the same act.

Later on, however, self-knowledge can be dissociated from objective knowledge, when the subject considers its own previous acts of direct or objective knowledge in properly reflective acts. An explicit and distinct knowledge of the self and all its aspects is obtained by reflective acts of this kind.[6]

§ 3. The Act of Knowing

This twofold knowledge (objective and reflective) constitutes an act of the subject. Authors usually speak of the *act*

6. It was concerning these reflective acts that Saint Thomas wrote: "Alius est actus quo intellectus intelligit lapidem, et alius est actus quo intelligit se intelligere lapidem" (*Summa Theologica*, I^a, qu. 87, art. 3, ad 2^m).

of knowing, and we ourselves have used this term at different times in preceding pages. Now we must determine more exactly just what use can be made of this term "act" in our description of the immediate date of consciousness.

In the Aristotelian and Thomistic tradition, *act* is opposed first of all to *potency*: act and potency are two basic modes of the real. "Actus et potentia dividunt ens." Potency is a determinable reality which is capable of becoming other than it is; act is a determined reality. In a derived and more special sense, *act* is opposed to *subject*, when we take subject to mean a reality which is already constituted, already determined, but still capable of, still "in potency" to, a reality, a further act. In this last case, act signifies more precisely the *second act*, since the subject is presupposed as an existing and determined subject, and therefore as the *first act* (existence can be called "act" with respect to the possibility or capacity for existing, which would then be considered a potency to act).

Now, provided that I leave aside the metempirical meaning which the ancients almost always gave to the words that we have just defined, I can say that my present knowledge shows itself immediately to be an *act* in both the senses mentioned. For on the one hand, the knowing self shows itself to be a tendency, a capacity, a function, in brief a potency for knowing.[7] The cognition itself therefore is a realization of this tendency, that is, the act of this potency. On the other hand, the conscious self or consciousness shows itself to be a reality which is both becoming and duration; it remains permanently the same, even though evolving constantly and growing continuously.[8] It is an identity which is able to overcome interruptions of consciousness (by sleep, fainting, and so forth). All this adds up to saying that the self exists

7. See above, pp. 99-100.
8. *Ibid.*, pp. 86-87.

in a stable and determined way, as a reality, as an existent thing, as a subject, as a *first act,* with respect to which the act of knowing must be called the *second act,* or a complementary act.

From the beginning of our epistemological analysis, we have recognized that the characteristic of duration or permanence belongs to consciousness. This characteristic belongs to consciousness because of the subjective function or because of the self, not because of the conscious presence of an object in which diversity and becoming (or successive diversity) predominate over unity and permanence. This is the sense in which knowledge is not simply identified with the *being* or *reality* of the conscious self or subject, but rather constitutes an *act* of the subject.

§ 4. *Immanent Activity*

Knowledge is an *immanent activity;* it is an actualization or realization of the self or subject. We apply the term "activity" to the becoming or movement which brings about this actualization of an already constituted and permanent subject. In other words, we apply the term to the further evolution of an already constituted and enduring subject. My knowledge is therefore an activity, and it is an immanent activity, that is, a movement which takes places in and which terminates in me. It proceeds from me (from my capacity, my tendency, my potency) and it remains in me (constituting me, making me myself). This is a new important characteristic of my knowledge. We must explain its nature further.

At first it might seem that there is no genuine immanence in my knowledge. Have we not described it as a "movement," a "tendency" of subject toward object, from the self to the non-self? Is it not the very model of transitive action? But if we look closer, we will see that there is movement and tendency precisely to the degree in which knowledge is not yet fully achieved, precisely to the degree in which there is curiosity and desire to know more. On the contrary, to the degree that knowledge is achieved there is a union of object and subject, possession of the object by the subject; and St. Thomas did not hesitate to call this a "unity" and "identity" of the knower and the known. The subject "lives" the object, it grasps the object in a mysterious way. Knowledge is therefore a strict immanence. It is this fact which enables my knowledge to be simultaneously a consciousness of self.

The strict immanence of the act of cognition is a basic thesis of Thomistic doctrine. This conception differs a good deal from the common sense view which emphasizes especially the transcendent aspect of knowledge. Common sense takes knowledge to be the apprehension of an exterior world which is independent of the self. It would be wrong to say that Descartes discovered the immanence of thought. What we owe to Descartes is a rather imaginative conception of immanence, a conception which is, after all, on the same level as the naïve realism of common sense. For just as common sense imagines without any qualifications that, from the very start, it grasps the world as independent of the self, so Descartes imagines that consciousness is a closed sanctuary, without any direct communication with the world. This sort of conception involves a double presumption: the postulate that a real world exists outside consciousness or beyond consciousness, and the postulate that consciousness is closed and isolated from the world.

As used in our epistemological analysis, the terms "objective reality," "object," and "non-self," always refer to the immanent term of the act of cognition. Perhaps this immanent term may show itself to be simultaneously transcendent. This is a later problem.

When we began our description of consciousness we noted that it possessed necessarily the threefold characteristic of *experience, affirmation* and *evidence*.[9] Now we can easily see that the immanence of the act of cognition is the basic condition for this threefold characteristic. For, in fact, this immanence makes it possible for an act to be simultaneously a knowledge of an object and consciousness of self, without the dualities of "object-subject" and "knowledge-consciousness" introducing any distance between the elements of the act, or prejudicing the immediate *presence* of the object to the subject and the conscious identity of the subject as knowing and as knowing itself. Here we can add some details to our previous analysis by noting that the act of cognition entails:—

(a) *A twofold experience*: objective and subjective. The subjective experience or the consciousness of self is a lived experience, an experience "from within." From this point of view, it is more intimate than the experience of an objective presence, although this last is just as immediate, immanent and evident as the lived experience. In fact, from the psychological point of view, the objective experience precedes the lived experience.

(b) *Two necessary affirmations*: These are entirely independent of any caprice or whim of the knowing subject; a necessary and inescapable affirmation of the object, and the affirmation of the self.

(c) *A twofold evidence*: of the object and of the subject. The evidence of these two presences together makes up the act of cognition: the objective presence which is immediate and undeniable; and the presence of the knowing self which is equally undeniable and certain.

9. See above, pp. 81-82.

CHAPTER VI

THE STRUCTURE OF CONSCIOUSNESS

ON BOTH its objective and subjective sides my act of knowledge shows a *complexity* revealing a definite structure. As the objectivity of the object grows weaker in the datum, image and concept, the assimilating action of the subject grows correspondingly stronger in perception, imagination, and conception. The act of cognition is completed in the judgment. This complex structure does not jeopardize the *unity* of the act.

§ 1. *The Complexity of Consciousness*

We have already seen that the basic structure of my consciousness implies an objective pole and a subjective pole. If we examine these two poles carefully, we will see that each of them involves a much more complex structure. How can we proceed to analyze this twofold structure? Aristotle had already noted that in human consciousness the objects show us the nature of the *acts* by which we grasp them, and the acts show us the nature of the *potencies* (faculties or capacities) which are their principles. From a purely descriptive point of view, we can say that in my consciousness the objective pole explains and determines the attitude which the subject will take. We have already noted this in a previous section.[1] Let us then analyze first this complexity on the part of the object which will serve as a guide.

1. See above, p. 94.

The objective pole of my consciousness is evidently very complex. If we tried to describe each of the objects occupying my field of consciousness as they chanced to attract my attention, we would never end. Furthermore, that kind of analysis would scarcely help us find the elements which really constitute our knowledge, that is, the elements without which there would be no knowledge, or at least no fully achieved knowledge. We must try to make a methodical analysis, we must try to distinguish the different categories or classes of objects which make up my act of knowledge in different ways and degrees.

This amounts to asking whether there are not several different ways of being "an object of knowledge," a "content of consciousness," a "non-self," or "objective reality." Certain simple facts indicate that there are. Take for example a "piece of white paper." At the present moment I actually perceive it, it is therefore a "content" of my consciousness. Now if I close my eyes, I will still continue to have this piece of paper in my consciousness. But evidently it is there in quite a different way than before. What is it that makes this difference? And this is not all. When I reflect on the experience that I have just had, I spontaneously assert, "this paper is white," or "this object is paper." In these judgments the attributes "white" and "paper" seem to have acquired a new status, for these same attributes can appear in other judgments and can refer to a number of objects distinct from the one I am considering at this moment. How should we understand these "universals," or these contents of consciousness, which can be attributed to many objects?

Let us try to explain these different kinds of objective presence a little further, beginning with that which seems most fundamental and most primitive, the corporeal datum.

§ 2. *The Corporeal Datum*

The term "datum" is taken here in a broad sense. It means every object which is simply present to the subject, which "obtrudes" on the subject, which seems to "constitute" the self in its act of cognition and not to be "constituted" by the knowing self. It therefore precedes any conscious elaboration by the subject. But here we do not claim in any way that this datum is given by any outside cause, or that it exists independently of the self. This datum has the following immediate characteristics:

(a) The datum is *real*, like all the elements of my consciousness, for it is not the non-being which is given to me as "red," "squared," "scented," "stinging" and so forth.

(b) The datum is *corporeal*, that is, *extended* or *spatial*. All its elements are "situated," they can be fixed with respect to one another in space. They appear either to coincide (for example, the color and the surface of this vase), or to be contiguous or juxtaposed, or to be distant from each other. Space (extent, extension or spatial exteriority) is then a new primitive datum of my experience. It is an original irreducible mode of being, which I know by immediate intuition.

An isolated datum is not immediately situated at a fixed point in space. Thus the precise localization of a sound or smell supposes a comparison of different data; it supposes the perception of certain repeated coincidences and an interpretation of these coincidences. I succeed in situating the "tick-tock" of my clock by noting the perfect coincidence between the rhythm of the sounds and the rhythm of the swinging pendulum. But the precise localization of these data is not what is important here. What is important is that all the objective data of my consciousness are some place, they occupy a "place" in the collection of corporeal or extended objects. This appears as an immediate characteristic common to all the objective data of my consciousness.

Not only are corporeal data "situated" with respect to each other, but they are situated with respect to the subjective pole of my consciousness. For the subjective pole itself is situated in the collection of corporeal objects. It is (according to a fashionable formula) a corporeal "self-in-the-world." Here is another piece of evidence which is immediate and undeniable. I may not understand how this "situating" takes place. It may remain a mystery for me. The exact localizing of bodies with respect to the self may raise serious difficulties. But none of these things can in any way change the fact which we just noted. We will come back to this point shortly.

(c) The datum is *temporal*. All its elements are located in succession, they are actually present to my consciousness; but they succeed other data which have disappeared. They constitute then an "after" with respect to a "before." They form part of a successive evolution, of a temporal extension or temporal exteriority. "Time" is also a primitive datum of my experience. The subject or the subjective pole of my consciousness is situated spatially with respect to corporeal objects. It is also subject to temporal succession, at least in a broad sense. Its acts succeed one another, its attitudes change, its attention and curiosity evolve when the objective pole of my consciousness evolves.

(d) The datum is *diversified*. It shows itself as a diversity. It shows a number of different aspects, determinations, or qualities. This multiplicity is made possible by the twofold basic multiplicity of space and time. We shall soon see another condition of this multiplicity.

(e) The datum presents a certain *structure*. In no sense

does it appear as a pure diversity or chaos. First of all, it has the twofold structure of space and time, and I am not aware in any way that I impose this structure on the datum. *A priori* forms of sensibility, in the Kantian sense, may perhaps play a part in the interpretation of the mechanism of knowledge, but they do not belong to an analysis of the conscious data. In addition, the datum has a number of other structures; all sorts of relations exist between the elements of the datum—relations of size, distance, similarity, contrast, attraction, sequence and so forth.

Since it is diversified and structured, the corporeal datum is always a complex object or a collection of objects: lights, colors, forms, odors, sounds, resistances. It is practically impossible for me to put myself in a situation where I would perceive only one object which would be simple and not subject to further analysis. Even if I fix my attention on a simple object as, for example, a point of light, I can never completely isolate it from its context. Furthermore, we must be careful not to confuse a *simple object* as we understand the term here, with a *thing*, as common sense understands it. A "thing" (a piece of chalk, a sponge, a rosebush, a chair) is a complex object. In fact it is a group of objects which appear to me to be connected, and which move together in the field of my consciousness. But the apparent unity or cohesion which this "thing" enjoys, does not authorize any immediate decision about the nature of that unity.

While still limiting ourselves to the description of the immediate data of consciousness, let us try to determine somewhat further the relation between the corporeal objects and the subject in my consciousness. A description of the way in which my own body is an instrument of knowledge is quite relevant here.

Some philosophers hold that our knowledge of the body, as an instrument of perception, is not an immediate knowledge at all. They say it results from a "system" built up by common sense or by the physiological and psychological sciences. This view however is equivocal. It is quite possible that at the beginning of my conscious life, I needed rather long experience to become aware of the very intimate union between the "knowing self" and the body that I now call "my body." But today so many repeated experiences have emphasized these bonds that I cannot possibly ignore them. An epistemological analysis which failed to consider this evidence would be unreal and artificial.

Let us see how this evidence reveals itself and obtrudes on my actual consciousness. We can note the following stages in the process of recognizing that my body is the instrument of my consciousness. First, there is always in my consciousness an *extended or corporeal objective zone,* a corporeal datum, whose characteristics we have just described. Secondly, I see that my consciousness is always and everywhere accompanied by a certain group of these corporeal objects. This *privileged group of objects* (my body) usually forms part of my actual field of consciousness, or, in any case, a simple focusing of attention will make it part of my actual consciousness. Thirdly, I find that there is a regular and constant relationship between certain kinds of objects and certain parts of my body. Thus all the luminous or colored objects that I see are related to the parts of my body or the organs which I call "my eyes." If I put a screen between these objects and my eyes, I abolish at the same time all the "lights" and "colors" in my field of consciousness. These facts by themselves would suggest that "my body" has *organs of different kinds,* and that if one kind of organ were lacking, a certain class of objects would disappear from my field of consciousness. This hypothesis is fully confirmed by a final fact.

Finally, I see that my body is really an *instrument of knowledge.* Not only does it always accompany my consciousness, as an object or content of consciousness, not only is it a condition *sine qua non* for having corporeal objects present in my consciousness, but it really forms part of the knowing subject as such. I know that I am present in my sensory organs as the knowing subject. I am conscious that I "perceive" lights and colors not anywhere at all, but in a very definite way involving my eyes and luminous or colored objects. "I" am present in "my eyes," I perceive in them and by them. I control them at least in a broad sense, for I can decide to open or close them, to turn them to the left or to the right, to fix my gaze on a certain object. In the same way I am conscious that I hear sounds, not at any place at all, but in "my ears." I experience tastes by "my mouth." I perceive odors by "my nose." I feel a sting or burn at a certain sensitive area of the surface of my body. In brief, the knowing subject shows itself to be a subject which is, at least in some way, a *corporeal knowing subject.* It is a subject which has corporeal perceptive organs and by means of these organs it can reach a world of corporeal objects.[2] These organs appear to me to be vitally united to my consciousness and to be living extensions of my consciousness.

Now we can better determine just how the objective datum is localized with respect to the subjective pole. It has a definite situation *with reference to the perceptive organ.*

2. Note once again that we are not yet affirming that this "world of objects" is *independent* of the subject.

The corporeal datum is therefore present to my consciousness through my body's sensory organs. Every corporeal datum is a certain "event" which affects one or the other of these organs. The situation which we have described at once raises new problems—although we are still on the level of pure description. Let us look at them briefly.

Is the datum a body which is *distinct from my body*? Not necessarily. Each particular case must be judged on its own merits. We will have to determine the respective roles of the perceived object and the perceptive organ. An important factor in this inquiry will be the mutual check which different perceptions can exercise on one another. Let us take some examples.

My eyes are open and I see the white sheet of paper over which my pen is moving. It is quite evident that I perceive a corporeal object, which is distinct from my body, and which is exterior and even distant with respect to my body.[3]

I can also perceive this same object at least partially—that is, without the colors—by touch. But then the situation becomes less clear and certain. On the other hand, the sensations of "resistance," "cold," and "glossy," certainly affect a part of my body, an organ of touch. These sensations certainly tell me about the presence of a body which is perceived by that organ as resistant, cold, and glossy. But on the other hand, it is not at all clear that this body may not be a part of my body. I need the added assistance of visual perception to know that a foreign body is present and to know that there is contact and juxtaposition of this body and my body.

With my eyes closed I perceive for an instant a point of

3. Note carefully that "exterior to my own body" does not mean "exterior to my consciousness," for everything that I "perceive" is evidently "in" my consciousness.

light, as if a spark had flashed in the back of my eye. This time I have every reason to think that no external body has intervened. The perception then must be explained by an event interior to my own body. (The physiologist will say that it is a question of a stimulation of the optic nerve caused by an internal stimulus).

In the same way I can experience a sharp pain in my elbow joint. I have no reason to think that this "pain" is a manifestation of a body distinct from mine. In brief, it is through the combined perceptions of sight and touch that I can distinguish my body from exterior bodies.

Is the *datum distinct from the perceptive organ?* When the datum is clearly distinct from my body it is evidently also distinct from the perceptive organ, for this is an integral part of my body. In the opposite case, the situation is not so clear. Then the datum appears as a modification of the perceptive organ, rather than as a body distinct from this organ. Thus a pain appears to me simply as a modification or new state of the organ that it affects.

In the case where perception tells me of the presence of a body distinct from mine, *how far does this distinction go?* Here we must be careful not to give a hasty reply. I can see that a certain body, distinct from mine, is contiguous to mine or juxtaposed to mine. I can see that it can be separated from mine, that it is more or less distant from mine, that this distance can change without causing any experience of discomfort to me. A more interesting fact is this: I see that a body which is perceived by several senses can cease to be present to one sense, without ceasing to be present to the other. Thus I can see, hear and handle my "watch;" I can continue to handle it, and hear it, even though I close my eyes. Or I can continue to see it and to hear it, even though I stop handling it. Another fact: quite often I can "meet again" and "recognize" objects which had disappeared from the field of my consciousness and which reappeared there later with the same properties. In brief, on the level of my consciousness, bodies which are distinct from my body appear to be independent of my body in this sense that their whole behavior seems to be quite other than mine. Nevertheless, at this time I cannot make any definite statement about the precise nature of this independence. Perhaps there is some basic bond between the self (including "my body") and the corporeal realities which are or have been in the field of my consciousness? What is the nature of this provisional bond? Questions of this sort do not belong to epistemology, but rather to metaphysics, because they suppose that answers have been given to the most general problems concerning the conditions of reality and, in particular, the dilemma of monism and pluralism, the problem of substance, the problem of individuality, the dilemma of pantheism and creationism.[4]

To prevent any possible misunderstandings and to answer possible difficulties, it may be well to conclude our description of the corporeal data with the following remarks:

We have not yet begun our critique, nor have we as yet raised the question of the *value* of the corporeal datum as an element of knowledge; we have simply set forth a *factual situation*. We have told how the corporeal datum actually presents itself in our consciousness.

This short description however and especially the rapid examination of the questions concerning the role of the sensory organs, suffices to show us that the world of corporeal objects is particularly complex. But we do not have to explore every corner of this world in epistemology, because to construct a

4. See Noël, *Le réalisme immédiat*, p. 38.

general theory of knowledge *it is sufficient to bring out the basic and indisputable features of my consciousness,* namely, those which resist every attack by methodic doubt and all difficulties raised by the physicist or the psychologist. These basic features can be reduced to the following: The objective pole of my consciousness is made up of a collection of corporeal data which are present to the subject or the self by means of a series of sensory organs belonging to the subject's own body; these organs are principally those of sight and touch. The combined action of these two permits the subject to see very clearly that its condition is that of a self inserted in a corporeal world.

The fact that there are certain obscure zones remaining in my consciousness does not in any way affect this perfectly clear situation. Physics and empirical psychology clearly presuppose these facts of consciousness. They do not question these facts. The illusions which physics and empirical psychology denounce only confirm these facts. To question these facts as facts of consciousness really amounts to condemning oneself without reason to final scepticism and agnosticism in our knowledge of the corporeal world. Such an attitude has nothing to do with a genuine critical attitude.[5]

We cannot in any way reduce the presence of the corporeal datum to my consciousness, or the objective experience to a contact or shock between two bodies (the datum and the organ), or to some sort of modification of the sensory organ. In so far as it is present to consciousness and a content in consciousness, the datum is clearly the immanent term of an act of the knowing subject. Thus the bodily event is excelled by the fact of knowledge, and of consciousness. This first element of my complete cognitive act (correlative to the cor-

5. See *"Problèmes épistémologiques fondamentaux,"* pp. 488-490.

poreal datum, its objective term) is called *sensory perception* (sensation or sensible apprehension). Sensory perception is the cognitive act produced by the help of a bodily organ, capable of grasping a corporeal datum. By its sensory organs and in them, the knowing subject is on the spatio-temporal plane as a knowing subject. Hence in perception the scattering and multiplicity of the cognitive act are greatest, while immanence and unity are least. The multiplicity of different sensory organs contributes to this by introducing a great variety of perceptions into consciousness. We can see rather easily that the diversity of objective data parallels the diversity of sensory organs, that colors and lights, for example, are always perceived by the organs of sight, while odors are perceived by organs of smell, and so forth.

We have just noted that consciousness is on the watch even on the level of perception. I am conscious that I perceive. I know that I perceive. "Scio me sentire." Perception is a conscious act. This fact shows that, as a knowing subject, I transcend the corporeal datum. To appreciate fully what this transcendence means we must first see exactly what are the conditions of existence for a purely *corporeal* reality. A corporeal reality is characterized by the multiplicity and exteriority of its parts, therefore by the dispersion of its component elements. The qualities which affect a body affect its extended parts and so are themselves subject to spatial dispersion. The movements of a body are likewise subject to spatial conditions, either because the movement has a spatial character by its own nature (for example, in change of place, expansion, condensation), or because it affects the extended parts of the body (for example, qualitative alteration). Finally, activity originating in a body can only be conceived as a transitive action, that is, as an "influence" exercised by this body on surrounding bodies, an influence which is communicated through contact in space and the passivity that this contact implies. A being which would in any way escape these corporeal conditions would not be merely a body.

Now, in its cognitive activity my consciousness manifests a mode of being which cannot be reduced to the corporeal status at all. Sensory perception is undoubtedly a conscious act. Here the knowing subject already asserts his superiority over matter. An act entirely subject to spatial dispersion could not have the character of self-knowledge or consciousness, since this on the contrary implies a strict unity, concentration and immanence. Indeed if the subject were a purely corporeal reality, its tendency to the object could only be conceived as a local movement, a transitive action, making immanence and consciousness impossible. Furthermore, the spatio-temporal exteriority or the dispersion of the elements making up a body is incompatible with the unity and concentration which characterize the immanence of the cognitive act. Perception then appears to be an act which is tied up with the corporeal world, yet it transcends the corporeal in some way; it is to some extent, incorporeal, immaterial, or spiritual.

The conscious character of my perceptions allows me to distinguish in every perception between the *object perceived* and the *act* of perception, between the datum and the grasping of it. I see a light, I hear a sound, I taste a flavor, I feel a resistance, I suffer a sting, a burn, or cold. Of course this does not mean that the problem of the nature of that distinction is thereby solved. But I am conscious that every perception involves a twofold experience for me.

It implies first of all an *objective experience,* or the experience of an "object," of a "term" which defines, specifies and measures my act; the perceived "presence" of an object, phenomenon, or appearance which modifies my consciousness; the experience of a fact which is submitted to by the sensory organ, which obtrudes itself upon me, sometimes so forcibly that it causes pain or even destroys the instrument of perception (in cases of blinding, deafening, and so forth).

It implies also *subjective experience,* a lived experience, the consciousness of an act of the self which grasps, seizes, possesses, and assimilates this datum.[6] Later on we will see that it is this twofold experience of the real, involved in sensory perception, which assures to human knowledge its essential value. The later processes of the cognitive activity merely develop what was acquired in perception.

Complete knowledge must start chronologically from sensory perception. In more general terms, sensory perception causes the first awakening of consciousness. The credit for having emphasized this fact, which is so characteristic of human knowledge, belongs to the Aristotelian tradition: "omnis cognitio nostra a sensu incipit." [7]

I can now sum up the results of my inquiry in the following way: The corporeal datum is composed of all the objects of my actual sensory perceptions. The organs of sight and touch play a preponderant role in the grasping of this datum. Among other things, they enable me to distinguish my own body from the collection of bodies surrounding me, whether they be distant or contiguous.

6. On the notions of "presence" and "lived contact," see Noël, *op. cit.,* pp. 197-223.
7. Even the traditional formula, *Nihil est in intellectu quod non prius fuerit in sensu,* can be interpreted in a satisfactory way, as will be shown presently.

§ 3. *The Represented Datum or the Image*

When a sensory perception disappears, as for example when I close my eyes, the objects of this perception do not completely disappear from me. I still keep the memory, recollection, image, or representation of them. My consciousness is stocked with a great number of images, which are residues of my previous perceptions. They are present to me with different degrees of clarity or actuality, and to a certain extent I can by conscious effort reinforce this presence and bring a certain image to the fore in my consciousness. Compared to the datum which they represent these images show the following striking characteristics: (a) They are a real element of my consciousness. They present themselves to me as a mysterious residue of perceived objects, or of the corporeal datum which was previously perceived. They are in a certain sense substitutes or representations. They remain in my consciousness when the sensory datum has disappeared. (b) The images are corporeal, in the sense that they represent the corporeal datum with its spatio-temporal characteristics. (c) The preservation of the images does not depend on the functioning of the sensory organs from which they came. Thus visual images persist even when I am not using my eyes. (d) Finally and especially, the images always have an essential reference to the datum. When my eyes are closed and I evoke the image of my desk, what I represent will not be a double, a copy, or a model scaled down to the dimension of my brain, but it will be the desk itself as I see it when I open my eyes. In other words, the image presents itself not as an "object" which is known, but rather as a mysterious "means" of evoking the object in my consciousness without appealing to an external sensory perception.

These images also show us another element of our subjective activity, namely, the imagination. The term "imagination" can signify either the *act* of cognition which is determined by the presence of an image in consciousness, or the *power* of knowing by means of images.[8] This same power of imagination is called sense or imaginative memory, when taken as the power of conserving previously acquired images and calling them back to consciousness. But the activity of imagination is not limited to that. I know that I can construct new objects by associating already acquired images. Thus I can represent a "winged horse," a "flying man," a "golden mountain." I can even create the story of an individual's life, or a story of a nation's life. I can create literary works such as tragedies, epics and novels. To the extent to which these creations of imagination, or these products of the creative imagination, go beyond images obtained from sensory perceptions, they evidently do not have the representative function that acquired images have. These spontaneous products of the imagination do not present themselves to consciousness as means for knowing an absent object, but rather as objects to be known. They are, however, imaginary objects—consciously constructed by the subject. They have the kind of reality proper to such constructs.[9]

The task of describing the properties of the imagination and the laws which govern it in producing, conserving, representing and associating images, belongs to descriptive psychology. The development of these points lies outside our present scope. But we can note that the play of the imagination, especially its characteristic compositive function, enriches

8. Here we are not talking about the metaphysical entity which the ancients called the *virtus imaginativa* or the *virtus phantastica*, but only about the "capacity" for knowing by images, as it shows itself to consciousness in its acts.

9. Critical epistemology has to determine what that "kind of reality" is.

my conscious life, but also complicates it and at times confuses it.

Can we easily *distinguish an image from a perceived datum?*

We know that the modern critique of knowledge has strongly emphasized certain cases in which the knowing subject cannot control his acts effectively. So it considers the problem of distinguishing between the world of images and the world of perceptions to be one of the hardest problems in philosophy. As a matter of fact certain conscious states are very obscure: thus, for example, the disturbances caused by fear, or other emotions, the morbid states of elation, delirium, hallucination, semi-consciousness in dreams, and so forth. In these cases the knowing subject cannot distinguish or analyze the elements making up his actual conscious state. Does not this sort of thing throw doubt on *all* conscious states? How can I know that I am not dreaming or suffering a hallucination at the present moment?

The answer is very simple. I know it by making a deliberate examination of my consciousness. If I could make this sort of examination when dreaming or when suffering the hallucination, I would see at once what was happening and would stop dreaming or being deluded. But these psychological states are precisely states of confused or diminished consciousness in which deliberate reflection is impossible.[10] At the present time, on the contrary, I feel perfectly able to examine what is going on in me, able to control the activity of my external senses, and able to distinguish my perceptions from my fantasies; in short, I am conscious that I am not dreaming or being deluded.

Modern criticism's way of considering these problems fre-

10. See Gilson, *Réalisme thomiste*, pp. 197-199.

quently reveals a basic fault in method. To meet the requirements of the methodic doubt and to get the greatest surety in his inquiry, the philosopher should rely on a reflective, attentive and calm analysis of his own consciousness. He should confine himself to the clear indisputable elements that this analysis furnishes. For the time being he will leave aside those confused states of semi-consciousness which exclude the reflection and attention necessary for a serious examination. In his first steps then he will not concern himself with the states of consciousness of the dreamer, or of the man who is drowsy and distracted, or suffering hallucinations. Epistemology should be a work of methodic and critical reflection. The study of these states of consciousness contributes little to its development. Such a study should be reserved rather for positive psychology, either normal or abnormal.

An attentive reflective consciousness usually finds it easy to distinguish between the corporeal datum and images. There is far more difference between the world which is perceived and the world which is imagined than a mere difference of degree of clarity, definiteness of contours, coherence of elements, or other like characteristics. There is clearly evident a basic difference *in the way in which they are present* to consciousness. To perceive an object means to possess it as a datum of experience, as an actual content of my consciousness; to imagine the same object means to re-present it to myself; it means to evoke its image in the objective field of my consciousness in some mysterious fashion, knowing all the while that the object represented is not present. When my consciousness is awake I find no difficulty in distinguishing between a friend who is actually seen and the image of this absent friend, between stomach cramps which I actually feel and the memory of those I suffered the evening before, be-

tween the meal actually served to me and the one which I
represent to myself in imagination. In short, the act of perception is a *real* psychological act which reaches a content of
consciousness equally *real,* while in the case of the image I am
conscious of the fact that the real psychological act of imag-
ining does not have an *objective content which is actually
present.* I know very well that the image is a substitute for
an absent object, that it is the residue or the trace in my consciousness of previous perceptions.[11]

Our ability to distinguish between the corporeal datum and
the image, between the real presence and the representation, is
also related to our control over our sensory organs. When a
corporeal object is present to me without the corresponding
sensory organ being active, then it is clearly a case of an object represented by imagination. On the other hand, I can say
that every time that the presence of an object in my consciousness depends upon the activity of a determined sensory
organ, such as the eye or the ear, then it is a case of actual
perception. And in most cases we can easily determine
whether a certain sense organ is functioning or not.

We can also note that the abnormal conscious states listed
above can be subjected to a later check. The person can make
this check himself on returning to a normal state of consciousness. He can do it in many ways. Take the most usual
case—a dream. A sleeping child believes that he is on the
bank of a river, and a terrible hurricane throws him into the
water. If he were sufficiently awake to make even a short
reflection on his actual condition, he would realize that his
eyes are closed, that the wind is not blowing on his face, that
he is lying in bed, and so forth. But then he would automatically have ceased sleeping and dreaming, he would be

11. See *"Problèmes épistémologiques fondamentaux,"* pp. 488-490.

back in a normal state of consciousness. Now, this is what actually takes place. Just as the child is about to fall into the water, his agony arouses him from sleep and he realizes that he is in bed. He immediately distinguishes between what is actually given, and the images. He says, "If I had fallen into the water, I would have been soaking wet, I would have been drowned, I would not be in my bed. But perhaps some kindly person took me from the water and put me here? But that cannot be, because I awoke in bed while I was falling into the water, before I reached the water. Furthermore, my parents who were awake near me tell me that I did not leave my bed or room, that I did not open my eyes, and that the wind did not blow." So the child concludes that he was dreaming. In other words this whole "vision" was imaginary, it was caused by an association of images.

We have already seen that consciousness transcends purely corporeal realities even on the level of perception. This is even more evident on the level of imagination. Imagination is not only a *conscious* activity (like perception), but the fact that I know the absent as absent, the past as the past, and the future as the future, shows that I distinguish between the datum and the images. And this activity simply cannot be reduced to a purely bodily activity.

I can know the absent as absent, that is, precisely in so far as it is spatially inaccessible. I can think of Pope Pius XII in the city of Rome. It is true that these objects are "represented" or "made present" in me by images, but if everything were reduced to images, then I should know the objects as present. (This can happen at times, in dreams or other similar states, strong distractions, day-dreaming, hallucinations.) But to know these objects as absent means to know them precisely as *not present*. If we pause to consider what this denial of spatial presence implies, we will realize that it reveals a knowing power free from conditions of space.

The same thing could be said about my knowledge of the past as past (the life of Plato), or of the future as future (the year 2000). Corporeal images can help me to "represent" past and future events, or make them "present to me," but they cannot explain how I can know these events as *not present*.

§ 4. *The Abstracted Datum or Concept*

All the elements comprising the objective pole described up to this point are marked and affected by spatio-temporal or corporeal conditions. Sensation and imagination concern corporeal objects. But even on the plane of these acts, the datum is to some extent "assimilated" by the subject since these acts are conscious. The corporeal object, and still more its image, "live" in me. My possession of the object in perception is still superficial and precarious, for the object must lie within the operational field of my sensory organs. In imagination my possession of the object becomes more intimate and more stable, for I preserve these images within the immanence of the conscious self and I exercise a certain dominion over them. To a certain extent I can evoke them in my actual consciousness, combine them, and transform them as I wish. The final phase of this process of assimilation is reached by "abstraction" in the idea or concept. Here the datum takes on in full measure the immanence of the conscious self—it completely becomes my life, and since I am in some way spirit it becomes "spirit" in me.[12]

12. Here we use the term "spirit" in a psychological sense. My consciousness shows characteristics which transcend those of purely material realities, or "bodies."

In a very general sense abstract signifies "separated" or "isolated" (*abstractum* = drawn away). The object of a sensory perception can be said to be abstract in this sense, since color, for example, is an object "isolated" from other objects really united with it and forming together one same thing. Our vision separates the color of this piece of sugar from its weight, resistance to touch, roughness and taste. Even within the domain of a given sense, the subject's attention can be focused on one detail rather than on another, it can concern itself, for example, with the form rather than with the color. Taken in a narrower and more usual sense, "abstract" signifies "separated or isolated from the corporeal," that is, from the spatio-temporal, freed from the corporeal conditions of space and time (*hic et nunc*). Are there any "contents" in my consciousness which are abstracted in this more precise sense?

Different philosophical groups have denied that any abstract representations exist in us. They take the ideas to be only "schematic images." This view was especially defended in the materialist and positivist circles of the nineteenth century. According to them, the idea of man, for example, would be an image which is so vague, blurred, loose and impoverished that it can now represent any man, big or small, fat or thin, white or black, and so forth. They say that the idea of triangle is a vague representation, a pattern which is so blurred that it is neither a right-angled triangle, nor an isosceles triangle, neither a large nor a small triangle, neither a red nor a blue triangle. Now, in reality there is nothing in common between the concept and the schematic image, except that the concept is somehow also a means of "re-presenting" a datum of experience to myself.

To see exactly what a concept is and how it differs from

the image, we can start by describing first the basic concept which dominates all the life of the mind, and then the two great categories of concepts which proceed from it.

The Concept of Being or Reality.—We know already that being is the *primum notum.* The "real" forms the object of our very first experience, of our very first evidence, of our very first affirmation: "something exists." This affirmation implies the presence of a concept, as we shall see. Let us suppose that we have some experience of a reality—that we perceive some blue datum. Now, I can stop perceiving it, without it ceasing to be present to me in the form of an "image," at least, as the vague, loose image of any object. Nevertheless this image still remains an *individual* image, situated at a certain place in the objective field of my consciousness, occupying a certain part of the temporal duration which envelops all the concrete contents of my consciousness. But now I spontaneously react to this datum and this image, and I see that, thanks to this object, I can have the *same basic experience* that I may have with any object. I can find in it the same fundamental value previously found in every other object. I state this discovery to myself, when I make the judgment, "This blue object is *real,* this object *exists.*" In the attribute or predicate of this judgment, the object is represented under a new form ("real," "exists"). This is no longer an individual representation situated *hic et nunc* (in time and space), because the same representation can be used to express any other object of experience. Thus I have transformed the individual and concrete object into a *universal* representation, that is, one which can be applied to an indefinite series of objects, one which is *abstracted* for this purpose from individualizing conditions. In short I have transformed this object into an idea or concept.

The Empirical Concept.—The real which is given in experience (whether subjective or objective makes little difference) is manifold or varied. To consider it only as a unity would be to consider it in a very incomplete way. Accordingly I am not satisfied with merely expressing the datum in terms of the general concept of *being,* but I also try to express in concepts all the *modes of being* which are given in my objective experience and in my lived experience. This effort gives rise to a great number of concepts which we call *empirical concepts.* In this way every element of experience can be expressed in a concept. Essentially this operation will always be the same as the one which gave us the basic concept of being. In fact, it only makes that first abstraction more precise. In the concept of being a certain datum of experience is conceived or represented as "real," as "being." In the empirical concept, this determined datum is conceived and represented as a "determination" or "limitation" of being, as a certain "manner of being," a "mode of being," an "essence," a "such," a "nature," a "quiddity." The only new conceptual element in the empirical concept is the referring or relating of a certain datum of experience to the basic concept of being. Thus the immediate meaning of the concept "blue" is a reality or mode of being which is specified by the object of this definite sensory impression. To form the concept "blue" means to represent a blue datum as a mode of being which has a universal value; it means recognizing that the experiencing of a blue object is the experiencing of a mode of being which can be shared by an indefinite series of concrete objects, of which this blue object is one particular case.

There exists a great variety of empirical concepts. We can distinguish the following principal groups. Some of these concepts are formed from *objective* or sensory experience (for example, the concepts of "body," "circle," "red"). Other concepts are taken from *lived* experience (for example, the concepts of "self," "tendency," "desire," "hunger," "anxiety"). Some of them are *simple*—formed by apprehending a simple object (for example, the concepts of "red," "sting," "cold"). Others are *complex*—arising from an apprehension of a complex object (for example, the empirical concepts of "house," "tree," "man," "cat," "broom," "triangle"). When a certain group of objects appears to me as a definite and stable whole, which comes and goes as a whole in the field of my consciousness, then I recognize a certain unity there. I take it to be a certain mode of being, a certain essence, a "thing," which I designate by a name, and represent by a concept. Finally, some empirical concepts represent an object taken *separately* (for example, "blue," "triangle," "cat"), while others express an empirical *relation* between objects (for example, the concepts, "distant," "larger than," "successive," "similar"). In short, all empirical concepts are of the same nature. When a datum of experience is conceived as a mode of being, when it is assimilated in the basic concept of being, then we get empirical concepts.

Elaborated Concepts.—Once the knowing subject has acquired concepts formed directly from experience, he begins to see that there are many *relations* among them. He continues his work of conceptualization by associating these concepts somewhat as the imagination associates concrete representations. This work of combining concepts and ideas gives rise to more and more complex ideas, and to ever wider conceptual constructions.

How is this process carried out? An example will show how it is done. We said above that the idea "triangle" is an example of a complex idea gotten by direct assimilation of a complex object. The sight of the triangular pediment of a building can give rise directly to the idea of triangle, that is, to the idea of a "certain way of existing," characterized by the geometrical form of this pediment. But let us suppose that I have from other sources the simple ideas of body, surface, plane, straight line, and point. All these have their origin in experience. Then by combining these simple ideas, I can construct the idea of triangle as a plane surface enclosed by three straight lines which intersect at three points. This idea of triangle is no different from the first idea of a triangle that I had, but it is clearer and more developed. It expresses the essence or the mode of being of a triangle better, by giving us in explicit fashion the notes which make it up. If I have a complex idea which was originally abstracted from a complex object, I can reduce it to an idea formed by combining simple ideas, if the complex object can be analyzed into its constituent parts. For then these parts can give rise to simple empirical ideas, which can be used to reconstruct the object on the level of concepts.

The nature of the given objects is not the only factor influencing the subject in the construction of ideas. There is also a certain amount of arbitrary choice shown in the elements which are combined, for the definition of a thing can be made from different points of view, especially when an artificial thing is involved. Depending on where his interests lie, the subject can emphasize some characteristics of the thing rather than others.

From this brief analysis of the "concept-forming" activity of consciousness, we can easily see what are the principal *marks* of the concept or idea.

(a) *The idea is a real element of my consciousness.* It is the real representation of a certain aspect, or certain value that I have found in the datum of experience, and which appears to me to be capable of being isolated from the individual, the particular, the concrete.

(b) *The idea is a content of consciousness* which cannot be reduced to the corporeal datum it expresses, or to the image on which it rests, for the idea is a *universal representation*. Every datum of experience is particular. It is situated among other data which it opposes. It is distinct from every other datum. Every image represents a certain datum, which is particular, distinct and situated in space and time, and however blurred and vague an image may be, it is always possible to imagine others like it which will be distinguished from the first in time or in space. The image can be simplified and schematized as much as you wish, but it will only grow poorer. It will never become anything other than a particular representation. On the other hand, the concept is a universal representation capable of signifying an infinity of objects. It cannot be in itself *multiplied*, but it can be *participated* in by an indefinite series of objects.

The analysis of human consciousness shows me that this universal character of our ideas cannot be denied. It is, in fact, clear that the idea "red" or the idea "triangle" appear to me to be not merely the representation of some particular object, but rather the expression and transcription in me of *any* red object or *any* triangular object whatever, which ever has been, is, or ever will or could be present in the field of my consciousness.

Where do I get evidence for this? What shows me that the idea can represent a number of particular objects? The experiencing of a number of "red" or "triangular" objects would not be sufficient of itself. This experience can help me to discover a real similarity among these red or triangular objects. They all share in this mode of being which I call "red" or "triangular," and which I then transcribe in myself by the concepts of "red" or "triangle." But I must become aware of the proper nature of these concepts in order to see this universal character. On the other hand, if I considered only the proper nature of the concept, this would not show me its universality. An examination of the content of the concepts "red" or "triangle" does not suggest that "red" and "triangle" are unique objects which cannot be duplicated. But this sort of examination by itself will not show me that it is possible to have many red or triangular objects.

This universal character of our ideas is shown by *bringing together the idea and the spatio-temporal experience.* My perception of space and time gives me the idea of purely numerical multiplication, because the essential divisibility of space and time implies that it is possible to have repetition and indefinite reproduction of the same object at different places and times. Furthermore, many experiences show that this possibility is realized, for I see various series of units, (for example, an avenue of poplar trees, a flock of sheep, a convoy of trucks, a box of matches, and so forth). In brief, every object I perceive appears to me to be individual or distinct from every other. Yet at the same time it seems *capable of duplication* in other specimens which would be numerically distinct.[13] The idea, on the other hand, appears to be essen-

13. At this point we do not have to determine whether "purely numerical multiplication" is actually realized on the level of "substances" and to what extent.

tially *one*, but with a unity which can be shared by or communicated to many individuals. It appears to be the unique representation or "law" (that is, the constant or unvarying expression) for an indefinite series of particular cases, or again, it appears to be a tendency evocative of an indefinite series of concrete objects which it represents in a certain way. The idea is *universal*, a *synthetic representation*.

This brings out one of the first functions of the idea; it enables us to *unify* an indefinite multitude of particular data in the immanence of consciousness. This function belongs in a preëminent way to the basic concept of being, since this *synthesizes* all possible experiences. The concept of being synthesizes not by imposing unity in an *a priori* way on a completely diversified datum, but rather by recognizing the basic unity shown by the datum in spite of its diversity. An ontological interpretation of knowledge could perhaps ask whether the unity which the datum has, as being, is not given to it by some unconscious activity of the subject which imposes a unifying form in some *a priori* way on what is diverse. But when we are merely describing the data of consciousness there can be no question of any such form.[14]

(c) *The idea is abstract,* that is, disengaged from the concrete spatio-temporal conditions that characterize every cor-

---

This problem belongs to metaphysics. It would be premature to discuss it at this time. It in turn will raise other thorny questions, such as that of the individuation of corporeal realities.

14. See J. de Vries, *Critica* (Freiburg im Breisgau, 1937), pp. 29-33, on the universal character of our concepts. Father de Vries also believes that he can talk about "singular concepts" (pp. 42-43). We believe that this is a result of an undesirable juxtaposition of intellection and perception. We can judge about concrete singular objects not because we have "singular concepts," but because our act of perception is already a properly human act. It is not a pure sensation such as we can suppose it to be in the animal (see above, pp. 119-20.) On the nature and role of concepts, see also Noël, *op. cit.*, pp. 17-19, 181, 292.

poreal object. This new essential quality of the idea is implied in the *universal* character which we have just analyzed. If the idea were a concrete content of consciousness, determined *hic et nunc* (here and now), it could not be universal, that is, *capable of being shared by an indefinite series of objects.* The operation of abstraction [15] consists essentially in seizing in a datum of experience either the value of being or reality, or some particular mode of this value, a mode of being, a quiddity, an essence. Or in other words, the operation of abstraction consists in isolating in this reality present to consciousness either the basic value (the idea of being) or a particular form of this value (an empirical idea). Sensory abstraction, or abstraction improperly so called, isolates one corporeal element from other corporeal elements; it impoverishes the datum. It is true that abstraction properly so called isolates some note from the spatio-temporal context in which it appears, but it does this to transpose that note from the realm of particular fleeting facts to the more intimate level of consciousness, and to give it a mode of existence which is immaterial, stable and universal. Abstraction properly so called is above all a developing of the datum and an enriching of the act of cognition. Every element of experience gains a higher type of existence when it becomes an idea, or acquires an "ideal" existence.

The fact of abstraction characterizes our human knowledge. Let us note well what it implies. On the side of expe-

15. To avoid all misunderstanding, note that we are speaking here only of the immediate data of consciousness, consequently the expression "operation of abstraction" refers here to that operation only in so far as it is conscious. The Scholastics were aware of this purely psychological meaning *(abstrahere est separatim considerare).* It is the only sense noted by Lalande in his *Vocabulaire,* Vol. I, p. 7: "Abstraction, action de l'ésprit considérant à part un élément d'une représentation."

rience it implies that the datum really possesses the values which the subject discovers in it. Ideas (different modalities of being) are incarnated in the matter. On the side of the subject itself, the operation of abstraction shows that the subject has a certain power of apprehending the value of being, or a capacity for discovering being and the modes of being which are hidden in the spatio-temporal world, or the world of lived experience.

Note that even those concepts which represent spatio-temporal objects are abstract, that is, freed from the shackles of fixed space and time. Thus the empirical concept of "cat" represents my cat as a certain kind of corporeal being; it represents the cat as having to exist by "nature" at a definite place and time, but the concept does not fix any place or time.

(d) *The idea always expresses either directly or indirectly an objective or lived experience.* To Plato belongs the credit for having emphasized the distinctive qualities of our ideas, and their transcendence over sensory perception. But Plato concluded that the ideas were completely independent of experience. He believed that ideas had their own subsistence, that they formed an incorporeal world of intelligible realities. This view is found in various forms in the whole Platonic tradition.

For its part, nominalism does not recognize the true value of concepts when it reduces them to mere *symbols*, that is, signs or labels representing a class of objects. It takes concepts to be only universal *words* bound by association to an indefinite series of similar images and evoking this series of images. Nominalism loses sight of the *meaning* of words. Influenced by Kant's distinction between empirical concepts and *a priori* concepts, modern idealists make the concept-forming activity into a spontaneous, *a priori* activity which is independent of experience. But these theories cannot be reconciled with the genuine data of consciousness. The Aristotelian tradition must be credited with having recognized the empirical origin of all our concepts. In my consciousness there is not a single idea which does not express an experience either immediately or mediately. The knowing subject does not posit anything which was not forced on it. It does not produce anything without the help of a datum. I have no innate ideas; all my ideas are acquired with the help of experience.

Now we can see the exact sense that ought to be given to the scholastic principle, *Nihil est in intellectu quod non prius fuerit in sensu.* Human consciousness awakes with sensory experience. The subjective or lived experience depends psychologically on the sensory experience, since self-awareness is had only when I know an object. Furthermore, the lived experience is primarily the experiencing of an *organic* activity composed of perceptions and emotions. My activity is never purely *spiritual.* So all my concepts without exception, that is, all my abstract representations, are *derived from concrete experience.* The only fault we can find with the traditional formula is that of using the term "sensus." The term "sensus" does not seem to embrace *all* our concrete experience.[16] It appears to neglect lived experience.

16. Here it is useful to note that the criticisms launched against the Scholastics by Descartes, Leibniz and other moderns, because of this principle *nihil est in intellectu quod non prius fuerit in sensu,* show a profound ignorance of Aristotelian thought. If we take the word *abstract* in the crude sense of "extract," it is certain that no concept is abstracted from the sensible. But no Aristotelian ever imagined that the ideas "came out" of sensible experience already completely formed, since Aristotelianism proclaims the transcendency of the intelligence with respect to sense, and takes the active intellect to be the active and immaterial principle of ideas. So the Scholastics felt no obligation to explain that at least the intelligence itself did not "come out of" the senses, or that the ideas of the soul and God did not previously "reside" in the senses. No one

Since it is the expression of an experience, the idea by its very nature refers to experience, that is, to the perceived or lived datum that it represents and expresses. Our attempts at abstraction tend to isolate the idea ("whiteness," "sonorousness," "irritability," "existence"), but the idea will lose all substance and sense if we try to take it independently of the datum from which it came and the concrete image which continues the experience. It is because it is essentially incomplete and "looks to" its object that the idea has an internal dynamism, which evokes the many individuals it synthesizes.[17] Besides, the idea is not the object of knowledge primarily; it is rather the act by which and in which the subject possesses the perceived object in an abstract way. The idea is called the act *by which* (*medium quo*) because the idea is naturally oriented to the object present to consciousness, which is the term of knowledge. The idea is called the act *in which* (*medium in quo*), for as soon as the act is placed it is to some extent conscious since it is a lived act in consciousness. As I become more perfectly aware of the idea, the idea itself becomes the reflex or indirect object of my intellection.

(e) *The idea has a stable precise content.* The *stability* of the idea results from its abstract character. Since it is disengaged from the flux of concrete experience the idea enjoys a value which is independent of any circumstance of time and place. Again, it is abstraction which gives the idea a precise content since abstraction isolates and emphasizes one determined aspect of the datum. But this precision is not

---

in the Middle Ages imagined such glaring blunders. These points were so elementary for the Scholastics that they did not hesitate to use daring metaphors in expressing the relationship between the sensible object and the specification of ideas. Perhaps this point could excuse the childish interpretations made by certain modern philosophers. See Gilson, *Réalisme thomiste*, pp. 200-203.

17. See above, p. 135.

the same in all cases. In the case of the concept of being and the simple empirical concepts, the precision is caused by the object. In the case of complex empirical concepts and elaborated concepts, we have seen that the subject's choice fixes their content at least in part. The subject's attention and interest will center successively on the several aspects of the datum, trying to discover its structure or nature more fully. The subject never stops forming concepts. He is always trying to form more adequate concepts. But each step in this effort can be expressed in a precise concept, which can be analyzed in a definition.[18]

The presence of these concepts or abstract representations in my consciousness shows me a new element in my cognitive activity, one which is distinct from perception and imagination. It is *intellection, thought,* or *intellectual activity.* The capacity or power of thinking is called the *intellect.*

Intellection is usually described by contrasting it with sensation. Sensation is taken to be a purely corporeal activity. Then intellection is defined in terms of its formal object, being, while the object of sensation is said to be the phenomenon or appearance. However, this way of presenting the case does not seem to conform well to the actual data of consciousness. For in myself sensation is already an experience of the real, an intuition of being. It is my complete human knowledge which should be defined as a capacity for being, as a power of

18. An example: Having seen a "chair," I can define it as "a rigid corporeal reality destined to facilitate the seated position of man." This is a definition which is *precise,* but *incomplete,* because it does not help me distinguish the chair from an easy chair, a sofa, a bench and so forth. Further experience with these new objects will lead me to complete my first notion which was in reality the more general notion of "seat." My enriched concept can now be expressed in another definition, also *precise* but richer than the first. This will be the true definition of "chair"—that is, one which belongs to each of the defined objects and only to them.

apprehending being as such and of recognizing the value of existence in any given datum of experience. Intellection is distinguished by the abstract nature of its contents. The intellect is the faculty of conceiving abstract ideas. Human intellection is essentially a "conceptive" or "conceptual" activity. Its role is to develop and synthesize the initial knowledge of the real begun on the level of experience.[19]

Now, the intellectual activity itself is very complex. Intellection properly speaking, or intellectual conception which we have just described, marks the beginning of an extremely rich and active development which plays a capital role in human knowledge. We will gradually see more of this development.

The transcendency of our conceptual activity with respect to purely corporeal realities stands out clearly at the end of this study. A purely organic activity would be riveted to the individual, to the *hic et nunc*. It could not account for my universal abstract representations. Neither could it account for my ability to conceive, at least in a hypothetical way, incorporeal objects.

§ 5. *The Affirmation or Judgment*

The Aristotelian tradition emphasizes the capital role of the judgment in human knowledge. The judgment (affirmation, internal speech, interior word, mental word) appears to be

---

19. In other words, human intellection is an *abstractive* activity. It is grafted upon a basic activity which is *intuitive* in character. This is the conscious perception which involves at the same time an intuition or experience of the non-self and the self, the apprehension of the one and the other as real. In a pure spirit on the other hand, intellection is necessarily *intuitive* because it has to perform in an eminent way the two tasks that perception and conception share in us, namely, the intuition of the concrete reality and synthetic or universal knowledge by abstract concepts.

the completion of the cognitive act. For with the judgment, consciousness and the subject's assimilation of the object reach their highest point. The subject becomes "conscious" of this "new possession of the object," and states to himself what this new reality is which he has acquired. What does reflection tell us about the judgment?

Every judgment appears to be a synthesis of two terms. These are called subject and predicate, when the judgment is written or spoken. What is the role of these two terms? Let us take the judgment, "This is white," as an example. Here the subject represents a datum of experience as *merely present* to consciousness, while the predicate represents a certain aspect of this datum, as *already assimilated by the conceptual activity of the intellect*. The judgment then points up the presence of a datum (by the *subject*, "this"); at the same time it opposes to this datum a concept which assimilates it further (the *predicate*, "white"); and it further expresses the basic identity of the one and the other (by the *copula* "is").

However, we cannot consider the identity of the subject and predicate to be a complete and absolute identity. It is true that we can formulate a judgment of pure identity, along the line of $a = a$. But this judgment is only an artifice of thought, a pure tautology. The "principle of identity" is not a judgment properly speaking. It can serve to show the *ideal term* to which human knowledge tends, that is, the identity of the conceptual act and the object; but it shows at the same time that if this ideal were reached, the complex act of judgment would no longer have any sense.[20] The synthesis

20. Thus Aristotelianism paid little attention to "the principle of identity." The "first principle" for Aristotle was the principle of non-contradiction. On the principle of identity, see A. Mansion, *"Sur la correspondance du logique et du réel,"* in *Revue Néoscolastique de Philosophie* (August, 1932), pp. 311-314.

made in the judgment supposes, then, a *partial non-identity* between the object and the concept which I have of it, a certain inadequateness that the subject claims to overcome by the affirmation.

In what does this inadequateness consist? We have already said that there are different levels in the assimilation of the datum by consciousness. The inadequateness consists in the difference between these levels. Thus in an immediate judgment, that is, in a judgment whose subject signifies a datum of experience (either perceived or lived), the subject will express the assimilation taking place on the level of perceptions or images, while the predicate will express the assimilation taking place on the level of concepts. ("This cat runs"; "This wall is white.") In mediate or derived judgments we can see a similar progress in the assimilation. ("Whiteness is a color"; "A color is a quality"; "A quality is a mode of being.") In such judgments the progress in assimilation is not had by advancing to a higher degree of immanence, but rather there is an advance in analyzing the datum, in bringing out better its content and relations. It is a progress which tries to understand the datum in an increasingly better way by relating it to its context and by relating it to the supreme unity of the basic intelligible "being."

The judgment is a synthesis, that is, an identification of predicate and subject, *because it follows abstraction which is an analysis*. The judgment, in fact, restores to the object what abstraction had separated from it. It corrects the imperfection of human knowledge by uniting as far as possible the concrete object and the conceptual activity of the subject. This amounts to saying that to be coherent every affirmative judgment must be "analytical," for unless the predicate were contained in the subject, we could not restore it to the subject by a judgment of attribution.[21]

The judgment appears to be the term and completion of the elementary act of knowledge. Later acts are only combinations of judgments. We must sum up the development of an act of human knowledge in the following way: The subject is first dominated by a concrete object whose presence in its field of consciousness attracts or provokes its attention; the subject then produces abstract representations of the object in the form of ideas (or concepts), according as its attention is drawn to this or that element of the datum—all sorts of factors, both objective and subjective, can help fix the subject's conscious attention; finally, when this new situation in consciousness has become clear, the subject expresses the result of the process. It does this in the affirmation or judgment, which is an active synthesis restoring to the object this or that aspect featured by the corresponding idea.[22]

21. It is therefore unfortunate to talk as Kant did of "synthetic judgments," and still more of "synthetic a priori judgments." The judgments that Kant called "synthetic a posteriori" also result from an *analysis* of the subject. But in this case the subject is a concrete reality instead of being an abstract concept as in "analytical" judgments in the Kantian sense of the term. To be able to state that "the cat sleeps," we must have found the attribute "sleeps" in the subject "cat." We must have seen the cat asleep. With regard to the "synthetic a priori judgments," we must reject them precisely because they claim not to be based on any analysis of the subject.

The ancients were much better advised when they distinguished between judgments "in necessary matter" and judgments "in contingent matter," judgments *per se nota simpliciter* and judgments *per se nota quoad nos*. See these classifications in logic. These distinctions do not answer the problems raised by Kant, but at least they help us to *formulate* the problem correctly and to avoid involving ourselves in false problems. For a critique of the "synthetic a priori judgments" of Kant, see Mercier, *Critériologie*, pp. 282-290.

22. On the nature of the judgment see also Noël, *op. cit.*, pp. 147-158.

§ 6. *The Unity of the Act of Cognition*

This complexity of the cognitive act does not destroy its unity. Many philosophical errors and false problems have been the result of philosophers losing sight of this unity of the cognitive act, either because they juxtaposed the elements or treated them as complete acts, or neglected some aspect of the complete act. So, for example, empiricism emphasized experience and neglected the conceptual activity. The idealist current on the contrary sacrifices experience, because idealism wished to emphasize the independence and spontaneity of thought with respect to the datum. As we conclude our analysis of the cognitive act we are in a better position to appreciate the structure and unity of this act. There are two general aspects to this structure. On the one hand there is a multiplicity of complementary components (such as perception, imagination, conception, affirmation) ; on the other hand there is a certain progress and becoming in the production of the complete act. It is on the level of perception that the act is most marked by spatio-temporal dispersion; it is in the judgment that it is most marked by the unity characteristic of spiritual immanence. But this unity is never perfect because it still remains a unity of composition, revealed even in the structure of the judgment itself by the duality of the *object* (the objective datum—either actual or represented by an image) and the *subject* (subjective activity). In other words, there is duality of the *objective term* present to the act, and the act itself. Consequently, there is a duality of knowledge and consciousness. In the act itself there is a duality of experience and conception, or a duality of the intuition of the concrete and the abstract representation. My knowledge is never "pure experience," without conception or thought, for as soon as my experience is conscious, it is translated into concepts. But neither is my knowledge ever "pure conception," or "pure thought," for the idea refers always and essentially to an experience which it expresses and signifies. If the idea is isolated from all experience, it loses all meaning for me.

Let us examine these different points of opposition more closely. What finally explains them all? *It is the fact that my knowledge is essentially assimilative.* Here we are not talking about the basic ontological conditions for knowledge. We have already noted that this question cannot be treated in epistemology. We are talking about knowledge as it appears immediately to itself in consciousness. *On this level it is an act which is dominated by an object. It is an activity marked by receptivity and even by passivity. It is a spiritual consciousness which, through corporeal organs, opens on a corporeal world.*[23] If my knowledge did not have this characteristic of being an assimilative knowledge, it would be simply self-consciousness, a perfectly immanent act, which would be both pure experience and pure idea, because this experience would be the consciousness of my spiritual act. But in my present status, my lived experience or my consciousness is always the consciousness of an activity which is both organic and transcendent to matter.

We must finally describe our complete cognitive act in the following way: On the level of the sense organism the knowing subject is dominated by the datum, that is, by the objects which obtrude on it. The subject submits passively to them, it "receives" them in its immanence. But that very fact implies that it reacts at once to this contact with objects by a

23. Let us not forget that we have not as yet explained the ontological relationship of this corporeal world to the self.

complex cognitive act, which begins on the level of the sense
organism (perception and imagination) and develops in a
state of perfect immanence (conception and judgment). The
progressive evolution of this cognitive act appears to be a
process of increasing assimilation, of increasing digestion of
the datum. And inversely, as we go from datum to image
and from image to idea, "objectivity" decreases. In other
words, the opposition between the datum and the subject,
which assimilates it in order better to possess it, decreases.

The characteristic feature of my knowledge is that *it is a
consciousness opening on a corporeal world, it is an immanent
act which unites in some mysterious fashion the reaction of a
bodily organ to the stimulation that it feels.* We cannot insist too much on these points, when we consider how much
the prejudices of idealism have beclouded these essential data.
The presence of mysterious or surprising aspects does not
destroy the evidence. And if I do not understand how consciousness can use an organ as an instrument of knowledge, I
am not thereby authorized to reject these immediate data and
to declare that the human consciousness is a "closed consciousness," bent back on itself, whose horizon is limited to its own
representations. Yet this is the picture which Descartes has
bequeathed to us. In the same way a longing for "intellectual
intuition" and "pure thought" does not justify expressions
which discredit or ignore the unity and characteristics peculiar to human knowledge. In other words, the brightest
point in the universe for us is not "thought in act," but
rather "knowledge in act," that is, *the complete cognitive act
as a synthesis of experience and thought.* Nor is it lived
experience rather than objective experience, for human consciousness is essentially "open" and assimilative and is naturally oriented toward the sense datum. It is the objective

datum which explains the cognitive act and, through that act, the activity or dynamism of the knowing subject. It is not natural to attempt to fix our attention on our lived activities alone. In fact, it is very difficult even to try to do so. When we try to conceive our acts and their hidden principles in so far as they transcend matter, we see that our concepts are still accompanied by spatial images. It is out of respect for the real conditions of human knowledge that Aristotelianism prefers to formulate its theory of knowledge in terms of objects and objective experience. For in an assimilative knowledge the object is first and dominant. Idealism on the contrary adopts an attitude which is non-human and artificial. It tries to practise an "angelicism" which is not within our reach.[24]

24. Much profit can be derived from an examination of the analysis of human knowledge which De Coninck tries to make in his remarkable study *L'unité de la connaissance humaine et le fondement de sa valeur* (2nd ed., pp. 17-46). Unless we are mistaken, this very original treatment is also a very penetrating one. From it we have taken several important suggestions.

Chapter VII

THE TOTAL ACTIVITY OF THE
KNOWING SUBJECT

THE elementary act of knowledge forms part of the knowing subject's total activity. It is only one of the factors in this many-sided activity in which we can distinguish three principal aspects, the cognitive activity, the appetite, and the biological activity.

§ 1. *The Integral Activity of the Subject*

We have already seen that the cognitive act is the act of a living being. My cognitive act is an immanent operation, contributing to the development and perfection of the living being that I am. This act is, then, not at all isolated; it is linked up with my other acts, it has a vital connection with my total activity; it is only one element or factor in this activity, or this constant evolution of which I am both the source and the beneficiary. We will soon have to determine the precise role which the cognitive act has in the life of the knowing subject, or in other words, what the finality of this act is. But we must first continue our description of consciousness by analyzing briefly the principal characteristics of the knowing subject's total activity as seen in consciousness.

§ 2. *The Cognitive Activity*

My cognitive activity is without any doubt the most conspicuous of all my activities, since it constitutes consciousness and is identified with it. The cognitive act which we have been analyzing up to now is but a link in an almost uninterrupted succession of cognitive acts. On the other hand, my cognitive acts are never simply juxtaposed like a series of heterogeneous images appearing one after the other on a projection screen. My conscious life is continuous. My cognitive acts are linked together, and they gradually blend together in the unity of my consciousness.

If we examine this evolution closely, we will see that it depends on two distinct factors: first, the changes which take place in the objective field of my consciousness (the appearance of new objects, the disappearance of old objects, and the transformation of objects); secondly, the subject's autonomous activity. The first of these factors is only another aspect of the corporeal datum's complexity. Not only does this datum present an infinite variety of characteristics, but it is also in a state of continual becoming. The second factor in the development of knowledge is the subject himself, for he is not an inert or passive spectator of this process. The subject actively promotes the progress of his knowledge, when he turns his attention to new objects, when he utilizes former knowledge to make his present knowledge more precise, when he tries to associate his images, ideas and judgments.

The principal phases to be distinguished in this activity of the knowing subject are the following: (a) *Attention.*—This is the direction of the conscious activity to a determined object. Psychology will study the laws and effects of attention. In epistemology we merely note that attention plays an important part in the evolution of knowledge and that attention is necessary for the critical examination of consciousness.[1]

1. In critical epistemology we will see that lack of attention is one of the principal causes of error.

(b) *Sense memory.*—We have already spoken of the power of the imagination to conserve the images of perceived objects [2] and to call these images back into consciousness. Psychology will try to determine the laws of sense memory and the influence which these past images have on actual perceptions. When we try to determine the value of perception in critical epistemology, we will have to take that influence into account.

(c) *Association of images.*—Here we are speaking of this process in so far as consciousness can follow it. It is obvious that I can construct new images by utilizing simpler images remaining from sense perceptions. I can represent a "golden house," a "winged man," a "dragon," and so forth. We have already noted some of the consequences that this creative function of the imagination can have in epistemology.[3]

(d) *Intellectual memory.*—Once ideas are acquired they can "remain" in consciousness. Even if they disappear from actual consciousness, the subject can recall them at least to some extent. Psychology tries to discover the conditions and laws of this intellectual memory, which conserves and re-presents concepts. (e) *Association of ideas or the work of conceptual construction.*—We have seen that the work of man's mind in forming concepts does not stop with the elaboration of empirical concepts, but that it also tries to group, classify and organize concepts by discovering their connecting relations. This work of association tends to produce *elaborated concepts,* which become richer and richer while trying to express objects which are more and more complicated. This work of association also tends to produce classifications of concepts or systems. We find the first example of this in the writings of Aristotle. The definition is the typical example of this work

2. See above, p. 123.
3. *Ibid.*, p. 124.

of conceptual construction, being a statement which locates an elaborated concept in a system of concepts and thus enumerates the elements which make it up. So when I define man as "a substance which is corporeal, living, sensible, and rational," I characterize man by a group of simpler concepts subordinated one to the other. I locate man in the traditional classification of genera and species. (f) *Reasoning.*—Now, just as the subject continues to combine concepts indefinitely, and thus construct more and more complex definitions or quiddities, so the subject also combines judgments in many ways. If we call every affirmation which refers immediately to a concrete object present to consciousness (or "represented" by sense memory) an immediate judgment, then we shall see that the intelligence starts from these immediate judgments to build up its mediate or derived judgments, and the systems of judgments which become more and more complex. In fact, a "science" is only a system of judgments relating to the same object.

The intellect is called "reason" or "discursive intelligence," that is, the faculty of reasoning, in so far as it has the power of combining its concepts and judgments. We can easily appreciate the capital place which reason holds in human knowledge, and consequently the importance of a critique of reasoning in the general critique of knowledge. The critique of reasoning presupposes an *analysis of reasoning,* that is, a precise description of the procedures used by reason in combining concepts and judgments. Descriptive epistemology could analyze reasoning to prepare the way for a critical appreciation in critical epistemology. But for centuries this analytical and critical study of reasoning has been taken care of by a distinct science, logic. This study has grown to considerable proportions. We will, therefore, follow the traditional arrangement of problems and reserve the analysis and critique of the reasoning processes for the third part of general epistemology. In these first two parts we limit ourselves to noting that this reasoning activity exists, and to formulating the critical problem it raises.

§ 3. The Appetite or Affective Activity

My cognitive activity appears to be part of a much wider activity, or of a much greater evolution of the self. It seems to be a "phase" of a basic dynamism pushing me to an ever greater perfection. My consciousness embraces much more than the activity of knowing. From the very beginning of our analysis, the self has appeared as a tendency, an appetite, a desire; [4] in fact, this appetite appearing as the appetite of knowing showed us the subjective pole of consciousness. Why do we have this desire for knowing, possessing, possessing oneself, unless it is that to possess and to possess oneself is to realize oneself more fully, to perfect oneself, to reach the greatest being of which one is capable? Why should we wish to perfect ourselves if it were not because this perfection implies satisfaction, enjoyment and happiness, while imperfection implies dissatisfaction, suffering and pain? To put it briefly, when I reflect on my cognitive activity, I discover a profound dynamism in myself, a tendency to greater being. This tendency is realized by a movement or activity coming from the self. Knowledge is only one element in this total activity or movement which tends to develop me completely. Knowledge is encompassed by a certain affective context from which it is quite distinct.

How can we define the appetite as distinct from knowl-

4. See above, p. 89, and pp. 99-100.

edge? Often these two elements of conscious activity are distinguished by representing them as opposed movements. The one would be a centripetal movement or *assimilation* of objects, the other a centrifugal movement or *tendency toward* objects. As a matter of fact, we can distinguish these two movements in my human consciousness, but when we consider the problem more closely, we see that they do not constitute the knowledge act and the affective act. We see that they are only preliminary conditions which are doubtless due to the imperfections of the subject which I am. To understand how original the cognitive and appetitive acts really are, it would be better to consider the term or completed state of these two movements. The two acts are two irreducible modes of being. The one act, that is, knowledge, can be characterized as "possession" or "presence." The other act, the appetite, can be characterized as "enjoyment," or, as the case may be, "pain" caused by the possession. The cognitive function is subordinated to a deeper and fuller function, the function of enjoying (or suffering). This new ingredient of conscious life is as original and irreducible as the element of knowledge. It is a primary psychological datum, and as such it is indefinable. We must live it ourselves to know what it involves.

The interior world of appetite or love shows a complexity which is even greater than that of knowledge. We can leave the task of making a detailed study of it to descriptive psychology. Here we can mention two aspects of this complexity which have an immediate bearing on knowledge.

1. The complexity of the appetite parallels the complexity of knowledge. At the level of my perceptions and my imagination there appear tendencies and acts of enjoyment of the same order, sense enjoyment, sense suffering, emotions, pas-

sions. At the level of thought appear tendencies and acts of enjoyment which are intellectual. The source of these is called the "intellectual appetite" or "will." These are the volitions or acts of the will which take the form of desire or aversion, joy or displeasure, acceptance or refusal, love or hate and so forth. Finally, complete acts of the appetite or complete affective states which we call "sentiments," correspond to complete knowledge. These imply both a sensible element and an intellectual element.

2. Another cause of complexity is the fact that the appetite can act either with respect to the object given, or with respect to the cognitive act itself. Some affective reactions concern the cognitive act itself. They correspond to the degree of perfection which the cognitive act has. Perfect knowledge (or what is taken to be such by the subject), the clear evidence of the object, the firm adherence of the subject (or certitude),—these cause a reaction of enjoyment, joy in knowing, and satisfaction for the subject. On the other hand, knowledge which is less perfect, less clear and certain, will be accompanied by proportionate reactions of desire, hope, impatience, or, in short, curiosity. Finally, obscure, confused, doubtful knowledge and conscious ignorance give rise to painful feelings of sadness, anxiety, anguish, and so forth. There are certain other affective reactions which are clearly related to the object known and not at all to the perfection of the knowledge which we have. Thus a knowledge can be perfectly clear, but if it is a knowledge of an aggressor, then it will cause reactions of fear, aversion, anger, displeasure and so forth, while a pleasing object will cause reactions of joy, desire, attraction. In these cases the knowledge of the object is only a condition, enabling the subject to possess and enjoy the object.

§4. The Biological Activity

The activity of self extends considerably beyond the spheres of knowledge and love. We have already seen that the self has its "own body." The body is a means of knowing and, as we have just said, it is also a means of enjoyment or suffering. These relations show that there is a *very intimate union between my consciousness and my body*. This body is really mine. It shares my unity and permanence. The continual changes taking place in it, needed for its well being and biological development, must be considered as elements of my total activity, or tendency to more being. Inversely, in so far as my cognitive and appetitive activities affect my organism, they should be looked upon as biological functions, contributing to the preservation and development of this diversified or organized body.

Organic or biological activities, even those affecting the nervous system and the organs of sense and feeling, become conscious to some extent only when accompanied by perceptions and feelings (acts of the appetite or the affective life). So processes of respiration, circulation and nutrition are only partially conscious. We do not have to explain here just how physiology can get information on the aspects of these processes which are not conscious. Here it is sufficient to note that knowledge is related to these biological activities in many ways, and mutual influence can be seen between them. On the one hand, knowledge depends in part on the condition of the organism, on the condition of the sense organs for example, and the state of the nervous system. It depends also on the influence which other organs can have upon these. Thus a stomach disorder can cause sensations of pain, heat, or irritation. It can even cause a lack of attention or a state of drowsiness, feelings like anguish and sadness. On the other hand, knowledge determines to some extent the activities of the organism. Thus attention and the accompanying nervous tension slow down certain bodily functions. Perceptions direct our biological movements—for example, the taking of food, movements of defense and flight when faced with danger, muscular exercise intended to stimulate certain functions like respiration and the circulation of the blood, and so forth.

Chapter VIII

THE FINALITY OF KNOWLEDGE

THE analysis of my knowledge shows me that in knowing I am seeking a certain end or goal, a certain good, a value. This end is a possession of being which will be as adequate as possible. This character of finality enables me to determine what is meant by truth and error. It also enables me to determine what the object of critical epistemology is.

§ 1. *The Fact of Finality*

The term of a tendency is called an *end, goal,* or *good*. When the tendency belongs to a conscious subject, we can also call the term a value. It represents a certain value for the subject; it is something sought after, something which has worth, something which is prized. As a conscious subject, I believe that knowledge is a good, a value, a source of satisfaction. I naturally want to know, and to know in an ever better way as far as that is possible. My curiosity is always aroused, it knows no limits. There is then a tendency to knowledge as such. It was precisely this appetite for knowledge, this inclination of the subject to the object, this curiosity, which enabled us to distinguish the subject from the object in the unity of consciousness.

But how is knowledge a good? When does it give me satisfaction? To what end is it directed? Here again an analysis of consciousness provides a very clear answer: I want to know because, for me, knowing means "possessing" the objects and "possessing myself"; it means enriching myself in a very original way (let us recall that "knowing" and consciousness are primitive irreducible data), but in a very real way, by whatever can be assimilated by consciousness.

This finality of my knowledge is a *fact*; it is a datum of my consciousness. Rightly or wrongly, I tend to a goal when I try to know. The goal is a certain "possession" of being, of the real, of *everything that exists,* whether it be the self or non-self. I want to possess being or the real *as it is;* I want to get the nature of things as well as my own nature; first to satisfy my curiosity, and then so that I may determine my conduct and attitude toward the things which are known.

§ 2. Difficulties

Now the very nature of the cognitive act raises grave objections to what is apparently the natural finality of knowledge. For if the act of knowledge (or actual consciousness) comes from a union of the objective datum and the subjective function, then there will be in this act a contribution from the object and a contribution from the subject. The ancients already expressed this in a well known formula: *Cognitum est in cognoscente ad modum cognoscentis.* For them, this was the application of a more general principle: *Receptum est in recipiente ad modum recipientis.* But if this is the case, can we ever know, by reflecting on the act which seems to be a compromise of the two elements, just what belongs to the object and what belongs to the subject? Is it possible to analyze this act and dissociate in it the element which is given and the element representing the cognitive function? What does a "perception of red" tell consciousness about the nature of the perceived object, or about the nature of the subject which perceives? In other words, how much light does knowledge give the subject about the nature, or even about the presence, of objects? Are objects anything else than contents of consciousness for the subject, contents whose nature is determined by the fact that they are contents of consciousness?

But there is another fact which seems both to confirm the finality of knowledge and to increase the doubts which we have raised concerning that finality. This is the fact of *error.*

Sometimes the conscious subject revises his knowledge because he thinks that it was previously defective or imperfect. He calls this imperfection "error." He says that he was "deceived." And to this defect which he considers error, he opposes a quality which he calls "truth." He considers a true knowledge to be one which is fully realized, one which reaches its goal. So the person who discovers that a piece of money is false after having taken it to be genuine, thinks that he has gone from error to truth. The same holds true for a person who gives up certain political, religious or scientific opinions which he now judges to be erroneous. Truth and error, then, express the *positive value* and the *negative value* (or lack of value) that the subject attributes to a certain act of knowledge. When the subject thinks that a cognitive act has reached its goal, the possession of a certain object, he declares that it is "true," otherwise he declares that it is "false." And since the act of knowledge is completed in the judgment, which fixes and expresses the attitude taken by the subject toward the object, the notions of truth and error get their full meaning in the judgment. So the question of truth can be put in the following way: Does a certain judgment give me a cognitive-possession of the affirmed object, and to what extent? I say that a judgment is true, when I believe that it is faithful and conformed to the objects. I say that it is erroneous when I think it is not faithful or conformed to the datum, that is, when it misses its goal.

§ 3. The Critical Problem

In the light of these remarks we can clearly see what the precise object of the critical problem is. We can formulate it as follows: What should we think of the cognitive subject's instinctive claims, or of the finality which he attributes to his knowledge? To what extent can this finality be realized? In other words, what are the potentialities of a knowledge such as mine? Or, just how far does this possession of objects and myself by knowledge go? Or again, can I get truth, and to what extent? Is error possible? If so, how and to what extent? If the cognitive act is a synthesis of an object and a subject, if it is formed by both subject and object, to what extent can it claim objectivity, to what extent does it give me the object as it really is? What limitations and reservations do we have to make?

The critical problem is, therefore, the problem of the value of knowledge expressed in terms of the finality that it shows. Let us note that, by placing the question of the value of knowledge in such thorough fashion, we also by that very fact raise a question about the value of the analysis of consciousness which we have just made. For this analysis is made through knowledge and is expressed in judgments. Therefore, if we see that a favorable solution can be given to the critical problem, the first result of this solution will be to confirm the meaning and value of the various assertions made in descriptive epistemology. These assertions will nevertheless have a certain meaning and value from now on, for they express judgments which the conscious subject will inevitably form when he wishes to describe the immediate data of consciousness as he sees them. I can ask what my judgments are worth, or what the data of my consciousness are worth, but I cannot in good faith doubt that there are data in my consciousness, that I seize them and express them in my judgments. To record this factual situation is the proper task of descriptive epistemology.[1]

1. See above, pp. 76-77.

Part Three

CRITICAL EPISTEMOLOGY

CHAPTER I

OBJECT AND METHOD

AT THE close of descriptive epistemology we indicated what the object of critical epistemology was. It is always a question of *my knowledge* as it reveals itself to my consciousness. The material object, then, is the same as the material object of the first part of epistemology. But this new study of my knowledge tries to go beyond simple description and simple analysis of the elements making up my consciousness, or simple "judgments of presence." It will try to determine the value and exact scope of knowledge. It will claim to formulate "judgments of value." Here it is no longer a question of merely describing my knowledge, but rather of criticizing and judging it. In the second part of epistemology there is a new point of view, a new formal object.

How does a judgment of value differ from a simple judgment of presence, or a descriptive judgment? This question immediately raises the problem of the method to be used in critical epistemology.

The method used in critical epistemology does not differ completely from the method described at the beginning of analytical epistemology.[1] We shall still use a method which

1. See above, p. 77.

is reflective and personal. Previously we made use of the methodic doubt to discover the elements which make up my consciousness. We shall continue to use it now to discover all the questions that can be asked about the value of my knowledge. However, the method of critical epistemology must introduce a new element, precisely because it is now a question of determining the value of knowledge. We must explain this point further.

We have already determined what a value is: A value is something which we esteem, which we seek after, which we look upon as good, as a desirable goal.[2] An absolute value is a good which is sought for itself, a final end. A relative value is a good which is ordered to something else as a means. The absolute value is sought for its own sake; it imposes itself, it should not be judged by anything else but itself. It is the norm which allows us to judge the relative values depending on it. To determine the value of an object, then, means either recognizing that it has an absolute value, or measuring its value with relation to an absolute value taken as a norm.

My knowledge reveals itself to me as an activity or tendency which is being realized. In this case, then, it is a question of determining first of all what the final end of my cognitive appetite is. This final end will constitute the absolute value in the order of my knowledge, and consequently it will be the norm or measure of all relative values. Then we shall have to evaluate all the aspects of my cognitive act in the light of this norm to see how far the act does indeed realize the end to which it aspires. This requisite norm must be found in my consciousness; otherwise it will remain inaccessible to me. Until I get more information, anything beyond my consciousness will have no sense.

2. See above, p. 159.

The new element characteristic of the method of critical epistemology will be the appeal to a norm of value.[3]

The plan to be followed in our critical epistemology now becomes clearer. Our first step will be to discover and determine the absolute norm which will serve to judge my knowledge; our second step will be to determine in the light of that norm the value of the different kinds of knowledge which I have.

We can now begin to see in what the critical study of my elementary cognitive activity consists. It will re-examine the data furnished by the descriptive analysis of consciousness, with the new purpose of situating and evaluating them with respect to a norm likewise furnished by the analysis of consciousness. It will interpret the data of that analysis in the light of what we perceive to be the ideal of perfect knowledge. It will then try to determine how far each aspect of knowledge realizes that finality, considering the conditions in which knowledge takes place and the factors which go to make it up.

But we have hardly formulated this program before the suspicion arises that this undertaking may be only a dream. The analysis of my consciousness shows me that, as a cognitive subject, I am seeking a final goal or an absolute value which is to possess by knowledge all the real as it is in itself. It is the ideal of a knowledge which would be unlimited and completely objective. But these pretensions seem to be excessive, incapable of realization, and in any case uncontrollable. First of all, how can I assure myself that I possess "everything

3. We say that critical epistemology is a normative science, not because it judges the value of knowledge according to a *norm* or criterion of truth, but because it tells what knowledge should be and what knowledge must avoid to realize its own finality. It points out, for example, how the subject should overcome error or illusion.

which exists?" Even more so, how can I know the real otherwise than as it is in me, that is, as a content of consciousness? Again, how can I know that this real which is known can exist in any other way than as a content of my consciousness? Even supposing that it has been proven that the real exists in itself independently of the knowledge that I have of it, is it not necessarily distorted by the very fact that it becomes an object of knowledge or a content of my consciousness? For if the act of knowledge results from the union of the subject and object, can we not say *a priori* that this act will always be a compromise between the two, that is, that it will always be *partially conformed* to the object, to the extent to which the object helped to realize it, and partially *not conformed* to the object, to the extent to which the subject contributed something of its own? Consequently, every act of knowledge would be partially true and partially false. But if we claim that we can determine what this dosage of truth and error is, what method can we use? Can we try to separate the objective element and the subjective element which make up the cognitive act? We know that consciousness itself would disappear when that separation was made.[4] Can we try to measure the difference between the object as known (*the object-in-me*) and the object as not-known (*the object-in-itself*)? But it is clear that any direct comparison between a known object and an unknown object has no sense, for we can only compare the known to the known. Can we appeal to an indirect criterion of truth, to some indirect way of measuring and controlling the objective value of knowledge? Can we conceive of any such criterion?[5]

We shall show that an absolute value actually exists in my

4. See above, p. 90.
5. *Ibid.*, pp. 46-49, 160-161.

consciousness, and that it can serve as a norm for evaluating the other elements of my consciousness.

We shall first give concise exact statements of the proposed solutions under the form of theses. We shall then develop and vindicate the theses in commentaries. There is no question here of giving strict "demonstrations" involving the mind's reasoning activity because we have not as yet evaluated those activities. All the affirmations of critical epistemology are immediate judgments. We have only to become aware of them to recognize their truth. The sole purpose of our commentaries is to help the reader to become better acquainted with them.[6]

6. On the method of critical epistemology see also *"Problèmes épistémologiques fondamentaux,"* pp. 485-487.

Chapter II

THE ABSOLUTE NORM OF KNOWLEDGE

WE HAVE now reached the most important and crucial point in our epistemology. The direction we take from here on will have a decisive influence on all our philosophy.

We have noted the conditions prerequisite for the absolute norm which we seek. I have access to this absolute norm *in the affirmation of existence* (being, in the sense of affirming the existence of something).[1] This affirmation can be expressed equally well in several ways: "Aliquid est," "Something is," "Something exists," "Being exists." Let us note at once that this affirmation coincides with the one which forced itself upon us at the very beginning of the analysis of consciousness.[2] Now we have to show that by this affirmation of being I really reach my final goal as a knowing subject, that is, the completely objective possession of everything which is.

Like every act of human consciousness, the affirmation of being presents two aspects or two poles: the act as such or the attitude of the subject, and the object of the act. So we must show that it has under both these aspects the absolute value that we ascribe to it, and that it therefore realizes the ideal of perfect knowledge. We shall try to establish this thesis in three steps.

1. In other words, we are not in the hypothesis of "absolute nothing". This is a first evidence.
2. See above, p. 78.

§ 1. Critique of the Affirmation as Such

Since the affirmation is the conscious expression of an object present to my consciousness, it has an objective value, that is, with respect to the value of the object that it expresses. It can therefore possess truth (or error), necessity, objective evidence and justified certitude.

As remarked above, the formal statements of our theses may seem rather succinct. Accordingly, we proceed to develop the implications of the foregoing thesis.

1. *The Objective Value of the Affirmation.*—The fact of affirmation is undeniable. I cannot sincerely doubt the fact that I formulate judgments, or that I affirm. No one dreams of doubting that, not even the sceptic. We saw in analytical epistemology that the affirmation completes the cognitive act. By it the subject takes a stand with regard to the object. He does this with full knowledge and complete independence. Without the affirmation there is neither perfect knowledge nor full awareness. In every instance, the value of knowledge depends upon the value of the judgment or affirmation. If the judgment had no sense or meaning, then epistemology would have to admit that it was bankrupt and impotent.

Now, I can ask what the value of the affirmation is, whether it does have any sense or solid foundation. Absolute scepticism and relativism deny that it has. For them the affirmation is a meaningless gesture; it is the result of an instinctive drive, the expression of a biological state, but it has no objective value.

We can note, first of all, an *ad hominem* argument which serves as an excellent introduction. It is that the sceptic can neither express nor defend his adopted position. For he can neither express nor defend his position without making affirmations and giving some objective meaning to his affirmation. But then he automatically refutes himself. The only position tenable for the sceptic, then, is to imitate the absolute dumbness of plants, as Aristotle already observed.

What actually happens in me when I formulate an affirmative judgment? Let us take any immediate judgment: "This is white." This judgment implies a very definite situation in my consciousness. On the one hand, there is the presence of "this" (a piece of paper, for example) in the objective field of my consciousness. On the other hand, there is an act, a reaction, a deliberate position, taken by the self in synthesizing "this" and the characteristic "white" as found in consciousness. The situation can be briefly summed up in these words: a conscious act expressing an object present to consciousness.

This situation does not afford the least opportunity for doubt, at least as long as I do not claim to go beyond it. For what could I doubt about? About the presence of "this"? About the presence of my act? About the fact that my act is the expression of "this"? There is nothing here that shows the least degree of obscurity or ambiguity. Everything happens in the full light of my consciousness. I am perfectly aware of what I am doing. I see that my synthesis is produced under the influence of the object which is present, and that therefore it has an objective significance. It expresses the object, it is conformed to the object. If I were to say, "This is not white," or "This is black," I would see at once that my act was not conformed to the object known.

To avoid all misunderstanding, let us develop somewhat further the exact meaning of this thesis regarding the objective value of the affirmation. When I say, "This is white," the subject of this affirmation is a content of my actual consciousness, and it is of this content that I affirm that it is white. I do not claim, then, that it is white in itself, if "in itself" means "independently of my consciousness." It is white for me, that is, as the objective term of my knowledge, or as it is given to me in my consciousness. But on the other hand, I maintain that as a content of my consciousness it is really given as a white object. My affirmation only records a situation which obtrudes itself upon me; my affirmation contributes nothing to the determination of this white object.

Thus the affirmation, taken as the conscious expression of a datum present to consciousness, always has a meaning, a significance, an objective import. As an element of knowledge it is worth what the object to which it refers is worth. It has value relative to the object expressed, provided that the expression is faithful. We shall return to this point shortly.

The objective value of the affirmation involves several important consequences, because it enables us to define in critical fashion a series of basic properties belonging to my cognitive act. We must say a word about these now.

2. *Truth and Error.*—At the close of descriptive epistemology we saw to some extent the sense which the cognitive subject spontaneously ascribes to the notion of truth and error.[3] Now our critical examination of the affirmation helps us to give a definitive meaning to these notions. *Truth is the conformity of the judgment to the object that it expresses;* error is the non-conformity of the judgment to the object that it claims to express. Truth then assures to the judgment its objective value, while error destroys it.

When we speak of "conformity," we suppose that there are two terms to the comparison, and for the conformity to be

3. See above, p. 161.

known both these terms must be known. These two conditions, duality and comparability, are realized in my consciousness when I formulate a judgment. There is a duality of the object present to my consciousness and the judging act by which I express it; there is comparability of object and act, since both of them are contents of my consciousness. The judgment is true if it attributes a character to the object which the object really possesses, if it expresses the object as it is given. The judgment is erroneous or not true in the contrary case.

Now, truth is already found in a somewhat rudimentary fashion in the idea or concept. Truth must be found there for the concept is necessarily the representation of an object of experience. A concept which would not represent anything would be a contradiction in terms. The concept therefore is always true, that is, conformed to the reality which it represents. But this conformity is as yet static and unperceived.

As soon as the subject becomes aware of this conformity, he expresses it in a judgment. Here the conformity is essentially dynamic or active, for it implies that the mind has made a decision and taken a definite attitude toward the reality. *The mind conforms itself in active fashion to the object known.* The judgment is in reality an act by which the intelligent subject takes a stand regarding the object known. Having seen some note in the object present to consciousness, and having expressed it by an idea, the subject now expresses to himself what he has discovered by affirming that the idea is really a note of the object or that the object really possesses this note.[4] Truth therefore is preëminently a quality of the

---

4. The negative judgment is not essentially different from this. It affirms that a certain note, represented by a certain idea, *cannot* be attributed to a certain object; that this object does not possess it.

judgment, since it is the judgment which restores the idea to the object and thus expresses the conformity of the one to the other. The judgment is, in a true sense, the knowing subject's own work, for the subject acts with full consciousness of what is happening in himself, and with full responsibility for the attitude which he takes.

So the judgment involves a risk, the risk of error. But how is error possible if the attitude of the mind which judges is determined, prescribed and dictated by the object present to our consciousness? If I am merely trying to express the real as it is given to me, how can I express anything else but that which is? How can my judgment fail to be conformed to the known reality? If truth is only the conformity of the judgment to the object to which it refers and which is present to consciousness, it would seem that it is very easy to have truth, and that error must be a rare failing, almost an anomaly.

But in reality daily experience shows me that I am constantly in danger of error, because different factors extrinsic to the object of my knowledge tend to make my judgments go beyond the real datum which should be the exclusive norm for my affirmations. Under the influence of these motives, I often form hasty judgments and attribute to a subject predicates which do not belong to it at all; these judgments then will be erroneous, that is, not conformed to the real. An attentive examination of the situation will help me recognize my mistake and correct my judgment.

The complexity, obscurity or distance of the object to be known can doubtless be the *occasion* of an error in judgment. According as I get away from the actual experience of a simple object which is clearly distinct from every other, my knowledge will have so much the less guarantee, and so much the more risk of error. But the true *causes* of error are found in the subject himself. We can list the following: [5]

(a) *The subject's haste and inattention*: He neglects to study the object attentively and to distinguish its proper characteristics before judging; thus he confuses a hare and a rabbit, a pear tree and an apple tree, and so forth.

(b) *The subject's temerity*: He presumes to make judgments which exceed his actual perception. Thus, he judges about the past, relying imprudently on his memory instead of checking its trustworthiness—for example, by consulting a book to find a date. He judges about the physical nature of an object, relying on his perceptions without subjecting them to necessary review—he states that a certain ruler "is" broken, when it "appears" broken to him in accordance with the law of refraction. He judges that a certain line "is" longer than another, when it "appears" longer to him because of the influence of the total perception in Müller's illusion. He judges that a certain chemical substance "is not" sugar, when he does not feel the sensation of sugar because of a disordered condition of his palate. He judges that a room "is not" sufficiently heated when a fever makes him shiver, and so forth.

(c) *The subject's confusion*: His feelings and passions interfere with his judgment. So, for example, love—it is said that "love is blind," it is at least biased—hate, desire, fear, anger, and so forth.

(d) *The subject's prejudices*: Convictions acquired previously through tradition or the influence of the environment,

---

5. These concrete examples are taken from ordinary life. They are simple illustrations intended to make the general doctrine of error easier to grasp.

and not checked, affect the evolution of knowledge by introducing false ideas [6] or false principles.

(e) *The subject's mistakes* in the logical connection of his judgments. Here belong the many faults of reasoning which will be unmasked in logic.

As we can see, the practical problem of distinguishing truth from error calls for intellectual asceticism and self-discipline. It is only by a constant effort of purification, detachment and disinterestedness regarding everything but the datum, that the subject will arrive at a calm and assured possession of truth which is his good. Since truth is the conformity of my judgment to the known reality, the measure of truth and the norm which dominates it can only be the object revealing itself to the subject, or *objective evidence.*[7]

3. *Necessity.*—We say that a thing which cannot not-exist is "necessary." The objective value of the judgment accounts for the quality of necessity belonging to every true affirmation; the affirmation imposes itself, it cannot be other than what it is, it is not optional, nor can it be changed to suit the subject. It is in the judgment that necessity appears

6. The term "ideas" used in this current expression really means judgments.
7. By a certain analogy with the truth and error of the judgment properly speaking, we can also speak of truth and error in the improper judgment implied in the animal's *conduct* or *practical attitude*. We say that the animal "errs" or "falls into error" when a partial or incomplete perception of a stimulus sets off a way of acting which does not fit the real nature of this stimulus. This is the case for the dog who pounces on a wooden bone, for the cat who tries to chew a mechanical mouse, for the hen which tries to hatch plaster eggs, for the bird that the scarecrow puts to flight. In all these examples the motor reactions of the animals were set off by visual perception which was not checked. Note that the "causes of error" in these cases are analogous to those that we remarked in the case of human knowledge: haste, temerity, the influence of passions (greed, fear, and so forth.) After a certain period the animal often succeeds in overcoming his "mistake," thanks to the check that new perceptions provide for his estimative faculty.

for the first time in my consciousness. The object is a fact—the subject is also for that matter. I have no reason for affirming that the object is necessary or that it exists necessarily. But given the fact that it exists and the fact that I become conscious of it, then I am forced to affirm its existence; it is impossible for me to deny this existence. The necessity of the affirmation, therefore, rests on the datum. This necessity emphasizes the dominant character of the datum. For the time being at least, it is a hypothetical necessity implying that if a certain object is given to me, then a certain judgment forces itself on me, and a certain affirmation becomes necessary.

The necessity of the judgment also entails at least a hypothetical universality. Since my assertion rests on the very nature of the object known, then every other consciousness which can know that object as it is given to me must accept my assertion as true. This assertion, then, has a subjective universality in the sense that it forces itself on all future subjects.[8]

4. *Objective Evidence and Legitimate Certitude.*—From the very beginning of our analysis of consciousness we have seen that all knowledge of the real involved evidence, that is, a certain clarity of being which forces itself on consciousness and expresses itself in the obligation which we feel to yield to the evident object when judging.[9] Both the objective character of the affirmation and the nature of truth justify and

8. The problem of *objective universality* is entirely different. The judgment is universal if the subject of the judgment is a universal concept, *synthesizing an indefinite number of particular cases*. The problem arises then of knowing how we can pass from the experience of one or several particular cases to a universal judgment or "law." We shall return to this point shortly.

9. See above, p. 82.

confirm this factual situation. For the affirmation is dominated and ruled by the object present to my consciousness. The clarity with which the object shows itself to my consciousness determines the content of my judgment.

This objective evidence of the affirmation gives rise in the subject to the affective state of certitude, that is, a state of partial satisfaction, rest and gratification of the appetite for knowing.[10] This is not a blind or hallucinatory feeling; rather it is fully justified precisely because it is based on objective evidence: I am aware that I make my assertion because I am dominated by the object forcing itself on me. I am aware that in my judgment I submit to the object as it is given to me. My confidence and certitude of not being deceived are based upon a perfectly clear situation: the stand which I take in my judgment is dictated by an objective presence which cannot be denied.

5. *Examination of Some Objections.*—It is well to close our critical study of the affirmation by stating and answering some difficulties.

If we admit that our judgment has objective value, does not this mean that we are accepting an initial postulate, that is, *our ability to know truth?* This controversy over the ability to know truth caused rivers of ink to flow in the nineteenth century. It appears to us to be the typical example of a false problem. I see my ability to know *by knowing.* I see my ability to judge objectively by judging objectively (just as I prove my ability to walk by walking, my ability to sing by singing). No postulate is needed for this.

Another difficulty: The sceptic declares that the judgment is uncertain, because no permanent object exists. Truth, he

10. Lack of evidence on the other hand will cause *dissatisfaction* or *uneasiness.*

says, does not exist. It changes unceasingly, like the real. Even though I admit that there is no permanence in the objects to be known, and even though I imagine an object which would be as fleeting and ephemeral as possible—a spark which would occupy the field of consciousness for hardly an instant—that would still permit me to make judgments which were true, in fact eternally true. For example, I could make judgments such as these: "A spark has been seen by me," "That which I saw was a spark," "A spark is luminous," and so forth.

But what of those critiques which talk about the non-empirical conditions for my judgment, that is, the unconscious factors which possibly help form the judgment and its object? Can the judgment keep its objective value in the face of these? Certainly. Let us take, for example, the judgment: "This is white." Now, whatever may be the conditions explaining the possibility of my actual knowledge or judgment, and whatever may be the factors explaining either how "this" is present to my consciousness, or how I can judge, all this will change absolutely nothing in the actual situation just described. I can imagine or conjecture any occult influence I may wish, any sort of "evil genius," any sort of instinctive urge as tending to distort the object or the subject's act, but the net result of all these hypotheses is still clear, that in my actual consciousness there is still "a white object" ("this"), and an act of judgment expressing it. This act has a meaning and an objective value. It has the mark of truth, since it is conformed to the object. It rests on objective evidence, and therefore has genuine solidity or legitimate certitude. We can easily see how important this doctrine is. It provides a basic refutation for absolute scepticism, relativism, subjectivism and pragmatism, since these systems pay no attention to the most essential and most evident properties of the judgment.

§ 2. *Critique of Being as the First Object of Affirmation* [11]

Being or the real, the first object of affirmation, imposes itself as the absolute value of my knowledge and as the final end of my appetite for knowing.

To elucidate this thesis, we may proceed to develop its implications in the following commentary.

The affirmation as such has an objective value, a value relative to the object. But what is the value of the object itself? First of all, what is the value of the object, when the object consists of being as such, or the real as such? This actually is the case in the affirmation "aliquid est" (something is, something exists). This affirmation imposes itself as the very first affirmation, the point from which all my judging activity must inevitably start. For if I do not affirm, at least implicitly, that something exists, I exclude all further affirmations, including the affirmation of my own existence. The subject of this first affirmation represents any being at all in so far as it is an object of experience. The predicate represents it under the form of a concept or idea. What is the value of this experience? What is the value of this concept?

1. *Critique of Being as the Object of All Our Experience.*[12] —The experience of being is as undeniable as the fact of the affirmation. "Experience" signifies immediate knowledge, the

11. To give a critical evaluation of being as the first object of affirmation means to show the value first of the *concrete realities* which are given in my experience, and secondly of the *concept* of being by which I express these realities.
12. That is, a critical evaluation of the real object or of the existing thing.

immediate presence of the known to the knower. Experience is the first original form of knowledge, for indirect or mediate knowledge supposes by definition an antecedent direct knowledge. When we explain the terms in this way it is evident that I have experience of the real, for the property of "reality" is essential to every object of experience. An experience which would not be an experience of a reality would be an experience of nothing. All my experiences are, therefore, experiences of the real, that is, immediate perceptions of the real, perceptions which are brought about by the presence of the known to the knower without any intermediary. Every intermediary which might be imagined to explain the knowledge which I have of the real would still be real. It is therefore impossible to throw doubt upon the experience or the immediate knowledge which I have of the real. This experience will remain the same, no matter what unconscious factors might have conditioned it, and whatever be the origin, basic nature or ontological status of the real which is present to my consciousness. What I record in fact is precisely the *conscious result* of all the conditions determining the existence of this reality and its presence to my consciousness.

The experience of the real can be called an "intuition," that is, an immediate apprehension of the individual concrete reality.[13]

We must insist again upon this important point that the real is given to us in an experience. I see that something exists, and that I exist, but I do not understand why something exists.[14] Let us recall also that the real is given to us in

13. The word *intuition* is here taken in the sense which Lalande (*Vocabulaire*, Vol. I, p. 398) calls "the most original sense of this word, the sense in which it can not be replaced by any other."
14. On the essential role of experience see Noël, *Le réalisme immédiat*, pp. 38-39,

any kind of experience, whether it be objective or lived. It does not make sense to speak of the lived experience or consciousness of self as a "privileged experience," for the objective datum is just as real and immediately present as the self or subject. Neither is there any sense in objecting that the objective datum might be only "phenomenal," as if a phenomenon were not itself something real.[15]

Taken as experience, my knowledge of the real implies and realizes the immediate union, the *real unity*, of the datum and the knowing subject. As we have just remarked, experience signifies immediate knowledge, immediate presence, of the known to the knower. Thus every experience implies, at least in some degree, a real or ontological identity of the knower and the thing known, for the immediate presence could not account for knowledge unless it itself also constituted that act of knowledge in some way. A simple juxtaposition in space would clearly not suffice. My experience of the real is therefore the possession of a real datum by identity.[16]

Now, this experience of being is quite evidently safe from any illusion, confusion or distortion for the simple reason that being is not opposed to anything. Nothing can cause an "illusion" of being in me, nothing can occasion a "confusion" with being, or cause a "distortion" of being, for distorted being would still be being. *In short, the experience of being is an infallible knowledge. Its objectivity is absolutely guaranteed.*

167-170, 184-185, 192-196, 238-251; also Gilson, *Réalisme thomiste*, pp. 184-239.

15. See the criticism of Msgr. Zamboni made by Noël, *op. cit.*, pp. 186-196. Here we cannot distinguish between "phenomenal being" and "ontological being," or between a "poor notion" and a "rich notion" of being. All these distinctions are premature and uncritical, since being transcends all these categories. See also *"Problèmes épistémologiques fondamentaux,"* pp. 480-485.

16. See De Coninck, *L'unité de la connaissance*, pp. 103-122.

However, this experience is imperfect in many ways. The identity which is produced between the knower and the known is *superficial*. In objective experience the identity is effected by reason of a spatial relation between the object and the sense organ.[17] In lived experience, the identity is more intimate, but it is effected only on the level of secondary acts. It does not penetrate to the fundamental reality of the self. Again, the identity which is produced is *transitory*, for every experience is fleeting and soon gives way to other experiences. The identity which is produced is *limited*. It only extends to a certain group of data. Now, my continually changing experiences show me that my possible experiences extend considerably beyond my actual experience, and therefore that I am far from actually possessing everything that exists.

At this point my conceptual knowledge intervenes to develop my experience and to enrich it enormously by bringing out its full value.

2. *Critique of the Concept of Being.*[18]—We have seen that the concept of being or reality was the fundamental concept, and that all other concepts are but modalities of this primary concept. It is this concept which defines intelligence. The intellect is essentially "the faculty of conceiving being," "the ability to grasp the idea of being in any experience." Its formal object is being, or the real, in so far as this is "conceivable." [19]

17. This spatial relation always involves a "contact." This is quite evident for most of the sense perceptions; in the case of vision there is *conscious* contact only with the "illuminated medium." It is by this intermediary that the organ is in "spatial relationship" with the "distant" object. But here, as in the case of the other perceptions, the experience is "superficial" precisely because it belongs to the spatial order.
18. This concept of being enables us to express everything which exists, or any object which exists, by a mental representation.
19. See above, pp. 130, 141.

We have seen that every concept represents the transferring of a datum of experience to the sphere of intellectual immanence. This transference is also a development. But the concept of being has a very special relation to the experiences from which it comes. The idea of being represents or expresses a certain simple datum of my experience (for example, this sound, this light, this color); but it also expresses many other simple or complex data (for example, this oak, this man). In the case of a complex datum it also expresses adequately all the simple elements constituting that datum. Facts of this sort show us that the abstraction of the idea of being is of a very special kind.

Like all ideas, the idea of being is abstract in the sense that it is separated from the corporeal, the concrete, the individual. It is the transference of the datum to the level of universal representations.

At first sight, it also seems to be abstracted in yet another way, and even to be the most abstract of all ideas in the sense that it isolates the note "being" from the rest. It abstracts from all the elements which mark off one datum of experience from the rest. In its explicit signification, the idea of being expresses the different elements of reality in what constitutes their unity and indistinction. In this case it abstracts from everything which particularizes, diversifies, or opposes one real element to another. In this sense, it expresses the least possible determination and represents the highest degree of abstraction.[20] But this viewpoint of explicit signification is incomplete and therefore provisional, for it is clear that the note "being" is dissociated from the rest only by a trick of

20. We can easily see that the concept of being results from and expresses any experience at all. There can be no such thing as a "privileged experience" for our knowledge of being.

thought. In the datum, "being" is identified with all the elements making up the datum and with each one of them. Being then does not isolate anything, it does not abstract from anything Thus in its implicit meaning, the idea of being expresses the concrete real adequately with all its differences and modes. From this point of view, the idea of being is in no sense the result of an abstraction, if by abstraction we mean the consideration of a partial aspect of the concrete (*separatim considerare*). It is the confused but adequate representation, conceptualization, or conceptual transposition of the concrete real. It expresses all the elements of that real, formally and actually, and not merely virtually or potentially.

This double character which is essential to the idea of being is commonly called *analogy*: unity in diversity or proportional unity. It shows me the essential role which this idea has in my cognitive activity. To apprehend any datum as *existing*, as *being*, as *real*, means to discover *in it* a quality by virtue of which this datum is not opposed to anything, is not completely foreign to any other datum, but rather is related to every other datum, whatever be the differences and oppositions marking off one datum from another. Thus, when I have perceived an odor as "something," as a "reality," or "being," I must also apprehend any other datum (for example, a color, a sound, a resistance) as "being," as "real," as "something." Since I can apprehend all my experiences as unified by this common possession of being, by this real similarity in spite of diversity, or as properly opposing only non-being, I can now synthesize my experiences by transposing them into one unique concept, the concept of being, whose extension is therefore truly universal with respect to the different data of my experience.

Further reflection on the unity of my experience as expressed in this singular concept of being will develop this novel concept still more. Since any datum, in so far as it is being or real, is not opposed to anything, it is clear at once that the only condition required for a thing to be expressible by the idea of being, is that the thing not be pure non-being. On the other hand, the unceasing stream of my experiences and the constant appearance of new data in my consciousness suggest to me that it is possible that my experience (past, present and future) may not be the same as all possible experience. I can even conjecture that the real which I can know in an experience might not be the same as the totality of the real. For the time being, this is only a hypothesis. But the knowledge of being which is given to me in experience, permits me to state that *if there exists anything outside my experience, this "outside" can be and is adequately expressed by the concept of being*. Otherwise, it must simply be identified with pure non-being.

Thus we see a new property which is essential to the notion of being, its transcendental extension. In traditional terminology, a universal notion whose extension or universality surpasses or "transcends" the extension of all other notions is called transcendental ("transcendit species et genera"). Its universality is unlimited, it synthesizes all the real. Now the notion of being expresses adequately, though confusedly, everything which exists, the totality of the real, everything which is not pure non-being. To conceive any datum at all as real means that we implicitly know all reality, without any reservation or exception, for it means seeing that this datum has a place in the universal order, and that it is bound to everything which exists by a real resemblance. It means to possess in a confused fashion the entire universe beyond the limits of my own experience. "Anything beyond thought is unthinkable," states the idealist, and he claims to confine thought within the periphery of its own representations, but in reality anything beyond thought is unthinkable because the object of thought is *everything which exists*, and because beyond being there is only *non-being, the impossible and the unthinkable*.

As we can see, this transcendental extension of the idea of being flows immediately from our examination of its comprehension. Since its comprehension does not involve any particular determination opposed to other determinations, the idea of being does not have a circumscribed or limited content, and thus it represents everything which is not pure and simple non-being.

The transcendental capacity of the idea of being destroys the very roots of Kantian empiricism. Kantian empiricism would hold that the legitimate exercise of thought must stop at the borders of the phenomenal world, that is, the world of experience.

Finally, we shall see that the transcendental extension of the idea of being allows me to affirm the existence of an *absolute or unconditional reality*. I say that a thing which depends on another thing in any way is "relative" or "conditioned." I say that a thing which does not depend on another is "absolute" (*ab-solutum*, freed from, independent of), or "unconditioned." Thanks to this idea of being, I can represent to myself in a confused way everything which exists, and I can examine the necessary characteristics of this "totality," as a totality. Since this totality is not opposed to anything, I must affirm that it is not conditioned by anything; it cannot be relative to anything. It is, therefore, absolute or unconditioned. In short then, my idea of being which represents the totality of reality represents an absolute object which is not conditioned or caused. But an uncaused reality is a reality which possesses what it needs to exist (since it is a *reality*) without receiving it from the outside (since it is *uncaused*). It is therefore a reality which is "by itself," which is its own reason for existence, which imposes itself, is necessary of itself, which must be, which cannot not be. So, the necessity which we saw first as a property of the affirmation or judgment is now seen for the first time in the object known.

Let us note that this necessity of the real, although it is truly absolute, is nevertheless for me a factual necessity in the sense that I know it through a fact, and as a fact. In other words, since something exists, something exists by itself, for the proposition *The totality of reality exists by something else* is clearly self-contradictory; in other words it destroys itself. I know that an absolute object exists, I know that something is necessary, but I do not know why.

I have now all the elements I need to judge the value of my conceptual knowledge of existing things. This knowledge is grafted on my experience of reality, but it exceeds that experience very greatly. This excess is not due to some sort of *a priori* element, or some kind of "projection" into the datum of a value that it did not possess, but it is due to a development of the datum itself. In this operation, the intelligible object (that is, the datum as being) is not at all received in a purely passive fashion, for there is no question here of a purely corporeal transitive action. Nor is the intelligible produced by any *a priori* activity of the subject independently of experience (since the intelligible is given in experience). The intelligible is actively apprehended and assimilated by the intelligent subject. I am conscious that I am the active principle of my immanent concept in which and by which I express some aspect of the datum; there is nothing in the content of this concept which does not come from the datum. The Aristotelians of the Middle Ages were very correct in stating: *Universale materialiter est in rebus, formaliter est in intellectu.*

The following characteristics of the idea of being explain its preëminent value:

(a) The idea of being is a *perfectly objective representation* of the datum of experience. Not only am I conscious of the conformity between my idea and its object (since both are contents of my consciousness), but the analysis of this idea shows me that it is an infallibly faithful representation of any datum whatsoever. It is evident, in fact, that the idea of being cannot admit of any illusion or distortion, for it represents a value which surpasses all confusions and particularities.

In the first place, the content of the idea of being surpasses the opposition between the subject and the object, for both are beings. From this point of view, there is a perfect homogeneity between the knower and the known. Since both the subject and the object are, as beings, of the same nature and oppose only non-being, it is not possible for the object to be distorted by being received in the subject. The content of the idea of being, therefore, constitutes a value which is perfectly objective with respect to the cognitive act.

But the content of the idea of being also surpasses every other opposition and diversity, because being can only oppose non-being; the real can only oppose the non-real or the *nihil*. Now, it is clear that it is impossible to confuse that which is and that which is not. When I apprehend a particular object and try to discover its proper characteristics, or its nature, then I am exposed to confusion and illusions. It may be that

I will distinguish this object imperfectly from other objects. But this danger does not exist when I apprehend anything as *being,* for pure non-being cannot give rise to any illusion or confusion.

(b) The idea of being is the *adequate representation of its object,* since it represents not merely one partial aspect of it, but all the concrete reality without any possible exception.

(c) The idea of being is the *adequate representation of everything which exists.* Its extension is transcendental. To question this character of the idea of being is to contradict oneself, for it amounts to supposing that something could exist without being expressible by the representation "that which exists." Let us note in this respect that the transcendental idea of being permits me to go beyond my experience, not by affirming that something exists beyond this experience, but rather by giving me the power to legislate hypothetically for everything which could possibly exist beyond the domain actually accessible to me in empirical experience. This procedure is not peculiar to the case of the idea of being. The comprehension of an idea always enables me to state in *a priori* fashion that it will extend to all the objects which realize this comprehension. Thus, once I grasp what the comprehension of the idea "animal" is, I know in an *a priori* way that if I meet in reality something which fits this description, that object will fall under the extension of the above mentioned idea. The privileged character of the idea of being consists in this, that the nature of its comprehension (which excludes all limit or opposition except to non-being) allows me to conclude that its extension is *unlimited* or *transcendental.*

(d) The idea of being is the *representation of an absolute or unconditioned object.* This is a direct consequence of its transcendental character. Whether anything exists outside my experience or not, my idea of being will in every hypothesis express the totality of the real, that totality which by definition cannot depend on anything else.

In brief then, my conceptual knowledge of being gives me a *genuine possession of the whole universe, through the transcendental concept of being, a representation which is confused, but adequate and perfectly objective.* This possession is marked by properties which are entirely different from the properties of my experience of the real. That experience was intuitive, it involved a real identity with the object known. The concept of being is abstract, it excludes any real identity with the object, of which it is only an adequate, but confused representation. But on the other hand, in place of the superficial and transitory possession of a limited datum, the transcendental concept gives us a possession of all reality, that is, the possession of an unlimited and unconditioned object. This possession is adequate and permanent (in terms of the duration proper to intellectual immanence).

§ 3. *The Ideal of Perfect Knowledge*

The affirmation of being [21] realizes the ideal of perfect knowledge, the absolute value or final goal of my knowledge. This affirmation possesses a truth which is absolutely evident and absolutely certain. However, this ideal is realized in my consciousness in a very imperfect way. It follows that, while it gives me a norm which will allow me to evaluate the other elements of my knowledge, the affirmation of being leaves my appetite for knowing only partially satisfied.

21. The affirmation of being means the affirmation that something is or exists.

In the following commentary we develop the further implications of this thesis on the ideal of perfect knowledge.

1. *The Affirmation of Being as the Absolute Value of my Knowledge.*—When we began to study our knowledge in critical fashion, we fixed the cognitive subject's final goal in these terms: it was *to possess all the real as it is in itself*. This ideal of an unlimited and completely objective knowledge is realized in the affirmation of being.

I have, in fact, discovered in my consciousness a cognitive act which seems to me to have an absolute value. This act is the affirmation of being as such. It is, at least implicitly, the starting point for all my judgments. Why does it have an absolute value? Because it consists *in possessing an unlimited and absolute object by means of an infallible act*. This act implies an experience or intuition in which no illusion is possible, a conception in which no distortion is possible, and an affirmation in which no error is possible. All along the line there is perfect objective evidence, and fully established certitude.

The possession of all the real (that is, of an unlimited and unconditioned object in an infallible act, which can stand up under the most exacting critical examination)—is not this the ideal of perfect knowledge? It is impossible to go beyond this ideal either on the side of the object or on the side of the act.

2. *Value of Existential Judgments.*—This knowledge of the being [22] or existence of things is expressed in judgments whose truth is absolutely clear and certain. After what we

22. Knowledge of being is knowledge of the existent thing, knowledge of that which exists, knowledge of the real.

have said above, this last statement requires only a brief commentary.

(a) *Existential judgments.*—Our knowledge of being is expressed by a judgment, by an affirmation of being or existence. This affirmation can take different forms: "This is," "That exists," "This is real," "Something exists," "Everything which is given to me exists," "Everything exists," "The totality of the real exists," "The real as a whole exists necessarily and absolutely." In these different formulas we pass from a singular judgment to universal judgments bearing upon my whole experience and then upon the totality of existing things. The passage from the singular judgment, "This exists," to the absolutely universal principle, "Being exists," is made by the process of "transcendentalization." As we have seen, reflection on the content of the concept of being shows me its transcendental extension, and allows me then to posit the universal subject "being" (all being whatever, everything which is not nothing).

(b) *Truth.*—The existential judgments which we just formulated are adequately true, that is, they are adequately conformed to the object known, because the idea of being which is the predicate in them is the adequate though confused expression of the reality itself as indicated by the subject. Of course, as we explained in our analysis of the judgment,[23] this conformity does not amount to identity, since the idea is a conceptual transposition of the object which gives it a new presence in the knowing subject, a presence *ad modum recipientis*. But this lack of identity and this imperfect conformity do not at all mean that my knowledge is imperfect. For it is not my goal as a knowing subject to possess everything which exists by really identifying my-

23. See above, pp. 142-43.

self with everything. Rather my goal is to possess everything existing by assimilating everything in an immanent act of my consciousness, so as to grasp the universal order in the most perfect way possible for my kind of consciousness. This requires that the concrete datum be transposed to the level of my conceptual immanence.[24]

I know that my existential judgments are true, because reflex knowledge or consciousness enables me to compare my concept of being with the experience it represents and which the judgment expresses. This comparison, which is finally identified with the judgment, shows me that the predicate and the subject, the concept and the object of experience, are equivalent. It also enables me to determine the roles played by the subject and the object in my knowledge, and to distinguish the strictly objective significance of my knowledge from the *modus cognoscentis* or the subjective mode which unavoidably affects my cognition.

All these judgments possess the hypothetical or relative necessity common to all affirmations based on the presence of the affirmed object. The judgment which states that the totality of reality is absolute has not only this relative necessity, common to all true judgments, but it further states an *abso-*

24. Let us note in advance that it is only the knowledge of *oneself* that can be had by a perfect identity of the subject and object. The knowledge of a "non-self" by a consciousness is necessarily had through "representation," for the non-self cannot itself form the immanent act of this consciousness. When the non-self is a *corporeal world,* then the need for a representation is even greater, for no consciousness can know matter by "identifying itself" with it, or by "conforming itself" to the matter, under the pretense of perfect intimacy or union. Dispersion in space and time excludes consciousness. The creative Consciousness itself does not know matter by "identity." As far as our knowledge of matter is concerned, its *imperfection* consists precisely in knowing the material world in a passive way, by spatial contact—in other words, *putting itself as far as possible on the level of the material world.*

lute necessity, that is, the necessary or unconditioned existence of the object itself.

(c) *Absolute objective evidence.*—Those existential judgments which express my immediate and actual knowledge of the real enjoy the greatest amount of evidence. They have an evidence which is perfectly objective, that is, entirely caused and imposed by the object—by an object which is safe from any danger of illusion, confusion or distortion.

(d) *Absolute certitude.*—This perfect objective evidence gives rise in the subject to a feeling of absolute certitude, that is, a complete satisfaction of his appetite for knowing or possessing being. However, even though his possession is adequate, it is confused, and thus the appetite for knowing still remains active as curiosity, as a desire to clear up this initial confusion, and to develop all the richness of our initial knowledge.

3. *Imperfections of my Knowledge of Being.*—This ideal of perfect knowledge is realized in me in a very imperfect way. Indeed, the representation of the universe in my concept of being is extremely confused, and this confusion is cleared up only slightly by my superficial, limited and transient experience.

The affirmation of being realizes, in a sense, the absolute value of my knowledge. This is why it can serve as the norm or criterion for evaluating all the different forms of my knowledge. I have to see just how far each of them measures up to the ideal, or achieves the knowing subject's natural finality, which is the most perfect possession possible of everything which exists.

But I possess this absolute value in too imperfect a way for it to be able to satisfy completely my appetite for knowing, and this is the reason why the affirmation of being forms the starting point and incentive for new attempts to assimilate the real.

These last remarks involve a fact which at first sight seems paradoxical: the critical examination of the norm of knowledge itself. In the light of the ideal that the norm sets up, the norm itself is said to be imperfect. How can it evaluate itself, and thus in a sense go beyond itself? This is possible because the experience of being and the conception of being have complementary and opposed characteristics. In fact, a comparison of these different characteristics allows me to see their imperfections in the light of the others, and to foresee a way of knowing being which would exclude these imperfections,—one in which the experience would not be limited, superficial and transitory, and the conception would not be abstract or confused. In brief, it allows me to foresee a way of knowing being, where the ideal of perfect knowledge would be realized in a more perfect way than it is in myself.[25]

The same comparison between the characteristics of experience and conception enables me to state more precisely what the *modus cognoscentis* or *contribution of the subject* is in my knowledge of the real as such. We have already pointed out that this contribution of the subject does not necessarily imply an imperfection in knowledge or an obstacle to its objectivity. Ideal knowledge does not mean that the subject in order to know the object *as it is* must itself disappear in the object. But the ideal in knowing is rather *to possess the object as it is in the immanence of the subject.*

25. In this type of knowledge the duality of experience and conception would dissolve into the unity of an intellectual intuition, which would be both pure experience and pure conception at the same time. This ideal is realized in the knowledge of the angels and in an infinitely more perfect way in the divine knowledge.

In other words, knowledge is always and essentially an act of the subject. It inevitably bears the stamp of the subject. I can surmise that in a more perfect subject than myself the act of knowledge would be his act to an even greater extent. Such being the case I can ask what the *modus cognoscentis* is when I know the real as such, and whether it involves imperfections.

The answer to these questions will be found in the treatment given above of the characteristics present in my knowledge of being, whether taken as an experience or as a conception. All of them are due to the subject's nature. They show us both the subject's eminence and his indigence. His experience of the real is intuitive and varied, but it is superficial, limited and fleeting. His conception is transcendental and gives him a grasp on the absolute. But his representation of the universe is abstract and confused. The subject can make an affirmation which is adequately true, perfectly evident, and absolutely certain, but this affirmation again will be only a confused expression of the real. In short, the imperfections proper to an assimilative knowledge, which is both empirical and conceptual, do not hurt the perfect objectivity of my knowledge of the real as such.[26]

26. For a critical examination of the knowledge of being see also Noël, *op. cit.*, pp. 167-170, 239-255.

CHAPTER III

CRITICAL EXAMINATION OF THE DIFFERENT WAYS OF KNOWING

MY KNOWING activity is not restricted to affirming the real as such. Under some respects this knowledge is perfect, but it is also most indeterminate, and it cannot satisfy my curiosity. Experience puts me in contact with many different forms of being. I want to explain them by relating them to the transcendental unity of being. Indeed, the basic act of my intelligence consists in seizing being and conceiving being in any experience whatever, and therefore in apprehending every particular experience as a mode of being. This amounts to saying that by my intelligence I apprehend the real as being basically both one and diversified. The goal, then, of all progress in my knowledge and of all my curiosity will be to comprehend the real, that is, to take it as a whole (*cumprehendere*); to unify and synthesize the multiple; to discover the relations by virtue of which the multiple really forms a unity; to see how and why the elements of the real constitute a unity or an order.

Can such a project be carried out? What prospects does my knowledge offer in this regard? Of what value are the attempts that I spontaneously make to know the universal order?

To answer these questions we shall examine in order the conditions in which our knowledge of the self, our knowledge of the corporeal world and progress in knowledge by reasoning, take place. We shall conclude with some critical remarks on the role which memory has in our knowing.

§ 1. *Critique of Our Knowledge of the Self*

My indeterminate knowledge of the real can be made more explicit with the help of my knowledge of the self. This knowledge is both empirical and conceptual. It is expressed in judgments which are true, evident and certain.

Here again the formal statement of our thesis is extremely succinct. We shall, therefore, proceed to develop more fully its implications by a detailed analysis.

1. *Knowledge of the Self as a Development of my Knowledge of Being.*—The analysis we made of consciousness showed us a double experience, objective and subjective. Now, these two experiences are of equal value for my knowledge of the real as being. It would be wrong to consider the subjective experience as privileged, or as revealing being in some special way. But it is true that the subjective experience is much superior to the objective experience in helping me to get a more explicit knowledge of the modalities of being. First of all, the subjective experience or the consciousness which I have of myself is an intimate experience of my own conscious activities, grasped in themselves as they issue from the dynamism of the self.[1] Secondly, this subjective experience concerns an activity that transcends matter in part, and to that extent shows me a modality of being surpassing the world of bodies. Thus, from certain points of view, subjective experience will lead us further than objective experience. This is the reason why we study it first. Nevertheless, from other points of view the knowledge of the self presents difficulties

1. See above, pp. 101-107.

and obscurities which are peculiar to it. These we must not forget. My human consciousness is a consciousness which opens on the corporeal world. Its natural tendency or orientation is toward objects. Reflection on self requires an effort which becomes more difficult as the complexity of the "internal world" grows greater.

We have already seen that subjective experience gives rise to the concept of the self and also to other empirical concepts whose content is furnished by this experience.[2] These concepts can then be restored to the datum by judgments expressing the knowledge which I have of such or such a datum. Here are some examples: "The reality which shows itself in my inner experience is a knowing subject, or self"; "The self is a source of tendencies and desires"; "The self is the source or principle of feelings, sadness, fear, anger, desire, and so forth"; "The self is a principle of activity"; "The self is a principle of perceptions, imaginations, conceptions"; "The self is endowed with a body and with organs of perception." These judgments express various elements of my subjective experience in concepts.

2. *Value of Knowledge of the Self.*—What is the value of this empirical and conceptual knowledge of the self? Considered as an experience, my knowledge of the self coincides with my consciousness of my activities. Now, the consciousness of the self is a knowledge which is not only intuitive, but a knowledge which is had by a real identity of the knower and known. It is therefore a knowledge in which no distortion of the object by the subject is possible.

However, we can recall here that this consciousness of my acts gives me only a superficial, transitory, and limited expe-

2. See above, p. 132.

rience of the self. It is, however, less superficial than objective experience, because, although it does not reach the self in all its reality, it does apprehend the operations of the self in their inner reality. It is also less transitory because consciousness is not subject to the purely successive becoming peculiar to matter. It has a duration which, to some extent, triumphs over dispersion in time. But on the other hand, the lived experience is more limited than objective experience, because it does not extend beyond my strictly personal, interior life, while objective experience opens upon a material universe whose richness is inexhaustible. Furthermore, the extreme complexity of psychical life, the difficulty that we experience in making these introspective observations, and the absence of checks, make the lived experience a very delicate field for scientific research. If we have perfect clearness in the judgment, the act which completes the process of knowing, yet considerable obscurity exists in other areas of consciousness, in our perceptions, imaginations, feelings, instincts, passions and so forth.[3]

Let us note that, in our conceptualization of our lived experience, the empirical concepts have the same role as the concept of being. They transpose the empirical data to a plane of greater immanence, where my knowledge has a greater fixity and unity than it had on the level of experience. My experience, in fact, is always bound up with a perceived or lived spatio-temporal reality. Even my lived experience is always an experience of an activity which, while transcending matter in a certain sense, still remains corporeal and concrete. In the concept we are given a way of knowing which is freed from all individual conditions. In my lived experience I ap-

3. This explains why it is so difficult for the psychological sciences to achieve a level of perfection comparable to that of the natural sciences.

prehend modes of being which are realized there, but their value for my knowledge goes far beyond this or that particular realization, since I meet them again in many particular experiences. In brief, the conceptualization of experience serves to bring out the universal values realized in that experience, and consequently the principles of order and unity which correct the diversity of the real.

But now we discover capital differences between the concept of being and empirical concepts:

(a) The concept of being synthesizes all the real; its universality is transcendental. On the other hand, the empirical concept, by the very fact that it represents a particular mode of being, can have only a restricted universality. It synthesizes a group of elements or a class of data.[4]

(b) The concept of being synthesizes all the real, because the multiple discloses a basic unity. It synthesizes the multiple in spite of its diversity and even in its diversity. Thus we see at once that the unity of the concept of being, which is perfect if we consider the explicit content, must necessarily be imperfect if we consider the implicit but formal and actual content. In short, the unity of the concept of being is *proportional* or *analogical*. On the other hand, the unity of the empirical concept is *perfect* or *univocal*. It designates a particular element which is isolated from other elements by a true abstraction, a true separation. The empirical concept has strict unity, and if I can use it to express other elements of my experience this is only in the measure in which that same mode of being is realized identically in these new experiences.

---

4. The problem of the actual extension of these empirical concepts, and the real scope of the universal judgments to which they give rise, immediately presents itself. To what extent can these judgments go beyond experience? This is the problem of induction or generalization of experience—a problem which belongs to logic and to the critique of sciences.

(c) But then we see that this empirical concept can no longer be the adequate expression of the individual concrete reality. Unlike the concept of being, it cannot represent adequately any element whatever of the real, for, in fact, one element of the real can never be interchanged with another. One element is never completely identical with another, otherwise these two elements would coincide; the two elements are distinguished at least as realities. The univocal, empirical concept, therefore, can only be a partial expression of some experience or some group of experiences.

3. *Value of the Judgments which Express my Knowledge of the Self.*—However, if I succeed in getting an exact knowledge of the nature and scope of my conceptual activity, then the judgments by which I express my intellectual or conceptual knowledge of the data of my lived experience will be true, necessary, evident and certain judgments. They will not have an adequate truth, an absolute necessity, or an evidence excluding all possibility of error and doubt, as was the case for the existential judgments bearing on the real as such. But they will have inadequate truth, hypothetical necessity, relative evidence and certitude. They will have inadequate truth, because these judgments do not express the object adequately. Thus, when I say, "I am ill," the predicate expresses the subject only under one partial aspect. They will have hypothetical necessity, for the self is not an absolute value as being is. It is a fact and it remains a fact, subject to verification. Consequently the judgments formulated concerning it will have only hypothetical necessity. They will have an evidence and certitude dependent on the concrete conditions under which the judgment is made. In this case error is possible because of the complexity of the datum. Objective evidence and legiti-

mate certitude will be had to the extent to which the judgment is made in the best possible conditions—when, for example, the datum is actually present, when the datum is clear and simple, when the subject exercises attention and prudence. In this way the causes of error will be eliminated.

4. *Conclusion.*—We can now conclude: My transcendental but indeterminate knowledge of the real can be developed to some extent along the lines of self knowledge, using the lived experience or consciousness that I have of my own activity. This experience can be translated into univocal concepts which are only partial but still objective expressions of the real. Thus it can give rise to true and certain judgments.

The kind of knowledge which we have just examined has a characteristic imperfection, that of "conceptual dissection." Since each univocal concept represents only a partial aspect of the conscious reality, I am forced then to dissect my knowledge into a number of such concepts. Thus I end by representing reality's richness to myself through a conceptual transposition which always remains inadequate. However, this process will not involve any error in my knowledge, provided that I understand the exact significance of what I am doing.

§ 2. *Critique of Our Knowledge of Matter*

My indeterminate knowledge of the real can also be made more explicit with the help of my knowledge of matter or the corporeal datum. We should first examine the objective experience which is the source of this knowledge. My knowledge of matter is both empirical and conceptual. Rightly evaluated, it can give rise to judgments which are true, evident and certain when they express the most immediate characteristics of the corporeal datum. It can give rise to other judgments which, as they depart from the immediate data and attempt to interpret the nature of the corporeal world, become less and less perfectly evident and more and more only probable approximations of the truth.

Continuing the procedure we have adopted elsewhere in this work, we shall now present an extended commentary on the implications of this latest thesis.

1. *Knowledge of the Corporeal World as a Development of my Knowledge of Being.*—Objective experience, the experience of the datum which forms the object of my sense perceptions, shows me certain modalities of the real, and to that extent it allows me to develop my indeterminate knowledge of the real. When the thesis is proposed in this general form, it does not admit of any difficulty. No one will dispute an immediate presence. If I have a perception of "red" or "cold" or "noise," this is an immediate and undeniable datum, and since non-being cannot appear to me as red, cold, noisy, it is clear that "red," "cold," and "sound" are in some way modes of the real, real modes of the non-self, or of the self.

We have already seen that this objective experience, like the lived experience, is expressed in empirical concepts: the concepts of "body," "distance," "red," "sound," and so forth. In turn, these concepts give rise to judgments which restore them to the datum: "This is red." As long as these concepts and judgments express only the immediate experience, they will have the same value and weight as concepts and judgments referring to lived experience. For these concepts are abstract and partial, but still faithful, representations of the concrete corporeal datum present to my consciousness. I can see the conformity existing between these concepts and their object. I can restore the content of the concepts to the object by the judgment, and thus see the objective value and truth of this judgment.

2. *Necessity for a Critique of Perception.*—But an entirely new problem appears when I raise the question of the objective value of the sensory datum itself. For then we have to consider the conditions in which objective experience takes place, or the role which the sensory organs play as instruments of this experience. This new factor will profoundly alter the data involved here in the critical problem.

Here again we must state the problem in exact fashion. To doubt in our sense experience either the reality of the objects perceived, or the reality of the perceiving organs, would not make sense. There can be absolutely no doubt that I perceive lights, colors, figures, local movements, sounds, odors, resistances, cold, heat, tastes, stings, and so forth. These objects are not nothing. Non-being or the non-real cannot appear to me in the guise of color or sound. These objects then have a certain "reality." They are real contents of my real consciousness. It is just as certain however that these objects are perceived with the help of bodily organs which act as instruments for my consciousness.

We have shown above how we discover these organs; first, as objects among objects, and then as instruments of perception.[5] Finally, however close the relation between the datum and the perceiving organ may be, the knowing subject always makes a distinction between its act and the object, between perception and term perceived.[6] Critical epistemology does not question the immediate data of consciousness as such.

5. See above, pp. 112-14.
6. *Ibid.*, p. 120.

This cannot be done honestly. If in spite of everything we still try to do so, we merely push into a blind alley.

The critical problem concerning my perception may be formulated as follows: What kind of reality belongs to the objects which are perceived, and to the organs which perceive, and what bonds exist between these two realities? This problem involves several more detailed questions which can be reduced to the following: To what extent can I talk in epistemology about the corporeal datum's *"reality in itself"*? Granted that I can talk about it, to what extent do my perceptions show me the properties or nature of this datum as it is in itself, independently of its perception by this or that sense organ?

Here we encounter one of the most controverted points in critical epistemology where presumptions and ambiguities cause great difficulty. We believe that one definite answer clearly forces itself upon us, a solution which rejects all forms of idealism, from solipsism [7] to indirect realism. It may be called direct or immediate realism, provided that we distinguish this moderate or critical realism from all forms of dogmatic realism.

3. *Prejudices and Misconceptions.*—Before we undertake our critique of sensation *ex professo*, it is best to clear away some presumptions and misunderstandings. History teaches us to take this precaution.

(a) Philosophers have often distrusted sense experience because of various well known states of consciousness in which the knowing subject confuses the contents of his imagination with the data of his perceptions, states in which he confuses

---

7. According to this doctrine, the individual self would be the only true reality; everything else would be only a representation or dream.

the "represented" real with the "present real." This is the case in dreams, hallucinations, hysteria and so forth. Many critics were strongly impressed by these facts, and consequently felt themselves obliged to embrace scepticism in this domain of knowledge. They said it was impossible to distinguish an "image" from a "datum" with any degree of certitude. Others tried to extend the subjectivity belonging to the contents of imagination to the objects of perception. Since, in their view, the images are the products of imagination, why then should the perceived objects not be the products of perception?

The distinction of the perceived datum and the imagined datum is a problem which, strictly speaking, belongs not to the critical but to the descriptive part of epistemology. For, directly at least, it is not a question of determining the value of my knowledge, but rather of knowing how it is constructed. For the present it is sufficient to refer the reader to what has been said on this point in descriptive epistemology.[8] Here let us limit ourselves to noting that for an attentive and reflective consciousness the distinction of the sense datum from the images is quite easy and that epistemology does not have to concern itself professedly with the so-called states of diminished consciousness. Let us also note that, contrary to what is presupposed in the foregoing objection, images do not appear to consciousness as products of the imagination, but rather as contents of the imagination and as residues of previous perceptions. The activity of the imagination is limited to combining these residues and thus creating complex new images. But this work itself is unconscious. What I see on the level of consciousness is the appearance of new representations. These representations evoke real situations never given to me, and at

8. See above, pp. 124-27.

least in certain cases I am aware that I control the stream of these images to some degree by fixing my attention in a determined direction.

The question of distinguishing between the data of perception and images evokes only an indirect critical interest in so far as it shows that the value of knowledge always depends on the degree of attention, reflection and composure of the knowing subject. But these are general conditions needed to have a good "return" from knowledge. When they are missing, and especially when the subject is in a definitely morbid state of disequilibrium, all the immediate data of consciousness can be falsified. Then it will be a case not only of confusion between the perceived real and the imagined or represented real, but of loss of memory, loss of sensitivity, and even of loss of personality or dual personality. All this is equivalent to saying that the epistemology of human consciousness is a study of an uncertain and unstable reality.[9]

(b) The idealist reaction against traditional realism was directed very often against an exaggerated realism which held that in my sensations I reached immediately a world of substances distinct from myself. It was very easy for the critics to show that exaggerated realism's metaphysical interpretation of the corporeal datum was beset with difficulties, and that this view found it very difficult to solve the problem of individuality in the material world and consequently the problem of the distinction of substances. The claims made by

9. Concerning the realism of St. Thomas, Father Rousselot (*The Intellectualism of Saint Thomas*, English translation, Sheed and Ward, 1934, p. 74, footnote 24) writes: "The *resolutio in sensibilia* is simply a verification of the normal state of the thinking subject which is necessary for the validity of the judgment. In this way, the senses as a whole acquire a criteriology value. Sleep is distinguished from the waking state by the impossibility of this operation, since the sleeping person is unable to verify at the starting point the connection of his thoughts with reality".

our realism will be much more modest and restrained; it will certainly not lay itself open to criticism of the kind just mentioned.

(c) The greatest presupposition made by the idealist regarding perception is indubitably the famous "Principle of Immanence." Under the pretext that knowledge is a vital act, an immanent operation, an activity of the self which is consummated in the self, idealism decrees that the act of knowledge cannot have a transcendent term, that is, it cannot have as its immediate object a reality which would be distinct from the self. It therefore concludes that the term of the knowing act can be only a representation of the object to be known, whenever it is a case of knowing a non-self—a corporeal world, for example, distinct from the self.

Such an attitude involves a clear presumption. It presumes proven that the term of the cognitive act cannot be simultaneously immanent (a content of consciousness) and transcendent (distinct from the reality of the self). It arbitrarily claims that the real presence of a corporeal object in consciousness is unthinkable or—what amounts to the same thing—that a consciousness opening on a corporeal world is impossible. But this presumption is flatly contradicted by the very clear data of consciousness. Consequently the presumption should yield before the facts. The idealist metaphysic should accept the facts and conform itself to them.[10]

But when all is said and done, the difficulties arising from a genuine critique of sensation were what doomed the naïve realism of common sense. Ordinary men had already criticized their own sensations and were aware that numerous illusions occurred in sense knowledge. The critique of sensation,

10. For the representationist conception of knowledge, see Noël, *Le réalisme immédiat*, pp. 15-17, 43-44, 66-71, 77-96, 159-161.

however, was considerably developed by scientists, physicists, and psychologists, and pushed even further by philosophers. It tended to stress all the subjective and relative elements in our perceptions.[11] Their critique merits our closest attention, for it will help us to state the realist position more precisely by determining better just what are the possibilities of perception considering the conditions in which it takes place.

One final preliminary remark. The analysis of my consciousness reveals a world of perceptions which is extremely complex. It is true that my sensory apparatus is an aggregate which serves one and the same consciousness. My various perceptions complete and check each other. The physiognomy of the corporeal world as present to my consciousness results from a synthesis of those perceptions. But in this complex world all the elements are not of equal value. The various classes of perceptions do not have the same characteristics, nor can they all be checked in the same way. Within each class of perceptions I can experience the whole gamut of intensity and clarity. We must take this situation into account, for a general critique of knowledge, such as we are interested in here, should not allow itself to get lost in a detailed examination of all the aspects of sense activity.[12] Its role is rather to determine in broad outlines the cognitive value of perception. For that purpose it should base itself on those data of consciousness which are most undeniable. These are, on the level of perception, the objects of visual perception and the objects of tactile perception (taken in a broad sense). Taken in its essential features, my experience of the corporeal world can be reduced to a synthesis of these two groups of objects.

11. See above, pp. 40-49.
12. This will form the object of the special critique which should accompany experimental psychology, as shall be explained later.

4. *Critique of Perception.*—Now let us try to get to the heart of the question. We can take as an example the actual situation in which I am at the present time. In ordinary language, "I am seated at my desk in my study. I let my gaze wander over the oaken surface of this desk while my right hand follows the outlines of the surface and thus describes a large rectangle in space." Now, if I wish to describe my perception of the surface of my desk in epistemological terms, I shall say: "My consciousness opens on a datum which shows the following characteristics: it is real, corporeal (spatial and temporal), rectangular, brown, polished, resistent and cold. To perceive these characteristics, I need my eyes and also my hand or some other organ of touch—at least for the last three qualities." The situation which I analyze in this fashion involves three component elements: my consciousness endowed with sense organs—*the knowing subject;* the thing perceived, which is a synthesis of the different characteristics enumerated—*the object known;* and the conscious perception by which I seize this thing—*the act of the subject.*

Such being the case, we can now give a more precise statement of the critical problem concerning sensation. Does my knowledge of a corporeal thing [13] show me this thing as a reality in itself? If it does, then how much does it tell me about the proper nature or the properties of this thing as it is in itself? In short, what is the objective significance or objective value of perception? What can sense consciousness know in a truly objective way? [14]

13. I apply the name "thing" to a group of simple objects which hang together in my field of consciousness; for example, my "desk," this "armchair," this "cat." See above, pp. 110-11.

14. I apply the name "sensible consciousness" to consciousness (my human consciousness) in so far as it is equipped with sense perceptions. As we have seen, "consciousness" implies a spiritual immanence. If I have sufficient reasons for thinking that the animal does not have this spiritual immanence I should con-

Our answer to the first question could be put as follows: The visual and tactile perception of a corporeal thing—my desk, for example—shows me that there is present in the objective field of my consciousness a reality *in se,* if by that we understand a reality which is distinct from the subject (consciousness and its body) and which is not produced in any conscious fashion by the subject. But on the other hand, this perception does not show me a reality *in se,* if by that we understand a reality *subsisting independently of the subject's reality.* For in fact the thing which is perceived exists and is real, since I do perceive it. That which did not exist or which did not have any reality could not be perceived, or affect my sense organs, or occupy the objective field of my consciousness. I can ask whence this reality comes, whether it is dependent or not on myself, but there is no sense in contesting its existence. Furthermore, the thing which is perceived is distinct from me in so far as I am a consciousness and a body. By sight I perceive the thing as being distant from my body; by touch and sight combined I perceive it as being contiguous to my body. Finally, the thing which is perceived is not produced consciously by the subject. I have no consciousness whatever of producing my desk by my act of knowing or by any other conscious activity. On the contrary, my consciousness testifies that the thing forces itself upon me in a dominating unavoidable fashion, that it resists me, that I submit to its presence. Consequently, the mere fact that I cease knowing it cannot make the thing cease to be, since my conscious act of knowing does not posit but rather presupposes the existence of the thing.

----

clude that it does not have any "consciousness." Consequently I should define it as a subject which is equipped only with organic perceptions centralized by a nervous system, but without consciousness.

But on the other hand, my perceptions alone cannot give me a decisive guarantee that the thing has an existence independent of mine. This might appear probable enough, for the "conduct" of this thing seems to be completely independent of mine. I can move, walk around my room, approach my desk or go away from it, but my desk will remain unmoved and indifferent. I will find it again "in its place" when I return home. It does not seem to feel any effects from my illnesses. In the same way, my cat comes and goes, eats and sleeps, without my being affected in any other way than by the knowledge which I have of it. But this high degree of probability does not yet amount to a critically established certitude, and I have to admit that experience does not reveal immediately the ontological relations which things have among themselves and with myself.

In short then, my perceptions and especially my combined visual and tactile perceptions assure me that around myself— a consciousness endowed with a body—there exists a group of things which are distinct from me. I am not conscious of producing these things, yet I have a certain relation with them through my sense organs. Whatever be the origin of these things, and whatever be their ontological status (that is, their relations with the total reality), they undoubtedly have a certain reality in themselves distinct from mine.

Now we can take up the second question and begin to examine critically the various properties which these things have when I become aware of them. We already know what these properties are from descriptive epistemology. The corporeal datum is extended, temporal, qualitatively differentiated, and structured. For the present we can disregard this last characteristic, since it is only the result of the preceding ones. To what extent then do these properties belong to things as they are in themselves? In other words, to what extent are they really objective?

(a) *Extension or spatial dispersion* is a strictly objective datum. It shows me something of the inner nature of the object. For, in fact, on the level of conscious data there can be no doubt that the things perceived—for example, my desk—are in fact extended, that they actually possess parts which are external to one another. The same thing holds for my perceiving organs, because I see clearly that my body is extended. Consequently, consciousness bears witness that perception always appears to me as a form of knowledge which essentially involves a spatial relation between two extended realities, the sense organ and the object.[15]

We may inquire about the origin of this spatial character which affects the things and sense organs when I perceive. It certainly does not come from any conscious influence of the subject, for I have absolutely no awareness of ever conferring this spatial character on either my sense organs or on things. But it may be asked whether it could not come from some unconscious influence of the subject, either in the sense that the subject unconsciously produced his own body and corporeal things, or at least the extension of his own body and corporeal things; or in the sense that the subject naturally had an extended body and produced the other bodies, or at least their extension. First of all, metaphysical hypotheses of this kind are purely gratuitous. They cannot be refuted in epistemology on the basis of the immediate data of consciousness. From the critical point of view they are irrelevant, because they do not affect the complete objectivity of extension

15. In other words, the spatial or corporeal nature of the object appears to be a condition of the possibility of sensation. To be perceptible the object must be extended or spatial.

in any way. Even though the spatial aspect present in my sense organs or in things were the effect of some unconscious influence of the self, it would still remain true that these organs and things really possessed that spatial aspect in themselves, since they have received it independently of the conscious act of perception. Consequently, no matter what hypothesis is proposed regarding its origin, extension still belongs to the nature of the sense organ and things independently of my knowledge.[16]

This fact involves a very important consequence from the critical point of view. With respect to space, both the perceived object and the sense organ are *homogeneous*—of the same nature. In this instance, the *modus recipientis* coincides with the *modus recepti*. The hypothesis of possible adulteration of the object by the subject is excluded for that reason. To the extent that sensation is spatial, it consists in the seizing of a spatial object by means of a spatial organ. Nothing is simpler or more easy to check, particularly since spatial extension is a *common sensible*, that is, a property common to the objects of different senses. This fact makes many verifications and checkings possible. In other words, in this case the question of determining what the contributions of the object and sense organ are, does not occur. *When knowledge of the corporeal world acquired by corporeal organs is considered to express knowledge of the corporeal characteristic itself, then this knowledge is necessarily objective.*

My desk is therefore extended, extended in itself. Its very nature is to be extended. Its front edge is "distant" from its back edge—entirely apart from my awareness of it. This

---

16. Thus we see that the Kantian theory of *a priori* forms of sensibility has no place in epistemology. See *"Problèmes épistémologiques fondamentaux,"* pp. 491-493.

holds true for a subject like myself who perceives it by means of bodily organs, but it also holds true for any consciousness, human or not, which knew it. This fact would hold true for that consciousness because such is actually the case, because this is actually the kind of existence which this desk has. Let us note further that all this would still hold true even if we supposed that this desk had no existence independently of my consciousness or independently of an absolute consciousness —for example, in the hypothesis of monism. Even then this desk would be no less real and no less really extended.[17]

(b) Is the *extension in time*, or the successive character of perceived events, a characteristic which affects corporeal things independently of my knowledge? Let us note first that a perception of the extension of things in space in no wise implies an immediate perception of their temporal character. Seeing a piece of iron or wood does not show me anything "successive" in these objects. On the other hand, I can very well perceive the "successive" character of my inner acts without discovering any "spatial" character in them.[18]

Considered as conscious facts, the objective pole of my consciousness, particularly the corporeal datum, evolves just as certainly as the subjective pole. The perceived objects succeed one another in my field of consciousness. Sometimes this happens in a sudden change—for example, when an electric bulb

17. A desk is, therefore, "extended" for God and for pure spirits just as well as for me, even though God and pure spirits do not know it by means of organic perceptions. In the same way, there is a "distance" between Brussels and Louvain, even for God who does not have to "travel" it. We apologize for insisting on these evident points, but they have been questioned before by intelligent men.

18. We must not carry over to epistemology or psychology something which, because of its method, holds true only for physics. From the fact that it is impossible to dissociate space and time in a system of physics, it does not follow that these characteristics are never separable in our knowledge.

burns out; sometimes in a slow evolution, as when day gives way to night. The subject's acts (perceptions, imaginations, feelings, judgments, and so forth) succeed one another in like fashion. But change seems to affect the objective pole to an even greater degree, since duration, permanence, or "continuity," is a distinguishing mark of the conscious self.[19]

But still keeping to the level of conscious facts, there are cases where changes of this sort in the objective field are clearly due to some change in the subject's attitude. Closing my eyes, for example, involves the suppression of all my visual data. When I take my hand away from my desk I suspend all the tactile perceptions experienced in the sense organ. On the other hand, I often have a very definite impression of being an unchanging witness to variations in the things perceived—when, for example, I look at a fly lighting on my desk and walking on it, or when I listen to the melody of a piece of music.

From such facts we can deduce the following critical principle: To be able to attribute to the perceived datum changes which seem to affect it, I must first of all ascertain that the states of the subject and its perceiving organs have not been altered. To the extent to which I can establish that fact, I can say that the perceived quality of succession can come only from the datum itself.

But how can we show that the subject has not varied, or that a change appearing in the objective datum is not due to some alteration in the subject?

To do this we have to make a detailed comparative study of our perceptions, using different classes of perceptions to check one another. If corresponding changes occur in the fields of several senses this will normally reveal a variation in

19. See above, p. 104.

the thing perceived. Thus the tick-tock which I hear, the movement of the clock's pendulum which I see, and the recurring contact which I feel between the weight of the pendulum and my stationary finger, all correspond strictly. This convergence leads me to say that these three phenomena are due to the action of one single objective cause on my different sense organs.

This critique does not properly belong to general epistemology, since it represents a specialized critique carried out in function of all the data of empirical psychology, and psychology's laws governing the biological and psychological conduct of the knowing subject.[20] It is true that this critique never gives us absolute certitude. It gives rather practical certitude, often only a simple probability which is based upon frequent repetition of the same experiences, and depends upon a continuous checking by successful action.

This conscious revelation of the nature of perception in consciousness helps me see how my critique of the perception of change and temporal succession will develop. We know that every sense perception involves a corporeal datum and a corporeal organ united by a spatial relation.[21] We know that this meeting in space is expressed in me by means of a new conscious act—perception. The situation immediately suggests an interaction between the two bodies involved, that is, a twofold transitive action or mutual influence between the two agents. But transitive action implies movement and succession. Consequently, if perception results from an interaction of datum and sense organ, then every perception

20. As examples we can list the phenomena of accommodation, the influence had by the laws of the Gestalt on the structure of the datum, the role of our ordinary biological activities (breathing, pulse) in our perception of time.
21. See above, p. 215.

will essentially involve a temporal change in both the datum and the organ.[22] From this point of view both the subject and the object are only relatively immobile. If, however, we consider the subject's whole field of perception, then this critique of our perceptions enable us to state that most of the changes produced there are due to the evolution of the world of data or things. The most important changes due to the subject's intervention would be those coming from some interruption in the use of this or that organ—for example, in cases of blindness, deafness, loss of sensibility regarding smell, touch, taste, the placing of a screen before the eyes, and so forth.

(c) Keeping to the level of conscious facts, we can say that corporeal things clearly possess *different determinations* which help us to distinguish one thing from the other. The total object of my perceptions is the corporeal world. This cannot be reduced in any way to a homogeneous or undifferentiated extended mass. On the contrary, the corporeal world exhibits an infinite variety of aspects, qualities, or "determinations." Each element of the extended universe has its own distinctive properties and characteristics. Each element has the power of causing qualitatively different perceptions in me.

Now, do these qualities belong to the datum apart from the knowledge which I have of it ? Do they affect it in itself, that is, in what constitutes it as a reality distinct from me and independent of my conscious activity? [23] Are they truly objective and to what extent?

22. This interpretation of the phenomenon of perception in terms of the *interaction* of datum and organ belongs to the *special metaphysics* of man, or *philosophical psychology*. We mention it here by anticipation to bring home the complexity of the problem of the perception of change, and to show why the general critique of perception cannot provide an adequate solution.
23. See above, p. 213.

Our answer must be qualified by certain necessary distinctions. I am in no way aware that I produce these qualities by any action on the datum. On the level of consciousness these qualities are data; they force themselves on me; they are objective in the same way as the reality of the object, or its spatial extension, is objective.

But may it not be that these qualities are produced by the self in some unconscious way? The answer to that query has already been stated when we spoke about spatial extension. Even though these qualities had been produced unconsciously by the self, *the object really possesses them when I know it*. This is the only thing which matters in critique. The hypothesis that qualities are produced unconsciously is a metaphysical hypothesis which can neither be proved nor disproved in epistemology.

The only problem concerning sensible qualities which properly belongs in epistemology is that of knowing how far their objectivity could be endangered by the fact that they are perceived by means of sense organs, corporeal instruments of consciousness. At this point we have to introduce some new distinctions.

All the determinations or qualities which I use to distinguish objects belong virtually to the objective datum. For unless these differentiating qualities were due to the nature of the datum, any object could cause the perception of any quality. This is certainly not the case in my consciousness. This sheet of paper has in itself a determination which causes a perception of "white" in me rather than a perception of "red." Sugar has in itself a determination which enables me to distinguish it from a "sour" object or a "bitter" object. In short, the sense datum possesses these perceived qualities virtually, that is, it possesses them "in its power" *(in virtute sua*). In certain circumstances it can cause this perception rather than another in me.

Spatial determinations belong to the perceived object formally and absolutely. We can distinguish two categories of sensible qualities. The first class are determinations of extension as such. They constitute limitations of extension, they give different forms to extension. These determinations are, in fact, the geometrical forms of objects—their lines, surfaces and volumes. Then there are other determinations which cannot be reduced to this first class, or to the determinations of extension as such, for example, sound, light, color, heat, cold, tastes, odors and so forth.[24] We call the first group spatial determinations. We call the second group non-spatial determinations or qualities properly speaking.

These spatial determinations are the conditions which make perception possible. An unlimited or indeterminate extension could not be perceived. Extension is perceived only in its limits and through its limits. Every perception implies a spatial relation between two bodies which are spatially determined—the perceived object and the perceiving organ. Furthermore, the spatial determinations of the object are of the same nature as the spatial determinations of my sense organs. My sense organs serve as instruments for measuring the objects perceived. Thus, when I use my hand to measure the length of my desk, my perception amounts essentially to noting the spatial correspondence of my hand with each of

24. Some qualities present a very complex appearance. Thus, for example, in "roughness" we can distinguish a *geometrical* element (that is, the uneven surface which presents irregularities) and also a purely *qualitative* element (the disagreeable impression produced by the rough object). We could make the same distinction for other qualities as for example for the "soft," "liquid," "solid," "heavy," "sharp," and so forth.

the sections of that length. This kind of perception rules out any distortion of the object by the organ.

In many cases however our perception of these spatial determinations is influenced and distorted by the knowing subject's organic condition. Such distortion is possible whenever the perception involves something more than a spatial coincidence between object and organ. Cases of this sort occur especially in visual perceptions. When I check these perceptions by tactile perceptions of the same objects, I discover a number of optical illusions due to the physiological and psychological conditions in which the act of seeing took place. We will return to this point shortly.

When this subjective influence is eliminated, the perceived spatial determinations belong to the datum formally and absolutely; *formally*, that is, they belong in their characteristic form—my desk is really rectangular; *absolutely*, that is, entirely apart from any relation to a sense organ—my desk is rectangular in itself. It is not because I am looking at it that it is rectangular, but rather I *see* it as rectangular because it *is* rectangular.[25]

The non-spatial determinations, or qualities properly speaking, present themselves to consciousness in quite a different fashion. In this case there is no longer homogeneity between object and organ, but rather adaptation of one to the other. A certain object is adapted to cause a perception of "green" in me, and my eye is adapted to perceive that certain object as green. Another object is adapted to cause a sensation of "cold" in me, and my hand is adapted to feel that object as cold. How can I distinguish the roles played by the object and the organ in these different qualitative impressions? These

25. Thus it will be rectangular for every consciousness which knows it as it is in itself. It is rectangular then for God or for a pure spirit.

sensible qualities are in fact only the impression produced in
me by this or that object when it is placed in contact with
this or that sense organ. But there is nothing in the immediate data of my consciousness which would authorize me
to state that these qualities which I perceive belong formally
and absolutely to the objects; in other words, that the datum
is in itself "green," "cold," "bitter," "sweetened," "per-
fumed" and so forth, apart from any relation to my sense
organs.[26]

To bring out more clearly what our stand regarding the
value of sensible qualities means, we can contrast our view to
different positions examined by Father Gény in his *Critica*.[27]

According to *conceptionism*, the qualities which are perceived do not belong to the object, but rather to the representation or the conception of the object. This representation
alone is the immediate term of the perception. This theory
is a corollary of indirect realism, which itself comes from the
presupposition of the "walled-in consciousness." It arbitrarily
separates the (transcendent) object, or the "thing in itself,"
from its (immanent) representation. We have already criticized this presupposition [28] and we will speak of indirect
realism again shortly. We must say that the qualities are
properties of the object itself, but they are properties of the
object as it appears in a consciousness endowed with certain
sense organs.

26. See *"Problèmes épistémologiques fondamentaux,"* pp. 493-494. It is evident
that at this time I no longer say that "the qualities are *fully objective;* they
belong formally to the object" (p. 494), without adding "in so far as it acts on
me and I react on it."
27. See Gény, *Critica de cognitionis humanae valore disquisitio* (Rome, 1927),
pp. 210-235.
28. See above, pp. 209-10.

Integral perceptionism stands at the opposite extreme to conceptionism. Apparently many medieval scholastics held it. Father Gény himself still defends it. It holds that sensible qualities are completely objective, they belong formally to the object independently of any sensation; this body is, in itself, green, sweet, hot, and so forth. The modification of the sense organ causes it to share the qualities of the stimulus.

We believe that this stand betrays lack of a critical point of view. For these sensible qualities manifest the object as it appears in a consciousness possessing certain definite organs, but there is no ground for stating that these qualities formally belong to the object in itself.

Father Gény believes that anyone who rejects these two preceding views, will be forced to accept a third position which he calls moderate conceptionism, moderate perceptionism, or interpretationism. Interpretationism, like integral perceptionism, holds that objects are perceived immediately, but the perceived qualities result from a certain physiological elaboration in the same organ, and consequently they result from a certain subjective interpretation. This point of view is quite similar to the one which we ourselves have proposed. But the terms used in describing it do not seem to be too fitting, for they introduce a certain separation between the qualities and the interpretation by which or across which the subject reaches them: "Sensus igitur nostri qualitates sensibiles percipiunt *per* aliquam earum *interpretationem*; quod ex hac interpretatione resultat vocamus colorem, sonum etc. formalem." [29] Now in reality, no separation should be introduced; the quality "red," for example, is the modality under which a certain object appeared to a subject possessing a certain organ of sight, but the perceiving of this quality does

29. See Gény, *op. cit.*, p. 216.

not imply any "interpretation" at all on the part of the subject.

The critique of sensation which can be made in epistemology, or at the start of philosophy and the sciences, should properly end here. It should limit itself to the following statements which, though sketchy, are still of great value. By means of my sense organs the consciousness which I am has a spatial relationship with a collection of bodies or extended objects. These bodies are in themselves real, extended, temporal and qualitatively different from each other. All this is true independently of the knowledge that I have of them. In themselves they possess spatial determinations (geometrical forms) which sometimes coincide with the spatial determinations I perceive, but often they are more or less seriously distorted by my perception. Finally, qualities properly speaking, while belonging virtually to the corporeal objects, are nevertheless essentially relative to the organs of the subject, so that it is impossible to determine in direct fashion by any simple reflection on immediate data just what these qualities are in themselves.[30]

At the close of our critique of sensible perception, the corporeal character of sensation stands out as its dominant trait. Sensation is a way of knowing which is bound up with extension. It depends on a corporeal organ, it is conditioned by a meeting in space and time of stimulus and sense organ. From this fundamental characteristic all its other characteristics derive—for example, its *passivity* (the organ suffers a change or the shock of the stimulus); the partial *relativity* of qualities (the sensation depends on the nature and the psycho-physio-

30. Let us again note that epistemology cannot decide the question of the *ontological relationships* between the conscious self and its body and between them and other bodies.

logical properties of the organ); the *individuality* of the perceived object (it is a body situated in space and time, "hic et nunc"); the *primacy of the spatial datum* (this element is common to all the stimuli and to the organ; it is the condition which makes the sensation possible); the *intuitiveness of sensation* (it is an immediate view of the concrete, thanks to the spatial contact had between object and subject).[31]

To push our critique of sensation any further we would first have to appeal to the information provided by different positive sciences which study this field—physics, chemistry, physiology, experimental psychology, and so forth. It is quite evident that a physico-chemical study and an anatomical, physiological, and psychological study of the conditions for my perceiving, can help in determining the cognitive value of these different activities. Thus, in the case of visual perception it will be a question of showing the mysterious mechanism by which I can be related to a distant object and have the impression that I seize in this object qualities which belong to it exclusively: the "red," for example, which I perceive is not presented as touching my eyes, but rather as constituting an "object" located at some distance from my eyes. It will also be necessary to determine the role played by the medium and the light propagated in it: I have the impression that I see a "star," but astral physics tells me that the light rays emitted by that star have taken years to reach me. Finally, we must determine what psychological laws are involved in visual perception and try to explain certain facts present in exceptional subjects—for example, the presence of "eidetic images" in the visual field. After learning the conclusions of these different disciplines, we would have to determine what their methods and results are worth in a suitable special critique.

31. On the critique of sensations see Noël, *op. cit.*, pp. 5-7, 171-178.

This is not the time to undertake that task, but we can offer some easy examples to show how this special critique develops and what methods it uses to determine the coefficient of subjectivity in sensation—especially the contribution made by the *modus recipientis* in the perception of sensible qualities.[32]

We have seen that, except for the case in which a spatial determination is perceived by spatial coincidence with the perceiving organ, sensible qualities always result from a certain compromise between object and subject; direct analysis therefore cannot distinguish the influence which the subject has in the perception of these qualities. We can however make an indirect critical attempt at fixing a sensation's coefficient of subjectivity. Even in ordinary life men try to free themselves in different ways from the subjectivity affecting sensation. We must note that the various attempts mentioned differ in value.

Some of these experiments try to determine how different subjects react to the same stimulus. They succeed in discovering certain anomalies which are most frequently due to the defective constitution of a certain sense organ. Thus, cases of color blindness, myopia, deafness, paralysis of smell or taste, atrophies of the sense of touch, have been uncovered. This is really the same as saying that this subject does not perceive a certain class of stimuli, or that he perceives them only with great difficulty. Experiments of this kind also show that subjects vary considerably in judging the agreeableness or disagreeableness of certain tastes, smells, colors, figures and

32. We believe that these anticipatory remarks will help the reader to distinguish the different steps involved in the work of evaluation. Many misunderstandings could be avoided if more attention were paid to these indispensable distinctions.

so forth. But these experiments should make no claim to determine whether a given perception is more objective or less objective than another. The most they can do is to distinguish between "normal" and "abnormal" subjects by first applying the numerical standard, and then by appealing to anatomical and physiological data.

When almost the entire group of subjects agree about the properties of a certain stimulus, what value exactly does this "agreement of the majority" have? This agreement of itself does not imply at all that the subjects' perceptions are identical. The fact that twenty subjects may agree in declaring a certain object to be "green," does not mean that they feel exactly the same qualitative sensations when presented with this object. All of them distinguish this stimulus from other stimuli possessing different qualities for them. Then because of certain accepted conventions in social communication they have learned to designate this class of stimuli by the word "green." However, the similarity of their sense organs will justify my *conjecturing* that the different subjects should get similar impressions.

The fact that the subjects agree almost unanimously in their designation of the object's qualities, has above all a practical value. The agreement makes it possible to use these properties in defining or describing objects. From the critical point of view however this first type of experiment is of little value.

In other experiments perceptions obtained by one organ complete and make more exact the knowledge obtained by perceptions from another organ. Thus, taste enables me to identify a certain white powder which vision alone fails to distinguish from other powders having the same appearance.

Smell brings out the true nature of a certain greenish liquid which "at first sight" could be either a liqueur, a lotion, or an insecticide. Hearing helps us determine the kind of metal from which a certain piece of money is made. The sense of touch helps us distinguish a genuine relief from an apparent relief. In all such cases it is really a question of obtaining added information by appealing to new perceptions.

Other situations which at first sight are quite different can in fact be reduced to those that we have just described. Thus a straight ruler partially immersed in water appears to be broken at the surface of the water, while at my touch it still seems to be straight. In this case must we speak of error or illusion in vision? Must we say that touch "corrects" vision? Not at all. In reality, the difference between these two perceptions helps me discover a *physical law* showing me that the two perceptions strictly speaking do not concern the same object. The organ of touch is in direct contact with the straight ruler, while the organ of sight perceives it by means of light rays which are really deflected according to the law of refraction.[33]

But there are some other experiments which have more weight from the critical point of view. This is the case for the well-known illusions of weight. Two objects which have the same weight but which differ considerably in volume will not appear to be equally heavy. The illusion however will disappear if the subject be blindfolded. Another example,— the same object will appear to be heavier or lighter according as it is weighed after a lighter or heavier object. The optical

33. There could be question of error or illusion if I were to judge imprudently on the basis of incomplete data, and affirm that the ruler is really broken. See above, p. 175.

illusion of Müller-Lyer, the illusions due to contrast of colors or lights, and many other illusions are well known. A sick man with a fever will shiver with "cold" in a well-heated room, and the finest dishes will seem "tasteless" to him. All these examples point up certain *psychophysiological* laws such as, for example, the influence of expectation, of previous perceptions, of the total object, of the environment and so forth. To a certain extent these laws express the subjective coefficient or the factors which determine the *modus recipientis* of the sensation. Consequently, they indicate variations in perception arising not from some objective change, but rather from some change in the subjective or organic conditions. We can discover these factors by checking the perceptions of a given organ against other kinds of perception which do not involve those subjective factors.

Measurement methods are the most effective means of realizing this emancipation from psychological laws. We have already stressed the point that spatial properties have a privileged character. In them sense perception reaches an element which is completely objective. To protect our knowledge from illusions and subjective distortions, we can then try to identify and characterize objects exclusively in terms of properties which can be measured spatially and may therefore be easily checked or recognized by everyone. This is the function of measuring instruments such as the ruler, scale, thermometer and so forth.

The principal characteristics of these measurement methods are the following:

They try to reduce the intervention of the senses in our knowledge of objects to a minimum. This intervention is limited to noting a spatial correspondence. As we saw above, this minimum is safe from any psychological distortion. It is a datum which is fully objective. In this way it is easy for all the subjects to agree. They will readily agree that a thermometer reads fifty degrees, that a certain object measures fifteen inches, weighs seven ounces and so forth. This process of reducing our knowledge of all the diversity seen in the world of bodies to a matter of noting a spatio-temporal recording made by some material process means that we eliminate every subjective element—whether it be passionate, pathological or simply physiological in origin [34]—from our knowledge of the material world.

The measurements which we get, or the continuous quantity (exemplified by the column of mercury, the ruler, the angle formed by the pointer of a scale), can be measured and expressed in terms of discrete quantity or numbers—in degrees, inches, ounces and so forth. Thanks to this transposition, we can make our measurements more and more precise by further subdividing the panel of our measuring instrument. Furthermore, measurements when expressed in numbers can be treated by all sorts of mathematical techniques.

The measuring instruments will allow us to construct gradually a physical world whose elements and properties are defined by means of qualitatively different measuring methods, yet still in terms of purely quantitative relations. This physical world will be strictly objective, even though it does not exhaust all the reality of the corporeal world. Physics, then, gives me a knowledge of the corporeal world which is true, but incomplete or schematic.

We can now see how the critique of sensation leads us to distinguish the psychological object, the object in itself and

34. On this point see Renoirte, *Eléments de critique des sciences et de cosmologie,* 2nd. ed. (Louvain, 1947), pp. 107-127.

the physical object. The *psychological object* is the object which is immediately perceived. The *object in itself* is the object such as it is independently of all perception. The *physical object* is that aspect of the object in itself with which physical science is concerned. Physical science studies the object starting from the strictly objective elements of the psychological object, that is, its spatio-temporal determinations. In respect to these determinations, the psychological object and the physical object coincide. These determinations thus form a privileged object from the critical point of view.[35]

5. *Value of the Judgments Expressing my Knowledge of Matter.*—If my knowledge of the corporeal world takes account of this critique of sense perceptions, it will, like my knowledge of internal experience, lead to judgments which are *true, necessary, evident* and *certain*, at least when these judgments express characteristics immediately given in objective experience. Here we must repeat what was said above concerning the judgments expressing knowledge of self. The characteristics of inadequate truth, hypothetic necessity, evidence and certitude depending on the concrete conditions of knowledge, are all found again in the judgments expressing the data of objective experience.[36]

But in so far as I get away from the immediate data of experience and claim to state what the corporeal things are in

35. As we noted above (p. 222, note 24), certain qualities entail a spatial element, and so they can be subject to measurement from this point of view. Thus the qualities "soft" and "hard" imply respectively a certain ease or difficulty in changing the spatial relations between the parts of the soft object or the hard object. These relations, changes, and the force of cohesion of the parts, can be measured. In the same way, the qualities "glossy," "rough," "sharp," "pointed" and so forth, imply a spatial element of a physical order which can be measured.

36. See above, p. 203.

themselves independently of my perceptions of them, my knowledge becomes more inadequate and also more subject to error. More inadequate, because the knowledge of the physical world is a partial and schematic knowledge of the corporeal world, developed only in terms of spatio-temporal determinations.[37] More subject to error, not only by reason of the corporeal world's complexity, but also because I tend constantly to attribute to corporeal things in themselves characteristics belonging to psychological objects, that is, to things as perceived by me. It will be the function of the special critique of sensations and the critique of sciences to determine the exact scope of the non-immediate judgments, by which I claim to express my knowledge of bodies.[38]

It is worth noting here that the question of the "truth" of knowledge does not occur on the level of perception. Truth, or the conformity of the knowing subject to the known object, supposes that we can distinguish two contents of consciousness which can then be compared. On the level of perception, however, only one content of consciousness is present, that is, the perceived object or psychological object. We cannot speak of truth or error in perception as such.

But may I not talk of truth and error when I compare my perceptions to one another and check one perception by another? Does not this comparison tend both to distinguish the object in itself from the psychological object, and to pass judgment on the greater or lesser conformity of the latter to the former?

It is true that the critique of sensation leads to distinguish-

37. I know that the physical world is differentiated qualitatively, but I know these qualities only by the qualitatively different procedures which I use to measure them.

38. A great many current errors are due to confusing the object *in itself*, the *physical* object, and the *psychological* object.

ing the object in itself from the psychological object which is only relatively objective and conditioned by subjective influences. But this critique draws no conclusion regarding the greater or less conformity of the psychological object to the object in itself. It concludes that the two are *identical*, when the coincidence of organ and datum apprehends spatial determinations, or it concludes to a more or less marked *divergence* between the two in other cases. This divergence, however, is not an error in the strict sense of the word, for error implies some defect or failure of knowledge in its natural finality. But the very nature of perception determines that its finality will consist precisely in seizing objects as they appear to a consciousness endowed with certain organs.

The question of the truth of knowledge can be raised on the level of the judgment where it is possible to have a direct comparison between the act of affirming and the perceived object expressed by this act. On this level there are two contents of consciousness, and a relation of conformity can be seen between them. Sensation can be a frequent occasion for errors in judging because the subject tends to overlook the dosage of subjectivity in his perceptions and tends to attribute to the object in itself properties which he sees in the psychological object. In this way his judgment goes beyond the datum present to his consciousness and thus he falls victim to his own rashness.[39]

6. *Conclusion.*—At the close of this critical study, we may try to sum up the results of our inquiry. Like my knowledge of the self, my empirical and conceptual knowledge of the corporeal world undoubtedly enriches my transcendental but confused knowledge of the real by making it more explicit.

39. See above, p. 203.

These conceptual expressions of self and bodies have in common the imperfection of conceptual dissection (*morcelage conceptuel*). But my knowledge of the corporeal world has an added imperfection peculiar to experience realized by means of corporeal organs when used as living instruments of consciousness. None of these imperfections, however, excludes a true knowledge of what bodies are, either as perceived or apart from my perceptions. Although this knowledge is partial and superficial in its provision of strictly objective spatio-temporal elements, and although it is essentially relative in its provision of qualitative elements, yet it serves to put me in contact with the corporeal things surrounding me, and it enables me to reach a double goal. First, it enables me to build up a *system of knowledge* by classifying and measuring the data or phenomena, both in the psychological order and in the physical order. This constitutes the theoretic finality of our knowledge of matter, and it is this finality which is of special interest in epistemology. Secondly, it makes it possible for me to carry on my *practical activity* in the corporeal world. It enables me to distinguish objects, to recognize them, to grasp them or push them away, move them, to change my own position with respect to them, to enjoy them and so forth. This constitutes the practical or biological finality of this knowledge.

A sound critique of sensation will keep midway between naïve realism and scepticism. It will take account of the fact that sensation is essentially relative as regards qualities. It will also take account of the fact that there are profound differences among the various kinds of sensation (visual, auditory and so forth). It will also advert to the assistance which the senses can give to each other because the sense system is unitary. Because of this constant cooperation of my different perceptions, I can acquire a relatively rich and reasonably guaranteed knowledge of the corporeal world. Frequently an isolated perception will give me only very meager information about the object which is perceived.[40]

§ 3. Critique of Reasoning

My immediate knowledge of the real and its modalities as given in my experience is made more explicit through the intellect's discursive activity. The value of this discursive activity is ruled by the same norm as immediate knowledge. In discursive activity we can distinguish the real order which it attempts to express and the logical order in which it is expressed. Mediate knowledge can be expressed in judgments which are true, necessary, evident and certain.

The full meaning of this brief statement of the epistemological critique of reasoning will be grasped more completely in the light of the following commentary.

1. *Discursive Activity.*—My analysis of consciousness has shown me the existence of this discursive activity, which is the process of associating concepts and judgments. We could have given lengthy descriptions of the many processes by which my discursive reason associates the various elements of conceptual knowledge. Then, on the basis of that analytical study, we could at this point make a detailed critique of the reasoning processes and proceed to elaborate the "laws" of reasoning or the logical laws. But we have already noted that this twofold study (analytical and critical) of reasoning has

---

40. The added help of sight and touch enables me to see that a perceived odor is not merely some modification of my olfactory organ, but that it is a property of the liquid contained in a certain vial. When the vial is corked, I no longer perceive the odor. When the vial is opened, I will perceive the odor better by bringing the liquid closer to my nostrils.

for a long time formed the object of a distinct epistemological discipline, that is, logic.[41] At this point therefore we shall
merely give a general statement of the critical problem as it
concerns reasoning, and indicate our solution of the problem
in the case of the critical and normative science of logic.

2. *The Norm of Discursive Activity.*—The critical problem raised by the fact of reasoning can be formulated in very
simple terms. What is the value of the discursive activity of
my intellect? Or more precisely—how, why, under what
conditions, and in what measure, can this reasoning process
help promote my initial knowledge? To solve this problem
we must once again return to the absolute norm of my
knowledge, that is, the affirmation of being. Under what
conditions does reasoning help to make my knowledge of being—already enriched by the experience of the self and of the
corporeal world—more perfect?

The proper finality of reasoning is not to grasp the complexity or diversity of the real, which is the finality proper to
experience, but it consists rather in correcting the dispersion
of experience and reducing it as far as possible to the unity of
being or the universal order. Since the intellect is an appetite
for the real, it tries to grasp the real as it is, with all its real
diversity, but also with all the real relations uniting the elements of this diversity. As a capacity for the real, the intellect is by that very fact also a capacity for the relations in the
real. The reasoning activity is legitimate, correct, and it can
advance my knowledge when it makes my immediate knowledge of the real more explicit by bringing out the real order,
that is, the network of relations which unite the elements of
reality. It is illegitimate when it arbitrarily introduces into

41. See above, p. 153.

thought elements foreign to reality as given in experience. In other words, the reasoning activity must always respect the initial knowledge from which it starts.

3. *The Conceptual and the Real Order.*—But now things become more complicated. The order of the reasoning activity does not exactly coincide with the real order. It is in fact only a conceptual transposition of the real order. Indeed the original element found at the basis of all reasoning is the concept. Now, the concept is not a "double" of the datum of experience, it is rather a synthetic and abstract representation of it. Reasoning strives to build up a system of concepts, a conceptual order, which will be a transposition of the real order to the level of intellectual immanence, the plane of stability and unity.

If we suppose that the linking up of concepts is correct, what is the value of this transposition? It will have the same merits and imperfections as the concept itself. This transposition sacrifices the originality of the concrete thing or individual as such, it sacrifices every element in the spatio-temporal reality which cannot be expressed in abstract universal concepts. But on the other hand, it reduces the diversity and changing flux of my world of experience to the unity and stability of an immanent synthesis in my consciousness. It strives to give me possession of the real order in a final synthetic act. This final synthetic act must substitute for an initial synthetic act excluded by my nature. Thus we are led to distinguish in reasoning a twofold system of relations.

The relations existing among the concepts as such constitute the formal order of concepts or the logical order. It is one of the primary tasks of logic to search for and define the properties of concepts and the relations existing among them as concepts. This makes it possible to determine the correct procedures of reasoning by a method of analysis called "resolutio." In other words, it is a question of showing that a given rational process can be "resolved" into immediately known items and, therefore, only forms an "unfolding" of that knowledge. Thus, for example, the conclusion of a correct syllogism can be resolved into its premises because it is entirely implied in those premises. In an incorrect syllogism on the contrary, the "conclusion" is not a genuine conclusion. It is only an apparent one. It is a purely verbal conclusion based upon some play on words, usually upon the equivocal meaning of a middle term.

Once the general laws of reasoning have been established, the intellect can use them to express the real order or the relations existing among the elements of the universal order. In other words, it can use them to elaborate the conceptual transposition of the universal order, which is the ideal to which it tends. This conceptual synthesis will constitute a material order of concepts, an order suggested principally by the concepts' matter or objective content as expressing experience.

We can then distinguish three orders in knowledge: at the level of experience, the *real order;* at the level of conceptual immanence, the *conceptual order;* and within this latter, the *logical order* or the formal order of concepts.[42]

We must note very carefully that when we oppose "logical" to "real," we are no longer taking the word "real" in its primitive, transcendental sense. In that sense the "logical" is

42. On the relationship between the "real" and the "logical," see Mansion, *"Sur la correspondance du logique et du réel,"* in *Revue Néoscolastique de Philosophie* (August, 1932), pp. 305-340.

also "real." Here "real" signifies *the real which is independent of our conceptual transpositions;* "logical" signifies *the real which is transposed into conceptual immanence.*

4. *Value of Judgments Expressing my Mediate Knowledge.* —The mediate knowledge obtained at the conclusion of reasoning can be expressed in true judgments just as properly as can immediate knowledge. When obtained by processes conforming to the laws of evolution of discursive thought, such mediate knowledge is only the fuller expression of immediate knowledge. In that hypothesis, indeed, the conclusions reached by reason will have exactly the same objective value as the immediate knowledge of which they are the fuller expression. But we must never lose sight of the fact that the conceptual construct is a transposition of the datum, and for that reason has characteristics which the datum itself does not have. Furthermore, mediate knowledge, obtained by the discursive activity of reason, is marked by a new imperfection, that is, the distance which now separates thought from the real because of the various intermediaries introduced by reasoning.

§ 4. *Critique of Memory*

Memory, taken to mean a knowledge of the past as such, plays an important role in our conscious life. Its primary and essential function is to safeguard the unity and permanence of consciousness in spite of its unceasing change, and to make possible the perception of temporal succession. Its secondary function is to preserve for the subject the benefits of his previous experiences. In its primary function, memory offers the same guarantees of objective value that experience does. In its secondary function, its testimony is not entirely dependable unless checked.

This thesis incorporating our critique of memory in the light of the established norm of knowledge can be explained further in the following manner.

1. *Memory.*—It is very evident that if my knowledge were limited to the present, or to my actual perceptions and the consciousness of my present activity, my conscious life would be very markedly curtailed. But I have the remarkable power not only of conserving images and ideas which remain from former knowledge, but also of using these images and ideas to re-present past events to myself in such a way that I know those past events precisely as past. The most evident result of this persistence of the past in the present is that it safeguards the unity and continuity of conscious duration. Due to this persistence my conscious past continues to live in me, and I am aware that the conscious self in some way escapes temporal succession, since I remain myself throughout the various vicissitudes of time. By this fact I am also able to apprehend temporal succession itself and to synthesize successive phases of the becoming which I witness and which I dominate because of the permanence of the self. Finally, this persistence of the past in the present preserves for me the benefits of innumerable experiences had in my past. It saves me the trouble of having to learn over again a multitude of things whose knowledge I have acquired once and for all.

2. *Value of Knowledge of the Past.*—What is the *value* of this knowledge of the past as such? What guarantee of objectivity does it offer?

My *general* knowledge of the past as such, that is, my knowledge of the persisting yet successive duration into which I am plunged, possesses the same guarantees of objectivity as experience itself. Indeed, this general knowledge can be reduced to a twofold experience: inner experience, or the consciousness I possess of the unity and permanence of the active self; and my experience, both objective and subjective, of the succession of objects and the succession of my acts. In both cases it is a question of immediate, undeniable data which cannot be disputed. My consciousness of the active self is clearly not knowledge of an "instantaneous" existence, it is knowledge of a duration, of a permanence, and nothing outside consciousness itself can explain it. The succession of my acts is just as evident. Finally, the successive character of the corporeal datum is a fact which cannot be explained completely by the successive character of my acts. If in certain cases the evolution of the datum is determined by some subjective change—as when I successively open and close my eyes—yet in numerous cases the conscious subject as such has no part in the becoming which he sees.

On the other hand, my special or detailed knowledge of the past is liable to frequent illusion. My memory is often undependable. My recollections become blurred and changed. They become associated or confused with other memories. They are influenced by my present perceptions, expectations and feelings. If we accept the data of memory without checking them, we leave ourselves open to error. We can make this check every time the past event has left positive and undeniable evidence behind it. Thus I may believe that I remember the title of a book, but to check the retentiveness of my memory I can go and look at the book itself in my library. This special critique of memory evidently depends on the special critique mentioned above, since it presupposes the development of the psychological sciences which, among other things, study the conditions required for the functioning of memory.

Part Four

THE CONCLUSIONS OF EPISTEMOLOGY

At the threshold of philosophy, any possible study of my knowledge must be based exclusively on the immediate data of my consciousness. This study as a matter of fact makes only very modest claims. It limits itself to *describing* and *evaluating* some ordinary act of knowledge; for example, an act which is elementary yet complete, which involves at its source a two-fold *experience* (perception of an objective corporeal datum and consciousness of myself). This act completes itself in the *affirmation* which is the conceptual expression of the experience. Finally, at the end of my analysis and evaluation of this initial act, I began to realize the possibility of developing this immediate knowledge by the processes of discursive reasoning, which processes are studied and criticized in logic, the third step of epistemology.

Although these conclusions may appear to be very meager, they have a very considerable import and entail very valuable consequences. We must now gather them together and draw out their more important corollaries.

CHAPTER I

CRITICAL REALISM

§ 1. *The Nature and Value of Knowledge*

AT THE close of epistemology I can describe my knowledge as follows: *an immanent activity in which I perfect myself by the conscious possession of the objective and subjective real.* In this statement we can distinguish the following elements: the knowing subject, *I*; the act of knowledge, *an immanent activity*; the object known, this includes *the objective and subjective real*; the more remote finality, *that I perfect myself*; the more proper and proximate finality, *a conscious possession of the real.*

To measure the value or worth of this knowledge means to determine the extent to which the finality proper to it can be realized. This supposes that we have a precise notion of what that finality is, and also an exact appreciation of the potentialities which the cognitive act has for realizing that end.

The ideal or the end that I seek in knowing is the completely objective possession of everything that is. We have seen that this ideal is realized in a true fashion in the affirmation of the real, that is, in a true possession of the whole universe in an infallible and adequately true act. This confused knowledge is completed by the detailed knowledge of the modalities of the real, given to me by the experience of the self and the experience of matter. It is made explicit by reasoning.

However, this "conscious possession of the real," which I reach in my very first complete act of knowledge and which can be developed indefinitely, thanks to new experiences and reasoning, has essential limits and imperfections.

In the first place my explicit knowledge of the real is limited by my experience, and although I glimpse the possibility of indefinite progress in the enrichment of this experience, I have no grounds for thinking that a time will come when I shall have acquired an explicit knowledge of everything which exists. On the contrary, my experience appears to be superficial by its very nature. I seize surrounding bodies by contacts which are spatial in nature and therefore essentially "superficial." I grasp myself on the level of my "activities" without however getting an intuition of the profound reality of the self. Such facts lead me to think that my experience of the real will always remain inadequate in comparison with the real itself.

In the second place, the objectivity of my knowledge—the conscious possession of the real *as it is in itself*—is not perfect under every respect. Indeed this possession is achieved in and by an act which is immanent to the subject, and therefore follows the "mode" or "capacity" proper to the subject (*cognitum est in cognoscente ad modum cognoscentis*). As a knowing subject I manifest certain peculiar traits which endanger somewhat the perfect objectivity of my knowledge. These peculiar traits are my recourse to corporeal organs as instruments of knowledge and the abstract character of my synthetic representations. The first of these characteristics causes the essential relativity of sensible "qualities," while the second introduces a "conceptual dissection" and unavoidable inadequacy into my representation of concrete reality.

My knowledge is *perfectly objective* in three cases: when I experience and affirm the real, in which case there is a transcendental value which consequently surpasses all opposition of subject and object and excludes all distortion; when I experience and affirm my own lived activities, in which case there is an object seized by consciousness and an identity of subject and object is realized; when I experience and affirm *spatial extension, temporal succession,* and the *spatial determinations* which affect corporeal objects. These conditions are seen to be independent of the act of perception which reaches them.

My knowledge is *imperfectly objective* in three respects. Critical reflection on my cognitive act shows me that the subjective function clearly influences the constitution of that act at three points: on the level of *perception,* where perceived qualitative differences depend on the nature of the perceiving organ and on the psychophysiological tendencies of the subject; on the level of *imagination,* where data are reproduced, preserved and associated according to the laws proper to this organic faculty; on the level of *intellectual conception,* where data are transposed under the form of abstract concepts and a conceptual reconstruction of the universe is carried out in accordance with the logical laws proper to conceptual thought.[1]

In short, the basic imperfection of my knowledge consists in the *irreducible duality of experience and concept,* destined to complete one another mutually but never to be identified.[2]

On the level of experience, possession of the real is achieved by a certain identity of subject and object in the act. This is a superficial identity in the case of objective experience, which is a lived contact with corporeal reality. It is an intimate identity in subjective experience or the consciousness of

1. See "*Problèmes épistémologiques fondamentaux,*" pp. 493-496.
2. Father Rousselot (*The Intellectualism of St. Thomas,* p. 146) has noted this point already: "The ultimate reason for all the imperfection of knowledge may be reduced to the duality of man's medium of knowledge as contrasted with the ineffable unity of the real with and in itself."

my own activities. But in both cases the identity is achieved on the level of secondary acts and not on the level of my profound reality or permanent self.[3] This possession by identity therefore involves numerous imperfections.

The imperfections which mark my experience (that it is limited, dispersed, successive and contingent) are corrected on *the level of conceptual immanence,* which is a transference and development of experience. On this level I can acquire a knowledge which is transcendental (or unlimited), synthetic (or unified) and expressible in judgments which are necessary either with an absolute necessity (in the case of my knowledge of being), or with a relative hypothetical necessity (in the case of empirical knowledge of the modalities of being). In short, thanks to my conceptual knowledge of being, I am capable of possessing everything that exists, but this transcendental synthetic knowledge is still extremely confused. It can be made more explicit in two ways, by reference to experience and by reasoning, that is, by partial successive seizures of the modalities of the real.

All the elements of knowledge are not equally guaranteed. Scientific work should be based on elements which stand up under criticism. In human consciousness there are obscure zones, weak states and confused situations which we must admit we are not able to clear up. However, these do not in any way endanger the value of clear and distinct knowledge.

We have just spoken of the value of knowledge in terms of its proper and proximate finality. This finality can be called theoretic finality. Since every one of my cognitive acts is completed in an affirmation regarding the object known, my knowledge always has a theoretic or speculative finality, as a

3. Later, in metaphysics, we will note that the identity realized in the cognitive act is "accidental," not "substantial."

disinterested contemplation of the real. Looked at from this point of view, it is an end in itself, not merely a means.

But the description of my consciousness has already shown that cognitive activity forms part of a far more complex network of activities. Among these activities I have distinguished affective and biological activities. This description suggested to me that my knowledge is only one part of the total dynamism driving me on to full self-realization. From this point of view therefore knowledge should be considered as a *means* to the total perfection of the self or as a means to its final end. So we can raise the question of the *practical* or *vital finality* of my knowledge, and try to determine to what extent this remote finality can be realized. But it would be premature to consider this problem in epistemology. Indeed to make any treatment productive we would first of all have to determine what the nature and end of man are and what are the speculative potentialities of human knowledge. So doing we would then be able to show the role which knowledge can and should play in man's integral life. Epistemology, however, has neither the task nor the means of solving these preliminary questions. Epistemology merely furnishes knowledge with a solid starting point for its future conquests.[4]

4. The further development of philosophy will make it possible for us to distinguish different aspects of the practical or vital finality of knowledge. Thus in spite of their natural imperfections, my perceptions serve to give biological finality to my knowledge in so far as they enable knowledge to play a part in my biological evolution. They put me in contact with the surrounding corporeal world and with my own body. They provide me, as a living organism, with a means of orientation, distinction and defence with respect to the environment in which my organism develops. Everyday experience shows that this biological finality of my knowledge is realized in a great number of cases, but it also shows that the "perspicacity" of the biological subject is often at fault. Thus for example he may take starch to be sugar or chalk. My perceptions also make possible the esthetic or artistic finality of my knowledge, because they furnish the material elements for the constitution of the *beaux arts* and the

§ 2. *The Different Facets of Critical Realism*

The analysis and critique of my knowledge have emphasized that the real is the object of this knowledge and the goal of its finality. The real is the first and in a certain sense the only content of every experience. It is the object signified by the basic concept implied in all other concepts. It is expressed by the very first affirmation I make, "Something exists." The real therefore constitutes a value which is absolute not only with respect to the consciousness which apprehends it (I seize it because it is, it does not exist because I seize it, I do not "posit" it by seizing it), but the real is also an absolute value with respect to anything at all. Consequently, the real is the supreme norm for my knowledge and the final basis for its value.

An epistemology which reaches this sort of conclusion concerning the role played by the "real" in my knowledge can rightly be called a realist epistemology. No name could characterize this doctrine better than that of *realism*.

However, to eliminate certain regrettable confusions already existing and to avoid causing new ones, we must specify further the exact scope of our realism. Our realism entails not only a radical realist position, but also realist attitudes in more restricted fields. These particularized realist views really distinguish our position and are very important because of the consequences to which they lead. We must therefore define these different attitudes carefully and show the positions which they oppose.

---

development of esthetic taste. The ethical or moral finality of knowledge is rooted in the absolute value of the object of thought which alone can determine what the absolute norms of morality are in terms of the human person's final end.

1. *The Fundamental Assertion of Realism.*—The affirmation of the real is the basic assertion made by realism. To be a realist is to recognize first of all that something exists, that this fact is *known* to me, that it has a *meaning* for my thought, that it constitutes an objective *value which dominates my mind*. In short, to repeat what has become a classical expression, to be a realist is primarily to "consent to being."

Realism therefore recognizes the primacy of being or the real as such over thought as such. It holds that thought of itself is only a "function," a "power," a "potency." It maintains that the essential law of thought is that thought must submit to the real and is capable of doing precisely that.[5] The real or being has its own value entirely independently of the knowing function or activity. Man's consciousness feeds not on its own activity but on the real which forces itself upon consciousness. The real is the measure of knowledge. The function of the active subject is merely to bring out all the implications of the datum presented to it.

But perhaps the real which obtrudes upon me was produced by me in some previous unconscious state. Perhaps it was produced by a deeper unconscious self latent at the source of my consciousness. What then? We hold that the realist affirmation would still remain intact. Even though the real had been produced by an unconscious Subject (or by a conscious Subject—it makes little difference), the real would re-

5. This is the law of human thought, and here we are speaking only of human thought. But we can also state that it is the law of every "intelligence," that is, of every "faculty of being." In God, being and thought are identified. But since we employ many concepts to express the divine perfection we must say that the being of God has a logical primacy over the thought of God. We should rather say that God knows Himself because He is, and not that He is because He knows Himself.

main just as real as in any other metaphysical view. The realist affirmation belongs to the *epistemological* order. It is independent of any further metaphysical interpretation. It holds that *on the level of my consciousness* the real obtrudes on the knowing subject, and that to know is not to produce an object but rather to "possess" it, "embrace" it, "contemplate" it.

It is true that no philosopher ever brutally denies the basic realist assertion. No one claims that "Nothing exists," or that the proposition "Something exists" has no sense. But as soon as there is question of determining further what this assertion *implies,* or what precisely it *signifies,* then many philosophers go astray. To preserve his scepticism, the sceptic should doubt this realist affirmation, because he holds that no affirmation is stable and no truth is enduring. The relativist cannot admit that the affirmation of the real has an absolute value. The subjectivist will not recognize the objective value of the knowledge of being. Finally and above all, there is an important group of modern idealists who have been led astray by the "Copernican revolution" of Kant. This group rejects the primacy of being over thought and distorts the very notion of knowledge. "To know," for them, is essentially "to posit being." Here we put our finger on the most pernicious error of modern thought. This fundamental realist assertion is accepted by a considerable number of doctrines which do not accept complete realism. Here we can list Platonic idealism, empiricism, nominalism, Cartesian idealism.

We believe that we have shown sufficiently well that the fundamental realist assertion is safe from all relativism and scepticism. The denial of this realist attitude is contradictory. It logically involves the denial of consciousness itself.

2. *Metaphysical Realism.*—A first capital specification of the basic realist position is the following: Not only is being an *objective* value transcending the thought which affirms it, but being is also an *absolute* value. I reach this absolute value by means of my concept of being. This concept is transcendental. It represents adequately everything which exists. We call this new realist position "metaphysical realism," because it recognizes the basic metempirical or metaphysical value, and therefore posits at once the object of metaphysics.

Those who accept this realism evidently go beyond a number of historical philosophical positions: empiricism in all its forms (nominalism, phenomenalism, positivism and so forth), since empiricism rejects any pretense of going beyond experience; Kantian agnosticism which declares that all noumenal science is impossible. Realism also goes beyond idealism in so far as the latter renounces any attempt to reach anything outside purely formal or purely logical thought (thus for example, L. Brunschvicg). A transcendental idealism like that of Fichte or Hegel, however, can be reconciled with metaphysical realism, as can also Platonic idealism.

3. *Psycholgoical Realism.*—This is another form of the realist position. The real is always given to me in an *experience.* Seeing that something exists, I apprehend the real and affirm it as an absolute value. I can have a twofold experience: objective experience, which puts me in contact with the corporeal world; and subjective experience, or the experience of my own conscious activities. Consequently, metaphysical realism can be based either on subjective experience or on objective experience.

We call *psychical* or *psychological realism* the philosophical position taken by the person who admits the reality of his own conscious activities and the possibility of knowing them in a scientific way. Only a few philosophers reject this form of realism; materialism and positivism would oppose it in so far as they disregard the reality belonging to conscious life. Some defenders of absolute phenomenalism, who try to reduce the self to an epiphenomenon without any value of its own, might also oppose this form of realism. It is clear of course that every philosopher who rejects the basic affirmation of realism will automatically reject all particular forms of realism.

4. *Cosmic or Cosmological Realism.*—This final realist attitude consists in recognizing the reality of the cosmos or the corporeal world, the object of my sense perceptions. This realism thus admits that sensation and the empirical concepts connected with it have a certain objective value. It holds that man's consciousness can to some extent reach the *in se* of the corporeal world and acquire a certain scientific knowledge of it.

This cosmic realism evidently goes beyond the elementary *cosmic empiricism* which all philosophers probably share. No one, unless he is mentally disturbed, rejects the immediate data of sense experience as being entirely without solidity or entirely non-existent. To merit the name of "realist," however, we must recognize a *value in se* in the objects of sensible experience. While defending this basic value, cosmic realism can still admit of many degrees and variations, depending upon the scope and meaning attributed to the knowledge of the corporeal world's reality.

If we recall that the principal problems of philosophy (God, man, the moral life) are not affected by this question of cosmic realism, then we must admit that this problem is not primary. In fact, only one problem depends on it: whether a cosmology or metaphysics of nature is possible. The sciences of the nature and knowledge of the material world hold only a secondary place in the framework of a genuine humanism. In such a humanism primacy must be given to values which are properly human. On the other hand, cosmic realism is undoubtedly one of the doctrines characteristic of Thomism. At the same time it is a truth whose rejection will distort very seriously the physiognomy of man's consciousness.

The critique just made of our knowledge of the corporeal world allows us to specify the following distinctive traits of cosmic realism. This realism is:

Empiricist or dualist: Consciousness reaches the corporeal world as a datum of experience, as an object which is distinct from the subject or subjective function. The objective experience even precedes the subject's knowledge of himself, or consciousness properly speaking.

Intellectualist or spiritualist: The intellect is active and transcends matter. It reacts to this datum, seizes it and affirms it as a value in itself by the help of concepts and judgments.

Immediate or intuitionist: Sensible intuition puts the subject in immediate contact with a real object and consciousness is actively present in sense perception. Consciousness therefore can affirm as an immediately evident object the presence of a *reality* (the real stimulus) which is corporeal (located in space and time) and able to produce qualitatively different perceptions in me.

Moderate or critical: This realism makes allowances for the "subjectivity" of knowledge and all the imperfections which that implies in me—the relativity of sensible qualities, possible defects of sense organs and nervous system, imperfections in conceptual knowledge, limitation of experience. (Experience reaches only the superficial characteristics of a very small part of the corporeal world and of my conscious activities. With the help of these restricted data all our human science is constructed.) As a supplement to its general critique of knowledge cosmic realism will also include a detailed critique of sensation, imagination (memory, dreams, morbid states, creative imagination), empirical concepts, and the positive sciences. It is clear that in carrying out this program the alert critical sense which is equally opposed to every form of dogmatism and naïve realism [6] will be characterized by a certain dosage of scepticism, agnosticism, idealism and pragmatism.

Idealism in all forms is the principal opponent of cosmic realism. Idealism harbours a profound distrust of sense experience and would like to free thought from any dependence on the objective datum. Platonic idealism declares that the objective datum has no consistency. Cartesian idealism accepts the prejudice of the closed consciousness and terms the objective datum inaccessible. Hume and Kant call the objective datum purely phenomenal. Kant and a number of modern idealists say that the objective datum has no genuine objectivity. The same group call the objective datum unintelligible or irrational. Immediate or direct realism is also opposed to mediate realism or indirect realism, which would hold that perception terminates immediately at a representation of the object. Moderate or critical realism is opposed on the other hand to naïve or dogmatic realism which does not pay sufficient attention to the subjective characteristics of knowledge.

6. On the subject of cosmic realism and its different aspects the studies collected by Noël (Le réalisme immédiat) can be read with great profit.

Our investigation has led us to an *integral realism,* a defence of all the realist themes just discussed. It is a type of realism which lies midway between empiricism and idealism. Empiricism weakens knowledge by losing sight of the part which conceptual activity and the transcendental capacity of the intellect play in our knowledge. Idealism distorts knowledge by sacrificing experience. Realism on the contrary preserves both these characteristic elements of our human consciousness, a consciousness which is neither pure experience nor pure idea. Realism tries to synthesize all the elements which are worthwhile and lasting in empiricism and idealism. With empiricism it recognizes that human knowledge is essentially dependent on experience, on a fact, on a datum. On the other hand, it holds with idealism that thought is transcendent to sensation and that the act of knowledge is immanent. Thomistic realism does not result from a mere juxtaposition of these two opposed theses. It is a synthesis of the two, for it emphasizes the necessary unity of the cognitive act. On the side of the object there is a *real identity* of the perceived object and the conceived object. On the side of the subject there is a *real unity* of a composite act, because consciousness is present at every level of the knowing activity (in perception, imagination, conception and affirmation). Consequently this whole activity is "informed" and unified by consciousness.[7]

7. "Critical realism," such as we have defined it, is safe from Gilson's censures of this expression. See Gilson, *Réalisme thomiste,* pp. 36-40; Noël, *"Le réalisme critique et le bon désaccord,"* in *Revue Néoscolastique de Philosophie* (February, 1940), pp. 41-66.

§ 3. *The Method of Realism*

Most Thomistic thinkers would be willing to accept in substance the conclusions we have reached, and most of them would agree with us in holding to an integral realism. But there is much less agreement on the procedure to be followed in constructing a realist epistemology. To clarify our own position it may be useful to state the principal points of the method we have followed in our study.

1. The epistemological problem is the fundamental philosophical problem. Systematic philosophy should begin by examining this problem because it controls all the rest.

2. If we wish to express the critical problem in clear and adequate fashion, we must first give a methodic description of consciousness. Descriptive or analytic epistemology must therefore precede critical epistemology.[8]

3. The analysis and critique which we make in epistemology should have as its primary object our knowledge of the real or being, and more particularly our affirmation of being. As a matter of fact we must necessarily start from *consciousness, knowledge,* and even more precisely, *affirmation,* because for me all the real depends on the fact of knowledge. We must show the nature and scope of the knowledge-fact. I can speak of the real only in so far as I know it. On this point we can and should accept the method of the Cartesian *cogito.* Further, there is nothing clearer in my consciousness

8. Instead of describing all the elements of the cognitive act previous to any evaluation, we could simultaneously describe and criticize each of the elements, starting from those which are more basic. Thus we could start by describing and evaluating the affirmation as such, and then pass on to the description and evaluation of experience and the affirmation of the real, and so forth. However, we believe that it is better to describe first of all the cognitive act taken in all its complexity. This will help us in arranging the various aspects of the critical problem.

than the affirmation which expresses and completes cognition.

Moreover we must start from the affirmation of the real, for no object is more immediate or fundamental than the real. The real is given in every experience. It obtrudes itself. It justifies itself. It does not presuppose anything. It is presupposed by everything else. It constitutes an absolute or unconditioned value.

In other words we feel that we must reject every epistemology which would claim to start from the evidence of "first principles," or from a critique of "judgments of the ideal order," or from the value of "eternal truths." For the abstract order has no solidity of itself. It must rest upon the concrete, of which it is but an expression. Human consciousness must accept *factual* evidence, that is, the existence of some thing, before it grasps necessary relations or *de jure* evidence.[9]

4. *There is no such thing as a privileged experience of being*, for every sort of experience, whether objective or subjective, infallibly reveals something of the real to me, and in this real the absolute value of "existence." An epistemology which would throw doubt on the value of sense experience as an experience of the real, or which would tend to subordinate it to the inner experience of the self, would not fully respect the data of human consciousness.

5. The term "real" taken in its basic essential meaning is a synonym for "existing" or "being." Taken in this sense it

9. In this matter we differ from Mercier and many contemporary Thomistic critics who have lost sight of the capital doctrine of the *ens primum notum*. We can note signs of a return to the primacy of being in Maritain's *Distinguer pour unir*, pp. 137-263; Noël's *Le réalisme immédiat*, pp. 239-245; Gilson's *Réalisme thomiste*, passim. See also P. Rousselot's *The Intellectualism of St. Thomas*, pp. 35-37, where the author shows that the knowledge of certain *facts* can be more important than the knowledge of *principles*.

cannot be defined because nothing is more simple or clearer than being. On the contrary, every other object of knowledge must be defined in terms of being or the real, as a determination of being. Thus it is that the image, the idea, the abstract, the universal, the conceptual, the logical, cannot be defined by *opposition* to being or the real, rather they must be defined as *modalities* of being. Consequently we must not start from the ideal to define the real by opposing it to thought or consciousness. We should rather define the ideal and thought, starting from the real, describing them as particular modes of the real, which oppose other modes of the real.

Many philosophers seem to lose sight of this first transcendental meaning of the term "real." For them "real" is opposed to "ideal" or "imagined" or "thought"; the real is defined in a purely negative way as "that which is not posited by consciousness," "that which is independent of conscious activity," "that which is not a product of imagination or thought." From our point of view this procedure involves serious difficulties and it could even make the critical justification of realism very difficult.

6. For centuries every discussion of cosmic realism has been bedeviled by the injection of the problem of dreams and of other psychological states in which the subject confuses imaginary objects with objects of perception. We believe that the philosopher who undertakes a reflective examination of his knowledge should not be too much disturbed by these states of weakened consciousness. The critical reflection itself would suffice to dispel any illusion since the illusion affects the subject only when his psychological state excludes any such critical reflection. Reflective consciousness usually finds it easy to distinguish between the data of perception and products of

imagination. This distinction presupposes that I know that my own body is the instrument for different perceptions. Between the sense datum and image there is not merely a difference of clarity, distinctness or cohesion, there is also a radical difference in the way in which they are *present*; a reflective consciousness can easily note this difference. The task of distinguishing sense data from images belongs properly to the analysis of consciousness, not to critical epistemology.

7. Let us note finally that whether the corporeal world (the object of my perceptions) is ontologically independent of the subject which I am, is not a problem of epistemology. On completion of this critique, I know that the corporeal world exists around me. I also know that it is not merely because I know it that this world exists. Rather it forces itself on my knowledge and I have to admit its coactive presence. But this fact does not definitely settle the ontological relationship between the reality of the cosmos and the reality of the self. That is a problem which metaphysics must try to solve.

The ontological independence of the corporeal datum is not the only problem whose solution is wrongly sought in epistemology. If we are to meet successfully the difficulties entailed in a study of human knowledge, we must know how to arrange the various questions, and we must treat them in the order required by systematic philosophy. It will be worth our while then to complete what we have just said about the method of realism by giving a brief summary of the problems still unsolved at the completion of epistemology.

§ 4. *Further Problems*

Some philosophers will say that an epistemology like ours furnishes only apparent conclusions. Because these philoso-

phers do not find here adequate answers to the problems
absorbing their attention, they conclude that the solutions
given by epistemology to the problem of knowledge are incomplete and superficial.

Complaints of this sort are due to misunderstanding. It
is not the purpose of epistemology to answer *all* the questions
which can arise concerning the nature and value of knowledge. Rather epistemology is limited to making an analysis
and critique of the immediate data of consciousness, that
study of knowledge which is possible and necessary at the
threshold of systematic philosophy. Consequently epistemology gives only a solution in principle—a *fundamental* and
general solution—to the problem of knowledge, which solution must be further specified and developed by the later
progress of philosophical reflection.

The better to clear up this misunderstanding, we will now
list briefly the principal problems which still remain unsolved
at the end of a general critique.

1. The question of the "first principles," which is often
considered a problem of critique as well as of general metaphysics, is in reality a problem which pertains to logic, for
the principles of identity, non-contradiction, and excluded
middle, are the fundamental laws of thought and the first
principles of the logical order.[10] Consequently it belongs to
logic to determine their origin, nature and scope. If under
the heading of first principles we also group other laws besides the fundamental laws of thought as such, we then pass
from the field of logic to that of ontology, from first principles of the logical order to first principles of the metaphysical order. Hence the principle of intelligibility ("Every

10. See Mansion, *"Sur la correspondance du logique et du réel,"* in *Revue Néoscolastique de Philosophie* (August, 1932), pp. 311-318.

being is intelligible"), and the principle of causality ("Every contingent being is caused"), are metaphysical laws which belong to the field of metaphysics.

2. All the problems concerning the nature and value of the discursive procedures of reason such as the syllogism, deduction, and induction, fall within the sphere of logic.

3. The general problem of substance (Do substances exist? Can we know them?) and the general problem of causality belong to general metaphysics.

4. The same must be said for the problem of our knowledge of God or the method to be followed in deriving the attributes of the First Cause; the solution of this important problem belongs entirely to ontology.

5. The very important problem of the distinction of individuals, and the related problem of our knowledge of natures or quiddities, receives a gradual solution in general metaphysics and later in special metaphysics. By its evaluation of absolute monism ontology prepares the solution by finding place in the real order for the "multiple" and the "finite." The general doctrine of activity further specifies the conditions of existence for every finite being.

The proof of the existence of God and the critique of pantheism (or relative monism) complete the task of situating the finite being in the universal order. Then special metaphysics can base itself upon these general doctrines and try to distinguish finite individuals and specific natures in our world of experience. First of all it determines the personal character and nature of the self; then it goes on to discover other human persons, and to define individuality among animals and vegetables by analogy with man. It is true that special metaphysics cannot push its conclusions any further. It apparently cannot determine the "species" in the biological world, nor settle the problem of individuality and natures in the inorganic world. The positive sciences can make very definite contributions to the solution of these difficult problems.

Note carefully that the conclusions reached by general and special metaphysics regarding these matters will finally provide the answer to the problem of whether my perceptions reach realities which are *independent of me*.[11] We left this problem in abeyance in our treatment of epistemology. At the completion of metaphysics I shall be justified in giving an affirmative answer to this problem, because I shall see that I am a finite person and that I am one element in an order of finite created beings; I shall see that my perceptions put me in touch with finite beings (men, animals, vegetables, inorganic matter) which subsist independently of me but dependently on God.

6. The problem of the ontological interpretation of knowledge belongs to the special metaphysics of man (metaphysical anthropology, rational psychology). What is in question? Once we have developed the metaphysical doctrine of the finite being's activity (substance, power of operation, complement of this power furnished by surrounding finite beings, necessary intervention of the creative Cause at the source of the activity, the ontological finality of activity), we can then interpret his cognitive activity in function of this doctrine and determine the ontological implications of the fact of knowledge. The problem should be formulated as follows: Given the general doctrine of activity on the one hand, and on the other, that knowledge shows itself to be an activity of the self with the characteristics that we have specified in epistemology, how are we to understand the ontological na-

11. See above, pp. 90, 96-97, 110, 114 (note 2), 116, 148, 214, 226 (note 30).

ture and functioning of human knowledge? Again, what ontological principles are necessary to explain cognitive activity as it shows itself to consciousness?

To answer this problem psychology must first of all seek help from several positive sciences, in order to determine the physical and psychological conditions in which our sense perceptions take place. Physics, chemistry, anatomy, physiology and experimental psychology can help metaphysical psychology on such points as the physico-chemical nature of stimuli, the anatomy and physiology of sense organs and the nervous system, the empirical laws of perception. Metaphysical psychology then tries to determine the constitutive principles of cognitive activity, how the origin and evolution of knowledge can be explained, the kinds of causality which are at work in the process.

We can easily see that this question of the ontological interpretation of knowledge has meaning and can be answered only in the light of an already constituted ontology. *A fortiori* it supposes that the basic critical problem has been solved, since the possibility of metaphysics itself depends on the answer to that problem. We may add that the best-informed writers on epistemological problems have emphasized the capital importance of distinguishing the critical problem and the ontological problem of knowledge.[12] Many authors however regularly fail to distinguish these two problems. This is one of the most common reasons for the obscurity and lack of precision found in many works termed epistemological. In these writings we find mingled with properly critical analyses, observations concerning the absolute consciousness, the essence of thought in general, the active intellect and the substance of the soul. Such violations of method

12. See Noël, *op. cit.*, pp. 162-167.

may help to "pad" epistemology and give an appearance of profundity, but only by sacrificing logical precision.

The distinction between these two problems is sometimes badly understood. Some seem to think that the critical problem develops exclusively on the phenomenal plane, and that it excludes any observations which are "metaphysical" in scope. This view cannot be admitted; first, because it implies what seems to be a very arbitrary juxtaposition of the "phenomenal" and "metaphysical." But since being is a transcendental value, the phenomenon cannot completely escape its jurisdiction or lack all metaphysical value. Furthermore, critical epistemology does not exclude all metaphysical assertions but rather has to set forth and state the object of metaphysics, as well as the basic judgments expressing our knowledge of being.

The ontological problem is logically posterior to the critical problem, in the sense that it goes beyond the level of our immediate metaphysical affirmations and tries to determine the ontological conditions or implications of our knowing activity. An inquiry of this sort presupposes an epistemology and an ontology.

The ontology of knowledge cannot in any way weaken the conclusions of our critique. There is no point in saying that the ontology of knowledge excludes all intuition of corporeal reality, all presence of intellectual consciousness in perception and all influence of corporeal objects in causing our concepts. These are facts properly noted and evaluated in epistemology. The function of the ontology of knowledge is not to deny these facts but rather to interpret them. If the ontology of knowledge does not succeed in throwing full light on the mysterious processes of human knowledge, the obscurities remaining in its explanation do not in the least affect the initial fact which obtrudes itself and which we must try to understand.

On the other hand, if the ontological theory of knowledge can furnish a satisfactory explanation of the knowledge process it will proportionately supplement, develop and confirm the conclusions of our critique in a very important way. By showing the latent sources of this unique activity, it will determine much better the place which knowledge holds in man's total activity and in the universal order. In this way it brings out the deeper meaning of the facts which epistemology simply records, and confirms the results reached in critical epistemology.

7. Finally, we must note that all the special problems of critique and methodology pertain to the philosophy of the sciences. What is the value of physical laws, physical theories and induction in physics? What importance do chemical, botanical and zoological classifications have? What is the precise meaning of mathematical constructs? What is the "real" significance of irrational numbers, or non-Euclidean geometries? What are the laws of the historical method, and what value do they have? Is history a science? What is the significance of philological, economic, sociological laws? All these questions are still unanswered at the conclusion of general epistemology. They have to be examined by the philosophy of sciences.

Chapter II

THE PRINCIPAL ERRORS IN EPISTEMOLOGY

To AVOID delaying our exposition by frequent long digressions, we have deliberately refrained from considering the numerous errors committed in the course of time in the field of analytical and critical epistemology. Besides, it is always a touchy and dangerous thing to take the works of writers holding other views than our own, and to condemn in them theses isolated from the context which gives them their precise meaning. There is always the risk of error and misjudgment. But in order to avoid that pitfall, must we renounce every attempt to compare ideas or to make a critique? Must we adopt the misleading attitude of relativism, and declare that all systems are of equal value and that each of them is true from its own point of view? Or will we capitulate to a clumsy "concordism" which would hold that the differences between philosophers are merely superficial and their disagreements are only questions of words?

In medio virtus. In this matter we must adopt a position midway between indiscriminate criticism and complete toleration of error. Even a general treatise like the present one must make some mention of opposed views. Our treatment would be essentially defective unless we at least gave a brief indication of the difference between our position and that of the principal philosophers who have dealt with the problem of knowledge. The brief account which follows merely points out some landmarks to guide the beginner in his reading and to stimulate him to further reflection.

§ 1. *Errors Concerning the Essential Characteristics of Knowledge*

These errors are evidently the most harmful. The following are the principal ones.

Scepticism fails to recognize the true nature and significance of *affirmation*. For it does not recognize that every case of knowledge involves an object which reveals itself (objective evidence), which forces itself on the subject and compels a firm, necessary, certain and true affirmation. In a more radical sense scepticism does not recognize the absolute value of being, its absolute opposition to non-being, or the power of the human mind to grasp this absolute value in every known object, however transitory it may be.[1]

Relativism, subjectivism and pragmatism represent milder forms of scepticism, since these systems question whether affirmation has any objective significance and whether objective evidence has an exclusive role in determining true and certain judgments.

Kantian idealism and all the types of idealism which ally themselves with the "Copernican revolution," falsify the very essence of cognition by taking it to be an activity which "posits," "produces" or "constructs" its object. Let us recall that "to know" is an original datum which manifests itself to us in our own consciousness; it is there and there alone that we can reach it. Now, in our consciousness cognition is always a mysterious way of "possessing" the real, of "contemplating" it, of "surrendering" to it by "recognizing" or "affirming" what it is. The act of cognition is the "second act," a new "form" of the self, a "quality." It has nothing in common with the category of "action." It is true that my act

1. See above, pp. 96, 178-179.

of cognition must be "produced" or elicited; but this is only a preliminary condition, due to my imperfection, or to the fact that I am not by nature in the state of knowing. The ontological interpretation of my knowledge would have to show how it is that, although I produce my act, I still submit completely to the real which is to be known. In short, "to know" never means "to produce." If we describe knowledge as being in any sense a production, we shall be guilty of a dangerous equivocation.[2]

§ 2. *Errors Due to Depreciation of Thought*

Under this heading we must list all the varieties of empiricism; *nominalism* (conceptual thought has no genuine real significance); *materialism and sensationalism* (only matter exists and knowledge is reduced to sensation); *agnosticism* (it is impossible to know anything outside experience); *phenomenalism* (for us there exist only phenomena, sensible appearances); *positivism* (positive facts alone are the object of science); *Bergsonian intuitionism* (conceptual thought does not reach the depths of reality). All these systems fail to recognize the intellect's peculiar activity which develops the empirical datum and finds there not only constant relations which form the object of scientific laws, but also the absolute value of being and being's absolute laws which form the object of metaphysical knowledge.

2. The divine consciousness itself is not a "production" in any sense. The divine thought is not creative in so far as thought, but in so far as it is identified to the creative will. Even the creative will is not essentially a "production," since creation is optional. In so far as the generation of the Word is concerned, theology does not present it as identical with the Father's knowledge, but rather as the fruit or expression of this knowledge.

§ 3. *Errors Due to Depreciation of the Objective Datum*

This is the contrary of the preceding error. It sacrifices experience in favor of thought. This error is the common distinguishing mark of all forms of idealism from Plato to Brunschvicg. This fact justifies our using one name to designate systems which from other points of view are very different. All idealists try to free thought from any sort of dependence on the empirical datum. Taken as a whole, idealism is not so much a doctrine as an attitude; it is "the philosophical tendency which consists in reducing all existence to thought, taking the word 'thought' in the widest sense," while ontological realism "admits an existence independent of thought." [3]

Idealism originated from an excessive distrust of sensory experience (Plato, St. Augustine to a lesser degree, Descartes). Beginning with the fourteenth century a great number of philosophers adopted this attitude of distrust. The collapse of ancient physics and the advent of modern science left many men in a confused state of mind. The philosophers were unable to distinguish quickly enough the permanent values in traditional realism from outmoded elements. While a considerable number of thinkers were won over by the ideal of the new science and began the all too easy descent toward empiricism, others tried to save metaphysics by sacrificing the sensory. We witness then the advent of rationalism which had a brilliant career from Descartes to Wolff. Rationalism should be linked to idealism in so far as it claims to deduce all certain knowledge from principles which are evident *a priori*, independently of the data of sensory experience.

3. On the term "idealism," see Lalande, *Vocabulaire de la Philosophie*, Vol. 1, p. 318.

Starting from Kant, the "Copernican revolution" gave idealism an entirely fresh orientation. To an increasing degree, thought became the supreme norm of truth and the source of the real. As idealism increased its claims, it tended to substitute absolute Thought for the individual thought of man. Human thought became only a manifestation of that absolute Thought (Fichte, Schelling, Hegel, Gentile, and others). Thus we are led to distinguish two very different forms of modern idealism. We have *subjectivist idealism* (called "personal idealism" in English) "which tends to reduce existence to *individual* thought" (Lalande). This is a radical idealism whose extreme form is *solipsism*.[4] There is also *transcendent idealism* which claims to discover at the root of individual consciousness a *transcendent Consciousness* (Thought, Spirit, absolute Self), and which attempts to interpret the universe by starting from this principle. Some forms of this idealism bear a rather close resemblance to metaphysical realism, but there will always remain an essential difference between them regarding the concept of knowledge itself and the nature of thought.

Today idealism is a very widespread philosophical view. In certain philosophical circles it has even become a "postulate" or "presumption," a sort of philosophical "dogma" whose basis is no longer questioned. Several converging reasons apparently explain this fact. First, a concern for the independence of thought has been fostered by many tendencies present in Western civilization since the time of the Renaissance— humanism, for example, the right of private judgment, nat-

---

4. Personal or subjective idealism can also take milder forms. Such is the case when it recognizes the existence of an exterior world and a certain sensory "datum" independent of the activity of the subject, but declares that this datum is "irrational," unknowable for the intelligence, and therefore without interest for the philosopher.

uralism, liberalism, individualism and so forth. Again, the presumption of "representationism" or the "principle of immanence," has dominated the thinking of a great many men since Descartes. They hold that consciousness is immured within a world of representations; science can be only a system of representations; outside of that lies the unknown, the "thing in itself." They do not necessarily claim to reduce all *existence* to consciousness, but they at least claim to reduce all *known existence*. They do not see how the objective term of the act of cognition can be simultaneously immanent and transcendent with respect to consciousness. This however *is* the case for the objects of our knowledge. Even among those who admit a certain objective presence in sensory perception, the modern critique of sensation has created an unfavorable presumption regarding the critical significance of perception, and idealist literature readily emphasizes the inconsistency of the perceived object or the sensorial shock. Descartes was already greatly concerned about the "errors" and "illusions" of the senses. Even today the idealist tries to minimize the value of sense experience in order to justify his agnostic attitude. He claims that by sensory experience it would be impossible to get beyond the "sensation-event" (the transitory subjective impression), to arrive at a knowledge which would transcend individual "subjectivity." He claims that it would therefore be impossible to establish intellectual values and especially metaphysical affirmations on such a weak foundation. Finally, Kant's "Copernican revolution" kept its attraction for many men throughout the nineteenth century. It tended to propagate a view of knowledge incompatible with the basic assertions of realism.

If we wish to escape the snares of idealism we have to recognize first of all that we are men, with all the limitations which that implies. Every radical intellectualism, whether it be rationalist or idealist, has the merit of emphasizing the unique activity of the intellect and the transcendency of the spiritual. But it makes the mistake of disregarding the actual conditions of human thought and of claiming a spiritual independence not attainable by us.

We must therefore free ourselves of the immanentist presumption and accept the immediate data of human consciousness as they really are. For our human consciousness is a consciousness which opens on a corporeal world.

As far as the contributions made by sense perception are concerned, we must note that idealist criticism rests upon an artificial dissection of objective experience. The purely sensory does not exist for us any more than pure sensation does. What is given to me is a sensory reality. Now, the least reality —however transitory and superficial we may imagine it to be —suffices to show me the absolute value of being and the necessary character of every affirmation based on the object known. The least reality obtruding itself on me likewise forces itself on every other consciousness capable of perceiving it. Consequently, if I apprehend any reality whatever, this means that I breach my subjective limitations. I do not have to appeal to any *a priori* or any "large Ego" to provide a basis for my necessary and universal assertions. When we consider the imposing structure of the natural sciences, their marvelous results and manifold applications; when we feel overwhelmed by the immensity of the material universe and filled with admiration at the spectacle of the order and stability realized there in spite of its unceasing evolution; finally, when we recall that the revelation of these marvels depends entirely on our sense perceptions, we are led to conclude that sensory experience has far more stability than idealism admits, and we find it difficult to understand how a philosophy which is so poorly adapted to man and so lacking in "sense of the real" can get itself accepted by so many. The Kantian conception of thought, however, is perhaps the greatest obstacle to any conversion to realism. This is why idealism can only be overcome by getting back to a true notion of knowledge.[5]

We can consider Descartes the initiator of *indirect realism*. This view is still defended today particularly by certain Neoscholastic philosophers.[6] It is but a timid form of idealism. It in turn accepts the presumption of the walled-in consciousness, since it dissociates the transcendent object from the immanent representation. It holds that the immanent representation is the only immediate term of perception.

Any extended discussion of indirect realism would exceed the scope of this treatise. Here we must confine ourselves to a brief indication of *defects in method* which seem to invalidate the position of indirect realism. To be more concrete we shall take the exposition of de Vries as the basis for our discussion.

The author's principal argument is based upon a consideration of the illusions which we undergo in dreams. In dreams we perceive objects as extended, as exterior to us, as distant from us, and yet these objects do not exist outside our imagination. According to the author, this fact shows clearly that the perception of the "suchness" of objects (their size, localization, qualities and so forth) does not imply a perception of their *in se* existence. For him, critical examination shows only a difference of degree between objects of sensation and

5. On idealism in general, see Lalande, *op. cit.*, vol. III, pp. 64-67; Maritain, *Distinguer pour unir*, pp. 208-215; Gilson, *Réalisme thomiste*, passim.
6. See, for example, de Vries, *Critica*, pp. 99-108. This gives an interesting and penetrating exposition of indirect realism, as well as a critical evaluation of immediate realism.

images: objects of sensation are more vivid, clear, stable, and coherent than images. We must therefore conclude that sensory data do not immediately reveal themselves as realities existing *in se,* but rather as contents of consciousness or representations. This conclusion is further confirmed by the fact that things often appear other than they really are.

In our opinion this argument of de Vries contains several inaccuracies and serious defects of method.

1. I cannot perceive the "suchness" of an object without also perceiving its reality, for the simple reason that they are identified. It is the suchness which is real or which exists. Thus when I dream, I am convinced that I perceive real things with such and such characteristics, and I am just as much deceived regarding the suchness of the thing as I am regarding its reality. This is due to the fact that I confuse the *representation* of an object with the *perception* of this object, and this confusion is possible precisely because I am sleeping. The numbing of my consciousness prevents me from making the simple critical reflection which would allow me to see that my perceptive organs are inactive and that I am "re-presenting" a certain situation without actually "seeing it with my eyes."

2. There is much more than a mere difference of degree between the object of perception and the image. To a vigilant consciousness capable of reflecting, the imagined object's mode of presence differs radically from the perceived object's mode of presence. As the term of my perception the object is *present* by itself, while it is merely re-presented or re-called by the image. For a vigilant consciousness, there can be no possible confusion between seeing a person or landscape and recalling the same absent objects by imagination. If the least doubt still remains it is always possible to make an easy check

(except perhaps in certain extreme cases which have little importance from the point of view of a general critique). It suffices to see whether or not the presence of the object depends on the exercise of my sense organs.[7]

3. If things sometimes appear other than they really are, this is due to the influence of subjective factors in perception. But this dosage of relativity does not in any way exclude the immediate presence of the object as the term of perception.[8]

Thus no decisive argument has been proposed against immediate realism. On the contrary, immediate realism expresses the genuine immediate data of consciousness. By the corporate action of my sense organs, my consciousness opens upon a world of objects which are real, extended, distinct from my own body, and capable of producing qualitatively different impressions. There is no justification for the suggested dissociation which would consider perceived objects to be merely re-presentations of *other* objects not perceived, that is, objects "in themselves." To venture on this path is merely to push into a blind alley. It raises the famous problem of the "bridge" between the object in me and the object in itself, between the representation and the thing. This problem is insoluble for two reasons. First, we would never be able to prove rigorously that the world of my representations implies a corporeal world *beyond those representations,* a world which would be more or less similar to the one which I perceive, for my representations might be produced by an "evil genius," or more simply they might be an unconscious projection of the self. Thus the way would be open to the most radical kind of idealism: solipsism. Secondly, even if we supposed that starting from "representations" the existence of a corporeal world

7. See above, pp. 124-27, 207-09.
8. *Ibid.*, pp. 221-25.

in itself could be proven, we would never be able to determine how closely these representations correspond to the object which they represent, since by hypothesis any comparison of the model and image becomes impossible.

In reality there is no "beyond" for us behind the objects we perceive. It is *in* the perceived objects that we apprehend certain characteristics which are independent of perception as such, for example, their reality, their spatio-temporal extension, their capacity to produce qualitatively different perceptions. We are then in immediate contact with a real corporeal world. We have to accept this fact—perhaps mysterious but nevertheless evident—that we do meet the real in perception. It is indeed a real body that I knock against and which "resists" me. It is indeed a real wall which I "see." My sense organs are so many antennae by which I communicate immediately with the corporeal world surrounding me. Let us not forget, however, that the problem of the *origin* of this corporeal world and its *ontological relations* with my own body and consciousness remains whole and entire. General and special metaphysics must give an answer to that problem.

§ 4. *Kantianism*

Kant wished to rise above the antinomy of empiricism and rationalism. Situated at the confluence of the two streams of thought which since Bacon and Descartes have apportioned modern philosophy, Kantianism represents an attempt to restore the unity of knowledge. Kant however reached a solution which is much closer to rationalism than to empiricism.

"Critique," as Kant conceived it, does not exactly correspond to what we have called critical epistemology. Kant wanted to determine the *conditions under which scientific knowledge was possible.* He wanted to discover how human consciousness should be constituted for scientific knowledge to be possible. Accordingly, in spite of the "critical" appearance of his work, his attention was focused especially on the "ontological" problem of knowledge. An inquiry into the ontological implications of knowledge presupposes an epistemological analysis and critique. But Kant apparently did not realize the need of clearly establishing these epistemological preliminaries. After all, there is a good deal of unconscious dogmatism in the founder of "criticism," the self-declared adversary of all dogmatism. He not only fails to attempt construction of a fundamental epistemology, but he admits without argument the possibility of science and the value of its laws. The distrust which he showed for the "thing in itself" could in fact be extended profitably to the "forms," "categories" and other such entities which certainly possess no "phenomenal" quality. Finally and especially, the epistemology implied at the beginning of Kant's "critique" is based upon a fallacious presumption. Let us consider this last point in more detail.

Kant recognized the presence of a "datum" in human consciousness. Considered as a conscious "phenomenon" this datum is manifestly spatio-temporal and real. Why then did Kant not consider these characteristics to be properties belonging to the datum itself? Why did he make "time" and "space" *a priori* forms of sensibility, and "reality" an *a priori* category of understanding? He did this because of the influence of a phenomenalist presumption. Misled by the phenomenalism of Hume he considered the datum which presents itself to human consciousness to be a "pure diverse" lacking all internal structure and intelligibility. This automatically ruled out any conception of human consciousness as a consciousness which would *assimilate objects*. And since he refused to think of human consciousness as a *creative* consciousness (his successors were to take this stand), he imagines a consciousness *producing its objects by "informing" a datum which of itself would be formless.* The *"a priori* forms of sensibility" and the *"a priori* categories of understanding" make the "pure diverse" into an "object" of knowledge, that is, an object of sensory intuition and intellectual conception. Thus the Copernican revolution was complete. It was no longer the real which informed consciousness, rather it was consciousness which informed the real. Intellectual knowledge was no longer the fruit of an analysis (abstraction), it was rather the result of a synthesis (the union of *a priori* forms and the datum).[9] In this way the phenomenalist presumption had led Kant into a capital error concerning the very nature of knowledge; he sees an "action," a "production of the object," a "construction," in an act which is essentially "contemplation," "possession," "submission to the real." [10]

As a result, a presumption which had falsified the analysis and critique of consciousness on the epistemological level now led to an interpretation on the ontological level which minimized the role of the objective datum and gave too much importance to the subject's function. Kant's interpretation was doubtless very ingenious and contained many noteworthy suggestions, but it was nevertheless built on radically false presumptions. The implications of Kant's "critique" were

9. Sometimes it is said that Kant conceived abstraction as a synthesis, while Aristotle looked upon it as an analysis. But an "abstraction-synthesis" would be a contradiction in terms. We should say rather that Kant suppressed abstraction and replaced it by an *a priori* conceptualization, followed by an informing of the datum.

10. See *"Problèmes épistémologiques fondamentaux,"* pp. 481-483.

disastrous for thought; especially so was his rejection of metaphysics as science, and his agnosticism in theodicy.

§ 5. *Aristotelianism and Thomism*

The critical realism whose value and potentialities we have tried to set forth was formulated for the first time in the philosophy of Aristotle and experienced a brilliant renovation and deepening in the work of Thomas Aquinas. But the epistemology implied in Aristotelianism and the epistemology which can be disengaged from Thomism are not quite perfect. It will be to our advantage here to note the defects found in them.

As for Aristotle, the principal gaps in his epistemology occur in the field of our *knowledge of being*. Aristotle does not develop all the potentialities of this knowledge. For that reason his metaphysics is defective. It never arrives at the creative Cause and supreme Providence of the universe. On the other hand, *sensory knowledge* is not scrutinized sufficiently and the system of physics of Aristotle, built on very limited experience, involves a large number of unverified hypotheses.

As for Thomistic epistemology, we have to make special mention of the following imperfections: *Sensory perception* is not duly criticized; the characteristics which distinguish the *concept of being* are not stressed enough, even though Thomism far surpasses Aristotelianism in the field of metaphysics; his exposition of abstraction is cluttered with too many sensory images; the *conceptual order* is not always clearly distinguished from the real order; finally, the *unity of knowledge* often seems to be weakened by formulas which juxtapose sensation and intellection, the sensory object (the individual) and the intelligible object (the universal).

This brief summary of the principal historical errors in the field of epistemology may seem rather misleading to some readers. Younger readers in particular are easily disturbed by the "scandal of the history of philosophy," which presents a picture of repeated errors by the human mind. In contrast to this pessimistic view, other people are inclined to discount the errors of philosophers as much as possible. These men advance the most conciliatory interpretations, without bothering too much about historical objectivity. They simply cannot conceive that so many great thinkers might have worked for centuries in vain. They are convinced beforehand that the history of philosophy should testify to a continuous progress of thought.

Here again truth lies midway between the extreme views. Some progress has been made in the course of time, and it is very evident that none of the great philosophers whose names adorn the history of philosophy have worked in vain. But there is no proof that progress in thought always follows a straight line. On the contrary, history records a series of oscillations between extreme views gradually approaching the equilibrium of an intermediate solution. History also shows periods of decay in which thought disintegrates, and periods of renovation in which it gains renewed strength. Finally, it chronicles the periodic revival of certain doctrinal currents. The appearance of a new philosophy does not necessarily indicate a forward step; and it is quite possible that a brilliant but one-sided thinker may lead many generations of disciples into a blind alley. We must be careful not to confuse "original thought," or even "thought marked by genius," with "true thought." It can happen that a great philosopher may construct a system which is fundamentally false, false in a wonderfully clever way. The influence of historical environment, unconscious prejudices, lack of perspective or balance, insufficient information, a poor starting point, excessive confidence in a personal intuition that has not been properly scrutinized, all constitute so many factors which can help explain the failure of a great many ventures in philosophy.

CHAPTER III

THE VARIOUS FORMS OF SCIENTIFIC KNOWLEDGE

PROBLEMS relating to the classification of sciences, especially the key problem of the distinction between *positive* science and *philosophical* science, are often treated in a very superficial empiricist fashion. In reality, the fact that there are different forms of scientific knowledge stems from the nature of human knowledge itself—it is already implied in the conclusions of epistemology. In this chapter we wish to describe the epistemological bases for the general classification of sciences, even though this may mean some anticipation of later developments in knowledge.

§ 1. Logic

We already know that general epistemology implies a third discipline, that is, logic. This forms a complement to analytical and critical epistemology. The purpose of logic is to determine the general laws of reasoning. For that reason logic has an important function propædeutic to all other sciences, since they all use operations of discursive reasoning. Logic, therefore, forms a sort of *general methodology for scientific demonstration,* and for this reason Thomas asserted that it was the instrument of all the sciences.[1] We can no longer accept certain views which Cardinal Mercier held concerning logic. Mercier wished to make speculative logic the last step in the systematization of sciences. In his view, logical laws

---

1. *In Boethium de Trinitate,* qu. 5, art. 1, ad. 2[m]; qu. 6, art. 1, ad 3[m].

would be derived from observation of sciences, and in the meantime we would merely "accept them on trust." [2] This view is an indication of the empiricist tendency which marked the philosophy of Cardinal Mercier. But logic is really a normative science. It does not study the order which the sciences actually realize; rather it determines laws which impose themselves on discursive reason and therefore govern the development of the sciences.

§ 2. Metaphysical and Positive Science

The most serious defect in ancient and medieval classifications of sciences was undoubtedly their neglect of the distinction between *philosophy* and the *sciences*. Critical epistemology helps us to see how the distinction between these two kinds of science arose. Critical epistemology in fact prepares the way for a twofold speculative effort in *metaphysical* science and *positive* science.

We have already seen that reality shows itself to be both basically one (the aspect expressed by the fundamental concept of being), and extremely *varied* (the aspect expressed by our manifold empirical concepts). Since we cannot seize the extreme complexity of the real order or the unity of this diversity by one intuitive act, we are obliged to reconstruct the real order by a slow patient effort; we must try to unravel the manifold relations which go to make up the universe, which in turn explain the "how" and "why" of the unity seen in a confused way from the very start. There are two different ways of undertaking this task. We can start from unity as represented by the fundamental concept of being and try to explain diversity beginning with this transcen-

2. See Mercier, *Logique*, 7th. ed. (Louvain, 1922), pp. 28-31.

dental unity. This will constitute the metaphysical effort or the science of the general conditions of being as such. Or we can start from the diversity which is given and the empirical concepts expressing it, and try to discover increasingly general laws which unify more and more of the diversity. This is the positive effort represented by the many different positive sciences.

Thus, for example, our knowledge of the self can be developed in two very different ways. First, I can develop my knowledge of the self and my lived or conscious activities exclusively on the level of empirical concepts, and the experience from which they come. This would involve observation of lived experience, conceptualization and definition of these concepts, empirical classification of them, inquiry into the empirical laws manifested in conscious activity. Empirical psychology tries to give this sort of interpretation of psychological experience. This is a delicate and rather uncertain enterprise, for internal observation cannot be checked and the data of lived experience do not lend themselves to the application of the rigorous impersonal methods of a science like physics. We have already remarked that from this point of view lived experience is quite inferior to objective experience.

We can also try to develop this knowledge in an entirely different way. I can take my lived experience precisely as a reality, and then try to determine the mode of existence, nature and essence making up the self and its activities in the light of my knowledge of being. In this case, the intimate knowledge which I have of my unity, duration, activity, and at least partial independence, makes it possible for me to determine my "nature" or "essence" with a precision and certitude not obtainable in any other field. This holds true to such an extent that a knowledge of my own nature will be an indispensable requirement when I try to define other natures than my own. This second way of studying the self constitutes philosophical psychology or the special metaphysics of man.

Like our knowledge of the self, our knowledge of the corporeal world can also be developed in two different ways: either as an empirical synthesis of empirical data, or as an attempt to determine the essence of the corporeal world starting from our knowledge of being as such. The positive sciences of the material world try the first approach; cosmology or the special metaphysics of the corporeal world adopts the second.

Here we can give a brief description of the way in which the organization or general classification of positive science should be understood. Various principles of classification could be adopted, but the most rational principle is that based on consideration of formal objects, and consequently on the distinctive methods of the different sciences. The fact that our experience is twofold provides a primary natural principle of division into sciences of nature (in the broad sense of the term, *Naturwissenschaften*), and sciences of man (*Geisteswissenschaften*).

Within the first category we can distinguish two fundamental groups, the mathematical sciences and physical sciences. The mathematical sciences form a special group because of the peculiar character of their methods. Starting with an extremely simple "datum" they elaborate very complex conceptual constructs. There is in them a minimum of experience and a maximum of activity on the part of discursive reason.

The sciences of man likewise include two principal groups

—the psychological sciences (which study the psychical experience in itself), and the moral sciences (which study the manifold revelations of human consciousness in the conduct of individuals or human societies; the historical sciences, philological sciences, sociological sciences, and so forth).

The development of metaphysical science parallels that of positive science. Empirical science embraces a great number of positive sciences because the empirical aspects of the real are manifold, and although it is possible to reduce them to groups of homogeneous phenomena (such as "physical," "chemical," "biological" phenomena), each of these groups retain formally different characteristics. This then gives rise to different methods of scientific investigation. For this reason the ideal of reducing all positive sciences to one single science seems Utopian. Nevertheless, the fundamental intelligible aspect represented by the transcendental concept of being is strictly one. Metaphysics which has being for its formal object is therefore a science which is one and indivisible. It is philosophy par excellence, the first philosophy, as Aristotle called it, or philosophy in the strict sense.

In spite of its fundamental unity, however, metaphysics leads to a certain multiplicity when it tries to interpret the real. Once again this is due to the complexity of human knowledge. To illustrate this point we have to anticipate for the time being some later steps in philosophical inquiry.

Starting with the critical analysis of its unique formal object, metaphysics first tries to determine the conditions necessary for every reality as such. It then encounters the diverse, the multiple and the fact of limitation; it gradually uncovers the ontological constitution of finite things (composition, activity and order) and their essential contingency. Then the comparison of the absolute independence of being with the basic relativity of the world of finite beings causes the mind to make the supreme discovery of the creative Cause which is necessary of itself, transcendent to the finite world, and the source of all reality. This first synthesis constitutes general metaphysics or ontology.

But the mind of man seeks unity. A simple juxtaposition of the intelligible aspect and empirical data cannot satisfy it. It tries to get back to experience by starting from the laws of being. In this effort it has to contend with the duality which we have often mentioned—the duality of objective experience and lived experience, the perception of the exterior world and the perception of the interior or specifically human world. On the basis of these two forms of experience it is possible to have two very different methods of inquiry, and the duality which they introduce into knowledge is met at every level of scientific classification. It manifests itself prominently in metaphysics in the formation of a twofold special metaphysics, one of the corporeal or physical world, the other of the human or psychical world: the metaphysics of nature and the metaphysics of consciousness, cosmology and metaphysical anthropology, or metaphysical psychology. These special metaphysics are developed in function of general metaphysics as extensions of it. They try to supply ontological interpretations of the corporeal and human worlds as given in our experience.[3] This is not the time to specify further the na-

3. There would be a considerable advantage gained by placing the metaphysics of nature after the metaphysics of man. The traditional order resulted from the Aristotelian conception, true under many respects, which considered man to be one particular case among the beings of nature; consequently it looked upon psychology as a part of physics. But if we consider the privileged character which our knowledge of man possesses, resulting from the consciousness that we have of our own activity and our own personality, we realize that the metaphysics of man could assist greatly in our study of the corporeal world.

ture, methods or feasibility of these inquiries, which often raise very difficult problems. However, we may be permitted to offer some anticipatory remarks about the general structure of philosophy.

In the first place, natural theology is an essential part of general metaphysics. It constitutes the indispensable culmination of general metaphysics. To make natural theology a distinct discipline, which is then relegated to the last part of philosophy, means that we separate the derivation of the attributes of God from its logical basis. This derivation in fact is but the development of the proof of the existence of God, and this in turn is but the last step in our metaphysical study of finite being.

In the same way philosophical biology forms an integral part of cosmology or the metaphysics of nature, since living beings form part of the cosmos which is the object of sensory experience.

From the point of view of strict scientific classification, metaphysical anthropology or the metaphysics of man embraces the philosophical study of human nature and all forms of activity proper to man. Consequently it includes not only the classical problems of rational psychology (metaphysics of knowledge, desire and human substance), but also the metaphysics of behavior or moral action (moral philosophy or metamoral philosophy), and the metaphysics of production whether utilitarian or esthetic (the philosophy of art and the fine arts). Further development of human metaphysics has given rise to still more specialized disciplines such as the philosophy of language, education, law, religion, history (not of the historical sciences, but rather of the historical evolution it-

---

Many problems, particularly that of individuality, can only be solved by analogy with the case of man.

self), civilization and so forth. Note that all these disciplines try to give a metaphysical interpretation of individual or social human activity. For that reason these inquiries belong to the metaphysics of man.[4]

Finally, the distinction between theoretical philosophy and practical philosophy has no scientific basis or interest. Every science is theoretical, even though it take for its object the "practical," that is, human activity.

§ 3. *Philosophy of the Sciences*

Epistemology establishes the general principles of a critique and methodology of knowledge. But this twofold study must be continued through all our scientific work. Every developed science involves a special critique and logic which formulate and apply the general laws of critique and logic in a way appropriate to the proper object of this science. Thus metaphysical inquiry should be accompanied by a critique and methodology of metaphysical knowledge. Biology, arithmetic and history also require in their turn special critiques and methodologies. The philosophy of mathematics, for example, contains two parts: first, a critique of mathematical knowledge which studies the nature of mathematical concepts, principles and demonstrations, as well as the significance or value of the conclusions of this science; secondly, a logic or methodology of mathematics which as a continuation of

4. Here we do not have to take a definite stand concerning the feasibility of these philosophical disciplines of more or less recent date. To what extent do they possess the characteristics of philosophical knowledge or of any scientific knowledge? In any event, we feel that it would be better to free the metaphysics of nature and the metaphysics of man as far as possible from all elements which do not properly belong to their formal object. The basic principles of ethics, for example, are all too often lost sight of among rules of conduct which are somewhat relative and partially empirical.

formal logic will try to determine what processes of inquiry are legitimate in mathematics.[5]

In the field of metaphysics the object studied is on the whole very simple. The difficulty resides entirely in the manner of developing it. Here, consideration of the object is closely tied up with the critical and methodological reflection evaluating and directing the inquiry. On the other hand, in the field of positive sciences the scientist's attention is centered almost completely on the object of investigation. The methods used are determined to some extent by the object he is trying to grasp. A successful outcome and verifiable results are taken as guarantee of the validity of his procedures. In short the scientist is ordinarily a "pragmatist." He will usually leave to others, philosophers, the task of explaining the nature of his inquiries, methods and results. In other words, the philosophy of the positive sciences (critique and methodology of sciences) is almost always left to the philosophers or to some few men of science interested in the epistemological problems raised by their investigations.

The philosophy of the sciences constitutes an important branch of scientific inquiry distinct from both the positive sciences and the metaphysical sciences. Its compass is considerable.

§ 4. The Unity of Human Science

To what extent can man's science be unified? More particularly to what extent can the metaphysical effort and the positive effort be reunited?

This amounts to asking whether the various types of knowledge, explanation and understanding achieved in dif-

---

5. Here we are evidently not speaking of the methodology of teaching mathematics, but rather of the methodology of scientific inquiry itself.

ferent sciences, particularly in the philosophical and positive sciences, are sufficiently analogous to make it possible to reduce them to one single explanation of the real order. If we recall that all knowledge is a knowledge of being, of the modalities of being and the relations which those modalities involve, we realize somewhat that the various types of explanation achieved in different branches of man's science cannot be completely heterogeneous to one another; consequently the ideal of a unified knowledge might one day be realized. Philosophers and scientists have dreamed of this ideal of unified knowledge more than once although under very different forms. As a matter of fact certain signs might lead us to believe that the positive effort and the metaphysical effort are destined one day to converge and fuse in one single science. An examination of the work done by each would at once suggest the possibility of *rapprochement*. The sciences clearly strive after simplicity; their classifications, laws, theories, search for analogies, in fact, the whole scientific effort, are based on the ideal of getting a simple explanation and unification of the empirical order. Metaphysics, on the other hand, is constructed starting from being, the basic intelligible. It expands on contact with experience. It tries to assimilate experience while still preserving its richness and variety. In short, these are two opposite movements; one goes from the complex to the simple, the other from the simple to the complex.

However, we can still wonder whether the progressive *rapprochement* of the two systems will ever amount to a genuine union or fusion. To answer that question we would have to examine the conclusions reached by the various sciences, evaluating them in the light of the respective methods. Whatever may be said about that point, the philosophy of the sciences does to some extent realize the ideal of unity by trying to understand the work of the positive sciences in the light of epistemology.

By combining the different suggestions advanced up to this point, and leaving aside the theological sciences which constitute a completely different type of knowledge arising from Revelation, we can now form a general synthesis of the purely rational human sciences. The schema given on the opposite page may help us to form some general idea of such a synthesis.

We will notice that the same realities (the corporeal world and the world of consciousness) can form the object of a threefold study: a positive study, a metaphysical study and a noetic study (in the philosophy of sciences).

If in our schema we leave aside the positive sciences, we get a synthesis of the philosophical sciences, or philosophy in the broad sense, which embraces epistemology, metaphysics and the philosophy of science.[6]

6. Not long ago we noted that from the point of view of the Christian thinker, the supreme synthesis of human knowledge rests with theology. It pertains to theology in its capacity as the higher wisdom to attempt the final unification of all knowledge accessible to man. See Revue Néoscolastique de Philosophie (November, 1933), pp. 549-550.

SYNTHESIS OF THE PHILOSOPHICAL SCIENCES

I. EPISTEMOLOGY
- Analytical
- Critical
- Logical

II. POSITIVE SCIENCES
- Sciences of Nature
  - Mathematical Sciences
  - Physical Sciences
- Sciences of Man
  - Psychological Sciences
  - Moral Sciences

III. METAPHYSICS (Philosophy in the strict sense)
- General Metaphysics (Ontology)
- Special Metaphysics
  - Metaphysics of Nature (Cosmology)
  - Metaphysics of Man (Anthropology)
    - General Anthropology (Psychology)
    - Metaphysics of Behavior (Moral), of the Arts, Law, etc.

IV. PHILOSOPHY OF THE SCIENCES (Critique and methodology)
- Philosophy of the Sciences of Nature
  - Philosophy of Mathematics
  - Philosophy of Physical Sciences
- Philosophy of the Sciences of Man
  - Philosophy of Psychological Sciences
  - Philosophy of Moral Sciences

BIBLIOGRAPHY

THE bibliography which follows does not pretend to be exhaustive. It is offered rather as a list of supplementary readings for beginners, to stimulate further thought on their part, and to elaborate the very condensed treatment found in the present study. It is limited to texts of Saint Thomas, and to works having a Thomistic viewpoint, for eclecticism would indeed provide a very poor first introduction to philosophy. Furthermore, the works listed will provide the reader with ample additional bibliographical data.

The Principal Texts of Saint Thomas

Quaestiones disputatae de veritate (1256-1259). The first twenty questions form a valuable treatise on knowledge (human, divine, and angelic), including special problems such as those of the communication of knowledge *(De Magisterio)*, prophecy, ecstasy, faith, the knowledge had by Adam and by separated souls.

Summa contra Gentiles (1259-1264). *Liber primus,* Chapters 44-71 (divine knowledge); *liber secundus,* chapters 58-78 (human knowledge); chapters 96-101 (knowledge of the angels); *liber tertius,* chapters 33-63 (the beatific vision, the natural desire to see God, the goal of human and angelic knowledge). See also the treatise on the providence of God, chapters 64-110.

Summa theologica (1266-1273). *Prima pars,* qu. 14-17 (God's knowledge); qu. 34-35 (the Word); qu. 54-58 (angelic knowledge); qu. 78-79 and 84-89 (human knowledge); qu. 94 (the knowledge of Adam); qu. 106-107 (angelic knowledge).

De Vries, J., S.J., *De cognitione veritatis textus selecti S. Thomae Aquinatis,* Munster, 1933, pp. 66.

Works on Thomistic Epistemology

WORKS IN ENGLISH

D'Arcy, M. C., *The Nature of Belief*. London, Sheed and Ward, 1945, pp. 252.

Barron, J., *Elements of Epistemology*. N. Y., Macmillan, 1931, pp. xix+225.

Benignus, Brother, F.S.C., *Nature, Knowledge and God*. Milwaukee, Bruce, 1947, pp. xiv+662. See especially chapters xiv-xviii.

Bittle, C. N., O.F.M. Cap., *Reality and the Mind*. Milwaukee, Bruce, 1943, pp. x+390. (Includes an extensive bibliography.)

Bourke, V. J., "Experience of Extra-Mental Reality as the Starting Point of Saint Thomas' Metaphysics," *Proc. Am. Cath. Phil. Assn.* (1938), pp. 134-144.

Coffey, P., *Epistemology*. N. Y., Smith, 1938, 2 vols. (reprint).

Creaven, J. A., "Personalism, Thomism and Epistemology," *The Thomist*, 1945 (8), pp. 1-26.

Farrell, P., "The Portals of Doubt," *The Thomist*, 1945 (8), pp. 293-368.

Glenn, P., *Criteriology*. St. Louis, Herder, 1933, pp. xi+261.

Hawkins, D. J. B., *The Criticism of Experience*. London, Sheed and Ward, 1945, pp. 124.

Maritain, J., *The Degrees of Knowledge*. Transl. by B. Wall and M. Adamson, London, Bles, 1937; N. Y., Scribners, 1938.

McCormick, J. F., S.J., *St. Thomas and the Life of Learning* (Aquinas Lecture, 1937). Milwaukee, Marquette Univ. Press, 1937.

McReavy, Leo, "Louvain Seeks a Thomist Epistemology," *Clergy Review*, London, 1948 (29), pp. 238-251.

De Munnynck, M., "Notes on Intuition," *The Thomist*, 1939 (1), pp. 143-168.

Noël, L., "The Realism of St. Thomas," *Blackfriars*, Oxford, (1935), xvi, pp. 817-832.

Phillips, R. P., *Modern Thomistic Philosophy*. London, Burns Oates, 1934-35; Westminster, Md., Newman Bookshop, 1946, 2 vols., pp. xiv+346, pp. xii+400.

Reinhardt, K. E., *A Realistic Philosophy*. Milwaukee, Bruce, 1944, pp. xii+268.

Renard, Henri, "The Problem of Knowledge in General," *Modern Schoolman*, 1946 (24), pp. 1-11.

Rousselot, P., *The Intellectualism of St. Thomas*. Transl. by J. E. O'Mahony. N. Y., Sheed and Ward, 1935, pp. viii+231.

Ryan, J. K., "The Problem of Truth," *Essays in Thomism*. N. Y., Sheed and Ward, 1945, pp. 63-80, 369.

Smith, G., S.J., "A Date in the History of Epistemology," *The Thomist*, 1943 (5), pp. 246-255.

Sertillanges, A. D., O.P., *Foundations of Thomistic Philosophy*. Transl. by G. Anstruther, O.P. *(Cath. Lib. of Knowledge, xx)*. St. Louis, Herder; London, Sands, 1931, pp. 256.

WORKS IN FRENCH

Brunner, A., *La connaissance humaine*. Paris, 1943, pp. 430. (An original and broadly conceived study of critical problems, including the critique of the sciences.)

De Coninck, A., *L' unité de la connaissance humaine et le fondement de sa valeur*. Louvain, 2 ed. 1947, pp. 186. (Contains original and searching views.)

Gilson, É., *Le réalisme méthodique*. Paris, s.d. (1936), pp. 104. (A collection of five studies concerning the realist position.)

———— *Réalisme thomiste et critique de la connaissance*. Paris, 1939, pp. 242. Reimpression, Paris, J. Vrin, 1947, pp. 240. (The work attacks different compromises between Thomistic realism and Cartesian or Kantian idealism. Gilson's position is really very close to that of Msgr. Noël in spite of what is largely a verbal controversy. The work contains very valuable ideas concerning the primacy of the real, although "real" is taken here to mean "extramental reality.")

Maréchal, J., *Le thomisme devant la philosophie critique* (Le point
de départ de la metaphysique, vol. 5), Louvain, 1926, pp. 482.
(An attempt to compare Thomism and Kantianism; it treats
the ontology of knowledge rather than the epistemology.)

Maritain, J., *Distinguer pour unir ou les degrés du savoir.* Paris,
1932, pp. 920. English transl. by B. Wall and M. Adamson:
The Degrees of Knowledge, London, Bles, 1937; N. Y., Scribners, 1938. (A real *summa* of the problems of knowledge; see
especially chapter III, "Critical Realism.")

Mercier, D., *Critériologie générale.* Louvain, 8th ed., 1923, pp. 448.

Noël, L., *Notes d' épistémologie thomiste.* Louvain, 1925, pp. 244.
(A collection of articles.)

——— *Le réalisme immédiat.* Louvain, 1938, pp. 300. (A later
collection of articles, revised and completed by other unpub-
lished studies; a clear and penetrating study of the basic problems of epistemology.)

Picard, G., *Le problème critique fondamental.* Paris, 1923, pp. 94.
(An attempt to refute idealism by using the intuition of the
concrete self.)

Régis, L. M., *La critique néothomiste, est-elle thomiste?* in *Philosophie,* vol. II (Etudes et recherches publiées par le Collège Do-
minicain d' Ottawa, III), 1938, pp. 95-199. (An attempt to
determine which "neothomist" positions can really claim to
represent the view of St. Thomas himself. The author believes
that on the whole the position of Msgr. Noël is not genuinely
Thomistic.)

——— *St. Thomas and Epistemology* (Aquinas Lecture, 1946).
Milwaukee, Marquette University Press, 1946.

Roland-Gosselin, M. D., *Essai d'une étude critique de la connaissance.* Paris, 1932, pp. 165. (A very methodical and critical
study which was cut short by the death of the author. Besides
the introduction, only the first part has appeared. It treats
"intellectual knowledge and the general conditions for judgment." It overemphasizes perhaps the idealist prejudices.)

Rousselot, P., *L'intellectualisme de saint Thomas.* 2nd ed. Paris,
1924, pp. xliv+xviii+262. English transl. by J. E. O'Mahony:
The Intellectualism of St. Thomas. N. Y., Sheed and Ward,

1935, pp. viii+231. (Contains very penetrating insights into the nature of human knowledge; it studies especially the metaphysics of knowledge.)

De Tonquedec, J., *La critique de la connaissance.* Paris, 1929, pp. 565. (Contains a description and critique of knowledge, together with an analysis of the psychological foundations of logic.)

Van Riet, G., *L'épistémologie thomiste. Recherches sur le problème de la connaissance dans l'école thomiste contemporaine.* Louvain, 1946, pp. viii+672. (A very extensive historical and critical inquiry from Balmes to Brunner.)

Note: See also the bibliography given by De Vries in his *Critica,* pp. xi-xiii.

WORKS IN LATIN

Boyer, C., *De cognitionis humanae valore generaliter vindicando,* in *Cursus philosophiae,* vol. I, Paris, s.d. (1935), pp. 167-213. (Proposes an interesting theory concerning judgment; he considers scepticism particularly.)

Geny, P., *Critica de cognitionis humanae valore disquisitio.* Romae, 1927, pp. 416.

Maquart, F. X., *Metaphysica defensiva seu Critica. Elementa philosophiae.* Tome III, Paris, 1938, pp. 346. (A very thorough study; cites a number of contemporary authors.)

Naber, A., *Critica (ad usum privatum).* Romae, 1932, pp. 412.

De Vries, J., *Critica in usum scholarum.* Freiburg-im-Breisgau, Herder, 1937, pp. 176.

TOPICAL INDEX

knowledge, 121, 139; first principle was that of non-contradiction, 143, n. 20; Aristotelianism formulates knowledge theory in terms of objective experience, 149; first example of classifications of concepts or a system, 152; answer to scepticism, 170-171; Aristotelians of Middle Ages held the universal was materially in things, 189; first formulation of critical realism, 281; imperfections in his epistemology, 281; Aristotle and St. Thomas, 281

Assimilation of Datum: takes place on different levels, 144

Association of Ideas: produces elaborated concepts, 152-153

Attention: reflection needs attention, 151; value of knowledge depends on attention, 209

Augustine, St.: Augustine's principle for organizing knowledge, 4; put a theory of knowledge at basis of his system, 9; early scepticism, 55; held radical intellectualism or idealism, 56; Augustine and Descartes, 56; dominant traits of Augustinian Neoplatonism, 56; contributed elements of medieval epistemology, 59; distrusted sensory experience, 271. See **Neoplatonism;** *Cogito*

Averroes: climax of Aristotelianism among Arabs, 57

Avicebron: influenced by Aristotle, 57

Avicenna: influenced by Aristotle, 57

Bacon, Francis: developed empiricism, 65; and modern philosophy, 278

Bacon, Roger: see **Roger Bacon**

Bate, Henry: Neoplatonist, 66

Becoming: primitive characteristic of consciousness, 86

Being: experience of being is implied in consciousness, 82 sq.; essence of, 83; being the *primum notum,* 83, 92; Roland-Gosselin emphasizes primacy of notion of

being, 84, n. 3; primacy over knowledge, 94-98; Gilson emphasizes primacy of being, 97-98, 259, n. 9; Maritain emphasizes primacy, 98, 259, n. 9; concept of being expresses the fundamental value, 130, 180 sq.; the absolute norm of knowledge is to be found in the basic affirmation of being, 169 sq.; being the first object of affirmation, 180 sq.; experience of being is infallible knowledge, 182, 189; concept of being, 183 sq.; abstraction of concept of, 184-185; analogy of the concept of being, 185; transcendental extension of concept of being, 186-188, 190; concept represents an absolute reality, 190-191; experience and conception of being, 191, 197; concept gives possession of all reality, 191; affirmation of being the ideal of perfect knowledge, 191 sq.; value of existential judgments, 192 sq.; the process of transcendentalization, 193; imperfections of knowledge of being, 195-196; concept of being different from empirical concepts, 202-203; primacy of being recognized by realism, 251: rejection of this primacy most pernicious error of modern thought, 252; no privileged experience of being, 259; Mercier neglects primacy of being, 259, n. 9; Noël on the primacy of being, 259, n. 9; object of knowledge must be defined in terms of being, 259-260. See **Datum; Knowledge; Real; Realism**

Bergson, H.: principle of organizing knowledge, 4; description of Bergsonian intuitionism, 270

Berkeley, G.: empiricist, 65

Biological Activity: see **Activity**

Bodies: extended in themselves, 226. See **Knowledge**

Body, The: as an instrument of knowledge, 113 sq.

Boethius, M.: introduced Aristotle to West, 57

Böhme, J.: Neoplatonist, 66

Bonaventure, St.: influenced by Aristotle, 57

"Bridge, Problem of the": is insoluble, 277-278

Bruno, G.: Neoplatonist, 66

Brunschvicg, L.: extreme Kantian formalist, 71; opposes metaphysical realism, 253; his idealism sacrifices experience, 271

Cajetan: Thomistic realist, 72

Capreolus, John: Thomistic realist, 72

Cartesianism: see **Descartes, R.**

Causality: problem belongs to metaphysics, 263

Certitude: in Mercier's *Critériologie*, 13 sq.; in *Critica* of Gény, 16; legitimate certitude is caused by objective evidence, 178; in existential judgments, 195

Charron, P.: sceptic, 65

Chartres: School of Chartres influenced by Neoplatonism, 57

Classification: see **Science**

"Closed Consciousness": see **Consciousness**

Cogito: a first immediate fact, 80; in Descartes implies reality, 82; the *cogito* formula implies *aliquid* (reality) 93; method of the *cogito* should be used in epistemology, 258-259

Cognition: see **Knowledge**

Common-Sense: claims of regarding knowledge, 35 sq.; common-sense difficulties regarding knowledge, 40 sq.; common-sense claim to be a subject, 46

Concept: nature of, 128 sq.; differs from image, 129 sq.; empirical concept expresses a particular mode of being, 131; classes of empirical concepts, 132; association of concepts, 132-133; formation of elaborated concepts, 132-133, 152-153; concept is a real element of consciousness, 134; the concept is a universal representation, 134; principal characteristics of concept, 134 sq.; how universality of concept is shown, 135-136; concept synthesizes particular data, 136; possibility of singular concepts, 136, n. 14; concept is abstract, 136-137; the concept in Plato, 138; nominalism disclaims value of concept, 138; concept always expresses an experience and necessarily refers to experience, 138-140; modern idealists make concepts independent of experience, 138-139; Aristotle recognized empirical origin of all concepts, 139; concept is an act rather than an object, 140; has a stable content, 140-141; concept analyzed in the definition, 141; transcendency of concepts, 142; contains rudimentary truth, 173; all its content comes from the datum, 189; subjective experience can give rise to empirical concepts, 200; process of conceptualization brings out universal values, 201-202; analogy of concept of being, 202; difference between the concept of being and empirical concepts, 202-203; univocity of empirical concepts, 202-203; "conceptual dissection" entails inadequacy, 204. For concept of being, see **Being**. See also **Affirmation; Image; Knowledge; Thought**

Conceptionism: on the objectivity of qualities, 224. For moderate conceptionism, see **Interpretationism**

"Conceptual Dissection": entails inadequacy in knowledge, 204; is present in our knowledge of bodies, 236; results from abstract nature of our concepts, 246

Conceptualization: see **Abstraction; Thought**

"Concordism": holds that differences between philosophers are only superficial, 268

Concrete: abstract order must rest on, 259. See **Datum**

Condillac, E.: taught sensationalism, 65

Conformity: see Truth

Confusion: as cause of error, 175

Consciousness: immediate data of consciousness must be starting point of system of knowledge, 11; need of describing immediate data, 18; should be studied by the reflective method, 27 sq.; by an interrogative method, 31 sq.; constitutive conditions of consciousness, 34; common-sense difficulties regarding consciousness, 43; consciousness an indisputable reality, 50; its existence the basic affirmation, 78 sq.; consciousness and reality, 78 sq.; its unity is primitive, 79; consciousness is a primitive, irreducible datum, 80 sq.; implies intuition, experience, affirmation, evidence, 81-82; clearly implies reality, 82; primitive identity of consciousness and reality, 84 sq.; consciousness is a becoming and duration, 86 sq.; identity of self a fact of conscious experience, 87; basic structure of consciousness, 87, 108; complexity of, 87, 108; duality in, 88; duality a first datum, 89; nature of duality, 90; pure consciousness impossible, 90; dissociation of "to be" and "to know," 91-92; objective pole of consciousness, 94; analysis of consciousness, 101 sq.; basic immanence of conscious act, 107; the body as the instrument of consciousness, 113 sq.; basic and indisputable features of consciousness, 118; control of abnormal states of consciousness, 126 sq.; transcendency of consciousness shown in imagination, 127-128; Descartes' picture of "closed consciousness," 148: finality of knowledge is a datum of consciousness, 159-160; consciousness an uncertain and unstable reality, 209; implies spiritual immanence, 212, n. 14; evolution of

objective pole, 217-218; indirect realism presupposes a "closed consciousness," 224; unity and permanence safeguarded by memory, 241; divine consciousness is not a production, 270, n. 2; "closed" and "open" consciousness, 273-274. See Knowledge; Self

Constructs: kind of reality proper to, 123

"Copernican Revolution": Kant's new notion of knowledge, 70. See also Kant; Subjectivism; Idealism

Copernicus, N.: and empiricism, 65

Corporeal Datum: characteristics, 110 sq. See also Datum

Corporeal World: problem of origin belongs to metaphysics, 278; knowledge of world developed in positive sciences, 287

Cosmic Realism: a characteristic of Thomism, 255; distinctive traits of, 255 sq. See also Realism

Critical Epistemology: object of, 20. See also Epistemology

Critical Problem: precise object of, 162-163. See Critique

Critical Realism: see Realism

"Criticism": see Kant

Critique: meaning of term in this work, iii; different views on critique of knowledge, 10 sq.; Middle Ages recognized need of critique of knowledge, 59; critique of reasoning, 153-154, 237 sq.; critique of affirmation, 170 sq.; of being as the first object of affirmation, 180 sq.; of existential judgments, 192 sq.; of the different kinds of knowledge, 198 sq.; of knowledge of the self, 199 sq.; of knowledge of matter, 204 sq.; critique of sensation, 205 sq., 212 sq.; limited scope of the general critique of sensation, 226; development and methods of the special critique of sensation, 227 sq.; of memory, 241 sq.; Kant's conception differs from our criti-

principle of identity, 98; principle of not a proper judgment, 143; perfect identity had only in knowledge of self, 194, n. 24. See also **Aristotle; Maritain; Experience**

Illusions: in sensation, 230-231; optical illusions of Müller-Lyer, 231; illusions of memory, 243

Image: represented datum, or representation of perceived objects, not an object, 122; distinction from perceived datum, 124 sq., 208-209, 276-277; schematic images differ from concepts, 129 sq.; association of, 132-133, 152; schematic image always particular, 134. See also **Concept; Datum; Memory**

Imagination: notion of, 123; properties and laws governing, 123. See **Image; Knowledge**

Immanence: an important characteristic of knowledge, 105 sq.; Descartes' imaginative conception of, 106; immanence of knowledge a basic theme in Thomism, 106; true sense of principle, 187; idealist principle of immanence an untenable presumption, 210; idealist principle a prevalent presumption today, 273. See also **Descartes; Idealism; Knowledge; Le Roy**

Immediate Realism: see **Cosmic Realism**

Inattention: cause of error, 175

Independence: ontological independence of corporeal world, 116 sq., 233-234, 261, 264, 278. See **Datum; Knowledge; Object**

Indirect Realism: in de Vries, 18. See **Realism**

Individuals: problem of distinction belongs to metaphysics, 263-264

Induction: problem belongs to logic and critique of sciences, 202, n. 4

Intellect: as power of thinking, 141; its acts distinct from sensation, 141-142; notion and role, 142; all varieties of empiricism

neglect transcendental capacity of intellect, 257, 270

Intellection: see **Thought**

Intellectualism: in Plato, 53; radical intellectualism in Neoplatonism, 56; modern intellectualism starts with Descartes, 67; radical intellectualism in Kant, 70; merit and mistakes of radical intellectualism, 274

Intellectual Memory: notion of, 152

Intelligence: implication of term, 36; common-sense difficulties regarding, 42 sq.; discovery by Plato, 53

Intelligible, The: not produced by *a priori* activity alone, 188

Interpretationism: on the objectivity of qualities, 225-226

Interrogative Method: nature of, 33. See **Methodic Doubt**

Intuition: implied in consciousness, 81; notion of, 181; angelic and divine intuition, 196, n. 25

Intuitionism: influenced by empiricism, 65-66

John of Damascus, St.: theology inspired by Aristotle, 57

John of St. Thomas: Thomistic realist, 72

John Scotus Erigena: influenced by Neoplatonism, 57

Judgment: synthetic judgment in Kant, 70, 145, n. 21; nature of judgment, 142 sq.; an active synthesis, 144-145; notion of immediate judgment, 144, 153; notion of mediate judgment, 144, 153; judgment completes elementary act of knowledge, 145-146; truth a quality of judgment, 173-174; judgment an active conformity, 173-174; risk of error in judgment, 174 sq.; judgment entails at least a hypothetical universality, 177; subjective universality of judgment, 177; objective universality of judgment, 177, n. 8; non-empirical conditions for judgment, 179: value of judgments concerning corporeal world, 233-234; value of judgments expressing mediate knowledge, 241. See also **Kant; Affirmation; Critique**

Judgment, Existential: value of existential judgments, 192 sq.; notion of, 193-195; have hypothetical necessity, 194; have objective evidence and certitude, 195. See also **Being; Evidence; Knowledge**

Kant, Immanuel: his critical idealism is a subjectivism, 69; *a priori* forms, 70, 216, n. 16, 280; synthetic judgments, 70, 145, n. 21; belongs to the line of radical intellectualism, 70; doctrine led to agnosticism, 70; doctrine on knowledge, 70; his "Copernican revolution," 70, 273, 280· Noël on Kant, 70, n. 18; influence on 19th-century philosophy, 71, 273; used characteristics of subject to overcome phenomenalism, 101; distinguishes between empirical concepts and *a priori* concepts, 138; synthetic *a priori* judgments, 145, n. 2; refutation of Kantian empiricism, 187; *a priori* forms do not belong in epistemology, 216, n. 16; his "Copernican revolution" leads to rejection of primacy of being, 252; Kantian agnosticism opposes metaphysical realism, 253; regards objective datum as purely phenomenal, 256; Kantian idealism falsifies nature of knowledge, 269-270; his "Copernican revolution" gave new orientation to idealism, 272; his conception of "critique" differs from our critical epistemology, 278 sq.; description of doctrine, 278 sq.; dogmatism in, 279; accepts the phenomenalist presumption, 279-280; his capital error on nature of knowledge, 280; his doctrine implies agnosticism, 280-281; on abstraction, 280, n. 9. See also **Affirmation; Being;**

Judgment; Idealism; Subjectivism

Kantianism: see **Kant, Immanuel**

Kepler, J.: and empiricism, 65

Knowledge: systematization of, 3 sq.; the ideal of unity, 3 sq.; principles of organization, 3 sq.; scientific classification may be arbitrary or conventional, 6; rational systematization. perennial ideal, 6; every synthesis rests on a critique of knowledge, 8 sq.; difficulties in the study of, 25 sq.; reflective method of studying, 26 sq.; personal method of studying, 27 sq.; interrogative method of studying, 31 sq.; common-sense claims regarding knowledge, 35 sq.; common-sense difficulties regarding knowledge, 39 sq.; difficulties from psychology, 44; difficulties of scientist regarding, 44 sq.; difficulties raised by the philosopher, 46 sq.; determination of nature of knowledge, 46 sq., 91 sq., 245 sq.; value questioned by some philosophers, 46 sq.; is knowledge a mere epiphenomenon? 48; immediate knowledge distinct from indirect, 49; value depends on nature and purpose, 49; problem of knowledge, 51; utility of the history of the problem, 51; no synthetic theory in St. Thomas, 58; Middle Ages recognized need for critique of knowledge, 59; Kant's "Copernican revolution" regarding notion of knowledge, 70; two aspects shown by history, 73; description of knowledge starts with conscious reality or real consciousness, 78 sq.; evidences of fact first acquired by human knowledge, 83; knowledge as a modality of being, 91 sq.; primacy of being over knowledge, 94 sq., 96-97; finality of knowledge, 100, 143 sq. (see also **Finality**); knowledge and self-consciousness, 101 sq.; knowledge an act of the subject, 103-105; immanence an

fies the subject, 95; measures knowledge of non-self, 95; problem of ontological independence of the object. 96; means immanent term of knowledge, 106-107; dominant in assimilative knowledge, 149; difference between object-in-me and object-in-itself, 167; mode of presence of object, 182; necessity of object known, 188; existence of an absolute object, 188; objective value of sensory object, 206 sq.; perceptions alone do not show independent existence, 213 sq.; is there a privileged object in sensation? 233; the psychological object, the object-in-itself, the physical object, 232-233; sense of distinction between object-in-itself and psychological object, 235; problem of ontological independence belongs to metaphysics, 278. See **Datum; Thing**

Objective Evidence: see **Evidence**

Objective Presence: different kinds, 109 sq.

Objective Reality: means immanent term of knowledge, 106-107

Objectivity: difficulties in determining objectivity of knowledge, 160 sq. See also **Affirmation; Datum; Independence; Knowledge; Object**

Occam: see **William of Occam**

Ontologism: of Malebranche, 68

Ontology: problems of ontology or general metaphysics, 262-264

"Open Consciousness": see **Consciousness**

Order: various principles for ordering knowledge, 3; of logical derivation in geometry, 4; the conceptual order and the real order, 239; the logical order, 239-240

Organs, Sensory: functions of, 114 sq.

Parmenides: ignored multiplicity in reality, 52

Perception: common-sense difficulties regarding, 42; sensory perception is already a conscious act, 118 sq.; nature of sensory perception, 118 sq.; sensory perception is somehow incorporeal, 120; involves a twofold experience, objective and subjective, 120-121; critique of sense perception, 205 sq., 212 sq.; the critical problem concerning sense perception, 207 sq.; sceptical attitude to sensory perception, 207 sq.; view of direct or immediate realism on, 207 sq.; complexity of sense perceptions, 211; general critique should be based on visual and tactile perceptions, 211; critique of, 212 sq.; the independence of object, 213 sq.; comparison of perceptions helps determine objectivity, 218 sq.; made possible by spatial determinations, 222; distortion in perceptions, 223; positive sciences can assist the critique of sensation, 227; finality of perception, 235; sensory perception and idealism, 273 sq. See **Knowledge; Sensation**

Perceptionism, Integral: on the objectivity of qualities, 225

Perceptionism, Moderate: view on objectivity of qualities, 225

Peter of Auvergne: Thomistic realist, 72

Phenomenalism: in Nicholas of Autrecourt, 64; surpassed by first affirmation of epistemology, 83; its inadequacy shown by an analysis of consciousness, 89; absolute phenomenalism rejects psychological realism, 254; description, 270

Philo: Neoplatonist, 56

Philosophy: controversy concerning starting point, 9 sq.; proper order in teaching, 9; problems of philosophy of the sciences, 267; lessons of the history of philosophy, 282-283; distinction of philosophy from science shown by critical epistemology, 285 sq.;

INDEX OF PROPER NAMES

77751